The Civil Service
under the Conservatives, 1979–1997

'An excellent and very accessible book. It will be essential reading for all those interested in the fundamental changes which have occurred in the Civil Service over the last 20 years.'

Professor David Marsh, University of Birmingham

'Richards' analysis of the politicisation of the Civil Service is judicious and incisive. He provides the first convincing book-length account of the changes in the relationship between ministers and civil servants in the 1980s and 90s.'

Dr Martin Smith, University of Sheffield

'This study provides powerful insights into the changing nature of the British Civil Service. It explains and assesses the significance of the "can-do" philosophy that grew up in the 1980s. The book deserves a wide audience in the academic community and beyond.'

Professor Gerry Stoker, University of Strathclyde

'A fascinating study, not just for inhabitants and watchers of the Whitehall village but much more widely.'

Sir Peter Kemp, Second Permanent Secretary,
Cabinet Office 1988–92

The Civil Service

under the Conservatives, *1979–1997*

Whitehall's Political Poodles?

DAVID RICHARDS

sussex
ACADEMIC
PRESS

First published 1997 in Great Britain by
SUSSEX ACADEMIC PRESS
18 Chichester Place
Brighton BN2 1FF

and in the United States of America by
SUSSEX ACADEMIC PRESS
c/o International Specialized Book Services, Inc.
5804 N.E. Hassalo St.
Portland, Oregon 97213-3644

British Library Cataloguing in Publication Data
A CIP catalogue record for this book is available from the British Library.

ISBN 1–898723 63 X (hardcover)
ISBN 1–898723 64 8 (paperback)

Printed and bound by Bookcraft, Midsomer Norton, Bath
This book is printed on acid-free paper

Contents

Foreword by Peter Hennessy

O NE OF US is a phrase that will ring down the years as long as Margaret Thatcher and her premierships remain of interest to political scientists and political historians. The latter group in their careful, even pedantic way will carbon-date it, however, to October 1964 rather than May 1979 – to the arrival of the first Wilson administration rather than to Mrs Thatcher in her initial incarnation. George Brown used it to question the senior Treasury officials assigned to his new Department of Economic Affairs, history will record, but folk-memory will have it ever more firmly fixed as the test Mrs Thatcher applied to what she saw as the decline-managers-cum-consensualists in the higher Civil Service bequeathed her both by her Labour and her Conservative predecessors.

It was a foolish, if understandable test for a conviction politician to apply – foolish because in constitutional terms civil servants are one-of-everybody's provided that 'everybody' had received the electorate's blessing at the polls. Equally foolishly, too many observers took at face value Mrs Thatcher's claim to have'changed everything' including her direct labour organisation in Whitehall. A handful of officials apart, knowledge of the breed plus supporting anecdote suggested that the watchdogs of continuity and due process had not turned into Mrs Thatcher's poodles. Senior civil servants may have settled for a quiet life and have failed to fulfil Hugh Dalton's job description of them as 'congenital snaghunters'. Mrs Thatcher was as difficult to interrupt as she was to dissuade. But anyone with any real knowledge of the senior British civil servant knew that he or she was almost the last person in the Kingdom to fall for what Victor Rothschild once called the 'promises and panaceas that gleam like false teeth' in the party manifestos.

That said, the question needed an investigator who could and would go beyond social anthropology and Whitehall lore. This

David Richards has done using both the political scientist's appetite for pattern-making and the contemporary historian's zest for placing the tape-recorder before those who were there and inviting them to tell it how it was. The result is closer to reality than anything that has come before. This book is a welcome and necessary antidote to those who, in the face of the Thatcher experience, speak hyperbole and display overreaction to this most mesmeric of Prime Ministers and her technicolour premiership. In place of hype, Dr Richards has brought reason and evidence.

Professor Peter Hennessy
Queen Mary and Westfield College
University of London
December 1996

Preface

IN SPRING 1989, a year after the publication of *The Next Steps*, Margaret Thatcher, Peter Kemp and a number of the Next Steps project team were involved in a meeting at a recently formed Agency, 'Companies House' in Cardiff, South Wales. A series of presentations were made in which officials painted a healthy picture of the progress the Agency had made since its formation in October 1988. Afterwards, Margaret Thatcher, in an aside comment to Kemp, enthused: 'there is no such thing as a bad civil servant, only a bad Civil Service.'[1] Implicit in this observation is that the Prime Minister had been much impressed by the officials she had met at Companies House that day. If this was the type of official who represented the new face of Whitehall (or what was now left of Whitehall), then, in her mind, the future for public service looked bright.

Given her enthusiasm about what she had seen during her brief visit to Cardiff, Margaret Thatcher may have suffered from a temporary bout of amnesia. Was this the same person who, in the early 1970s while Minister in the Department of Education and Science, had decided that her working relationship with her Permanent Secretary, William Pile, had reached such a nadir that she made a request to the Cabinet Secretary, William Armstrong, for Piles' removal? Likewise, when reminiscing about the 'dinner party' she hosted for her Permanent Secretaries in May 1980, she observed that: 'such a menu of complaints and negative attitudes as was served up that evening was enough to dull any appetite'. Was this also the same Prime Minister who, early in her first term, clashed with the official Donald Derx at a meeting in the Department of Employment and informed her entourage to 'never let me see that man again'?

Since the Conservative Government were elected to office eighteen years ago, it is clear that profound changes have swept through the corridors of Whitehall. An Executive Officer recruited to the

Civil Service in May 1996 would have joined a vastly different organisation to the one his predecessor entered in May 1979. However, the crucial question to be addressed by this book is: are the personnel serving at SW1 today of the same type and character as those the Conservative Administration inherited in 1979?

Throughout the tenure of the Conservative Administration, academics and political commentators have regularly referred to the politicisation of the Civil Service. Appointments at the most senior grades in Whitehall, particularly those approved by Mrs Thatcher, have been cited as unequivocal confirmation of this notion. However, there has been no systematic analysis of this supposed 'bluing effect' on the senior Civil Service.

Between 1994 and 1996, I conducted a series of interviews with both retired and contemporary civil servants who worked day-in, day-out alongside both Margaret Thatcher and John Major. This has allowed me to compile fresh, primary data dealing with this vexed question. Such an approach demonstrates that there was no form of overt politicisation. However, during the last eighteen years, Whitehall has become a more personalised organisation.

This book provides a comprehensive analysis of the Conservative Administration's attitude towards the bureaucracy it inherited. It also examines the broader effects that their reforms of the Civil Service had on central government. In particular, it highlights the contradiction Mrs Thatcher faced on coming to office: she wished to transform an institution to which she was ideologically hostile, but discovered that many of its employees were highly talented and able officials. The interviews have allowed me to provide a fascinating and, on occasion, a very personal insight into how the longest serving prime minister of the twentieth century operated behind the closed doors of Whitehall.

The book then goes on to examine the ramifications of the personalisation of the Civil Service for the Major Government and any succeeding Government. This section concludes by contending that the whole notion of an impartial, permanent and anonymous bureaucracy may be assigned to history. In an era when more and more of the work of Whitehall is either being privatised or contracted out to agencies headed by powerful Chief Executives, the role and function of the mandarinate is rapidly contracting and may, conceivably, disappear altogether. It is ironic that at the end of an epoch in which civil servants like Bernard Ingham,

Charles Powell and Robert Armstrong became household names, we may now be witnessing the consignment of Sir Humphrey to a footnote in the institutional history of Britain. Thus, as the new millennium draws ever nearer, the book concludes by looking at some of the broader ramifications for future governments.

Acknowledgements

I T IS CUSTOMARY for authors to thank those nearest and dearest to them and I would not wish to stray from this path. Thus, to my family, in particular my parents, friends and those who have shared living or office space with me in recent years, I hope it was worth it.

There are of course those who have helped me shape this book into what is now before you. Although no one other than myself can be held responsible for either the content or any errors herein, there are a number of 'nearly culpables' whose names I must divulge. Most generally, the Department of Government at the University of Strathclyde and also the Department of Political Science and International Relations at the University of Birmingham have provided a sympathetic setting in which the bulk of this book was written. More specifically, a number of colleagues have provided invaluable assistance and time. They are: Martin Smith, Kevin Theakston, Gerry Stoker, Peter Hennessy, Colin Hay, Matthew Watson and Martin Rhodes. My thanks are also extended to David Marsh, both for setting me off down this path in the first place and for not being shy in coming forward when he had *anything* to say. Some things never change!

Finally, may I thank the numerous civil servants who afforded me both the time and patience to sit through what, more often than not, proved fascinating interviews. Without their assistance, this book would never have been written. The frankness, honesty and diversity of views they provided have helped me to disregard the Mandy Rice-Davies sentiment – well, almost.

For my Godson
Daniel

Introduction: There is No Such Thing as a Bad Civil Servant, Only a Bad Civil Service

THERE HAS BEEN NO systematic analysis of the mandarinate appointed by the Conservatives. The most detailed attempt to assess the notion of politicisation was carried out by the 1985 RIPA Working Group. However, despite informal Cabinet Office backing, the report they submitted managed to make only one substantive conclusion: relative to her predecessors, Margaret Thatcher had taken a much more hands-on approach to approving senior appointments. This book will fill the gap by providing both a quantitative and qualitative analysis of appointments to the two most senior grades in Whitehall between 1974 and 1996. In so doing, it will enable me to add substance to the rhetoric surrounding the alleged politicisation of the Civil Service after eighteen years of Conservative Government.

Chapter 1 examines the existing commentaries on the possible politicisation of the higher Civil Service by the Conservative Government of 1979–97 and, in particular, by Margaret Thatcher. Although, it is broadly accepted that Margaret Thatcher displayed a much keener interest in her senior civil servants than previous Prime Ministers, there is no consensus on the reasons for this change. Commentators were divided. Initially, some academics and journalist suggested that Margaret Thatcher had set out to appoint a new breed of senior civil servants who were sympathetic to the policies of the Conservative Government. By the mid-1980s, such arguments were increasingly regarded as too crude and simplistic. Instead, commentators argued that Mrs Thatcher wished to establish a mandarinate of can-doers and sound administrators. Although, this second, more subtle notion of politicisation appears more

convincing, it remained anecdotal and under-conceptualised. The
chapter argues that the whole notion of politicisation remained
underdeveloped.

Of course, any discussion of politicisation needs to be put in
the context of the desire by the Conservative Government and, in
particular, Margaret Thatcher, to transform the culture and make-up
of the mandarinate. For this reason, chapter 2 traces the dynamic
evolution of Civil Service reform during the 1980s and 1990s. In
order to ensure the success of these reforms, it was essential for
the Conservatives to introduce a new breed of senior civil servant
to the highest tiers in Whitehall.

Any account of Mrs Thatcher's role in the process of appointments
must first explain how the senior appointments procedures operates. This is a procedure which, since the fundamental changes that
followed the 1968 Fulton Report, has largely remained shrouded
in secrecy. Chapter 3 throws light on these proceedings. Using
first-hand accounts from individuals who were directly involved, I
outline this process, providing both an 'official' view of the existing
system and an account of what actually happens when a vacancy
arises at the most senior levels in the Whitehall hierarchy.

Chapter 4 considers whether or not there was an obvious change
in the type of individual who was appointed to the highest grades
during the 1980s, compared to the previous Labour Administration
of 1974–9. It is very unusual for a civil servant in the senior open
structure to receive a promotional rise of two or more grades.
As such, I provide a quantitative and demographic analysis of
all promotions of civil servants to the two most senior grades
in Whitehall between 1974 and 1990. Here, the intention is to
establish whether, during the Thatcher administration, there was
a tangible change in the make-up of the mandarinate. The results of
this analysis suggests that first, there was no increase in the numbers
who received rapid elevation to the highest grades during the 1980s,
and second, there was no marked rise in outside appointments to
Whitehall. The traditional, promotional, patterns of the Civil Service
appeared to remain intact. However, this does not mean, *per se*, that
there is no resonance in a notion of politicisation; only a qualitative
analysis can comprehensively address this question.

This book uses two types of qualitative analysis. In chapter 5
the memoirs of Mrs Thatcher and her ministers are examined.
These offer a number of examples of occasions on which the then
Prime Minister directly intervened in the appointments procedure.
Indeed, in her own memoirs, Margaret Thatcher concedes that she

regularly intervened, arguing that there was limited benefit in directly attacking the structures of Whitehall. Instead, she felt that only by 'encouraging or appointing individuals' could progress be made. Her aim was to induce a revolution from above which would permeate down through the lower tiers in Whitehall. Ministers' views on politicisation are discussed, in particular the notion that Mrs Thatcher surrounded herself with a personal staff who had 'the commitment and belief to carry through the radical policies she believed the country required'. I conclude by suggesting that Mrs Thatcher used the normal process of sending high-flyers to the centre of the Whitehall village in order to single out those officials she believed displayed the can-do, managerial characteristics she wanted in her mandarinate.

Obviously, evidence derived from politicians' memoirs is tendentious. So, chapter 6 presents the views of senior civil servants of the period, collected in a series of interviews I conducted. The mandarins confirmed the fact that Mrs Thatcher had a greater involvement in the appointments procedure than her predecessors. However, they were unanimous in the view she did not try to introduce a set of individuals who could be deemed Conservative Party sympathisers. The issue was broader; she wished to change the culture of Whitehall which, she argued, had become 'flabby'. This involved altering the make-up of senior personnel in Whitehall. Thus, Mrs Thatcher chose officials with proven track records as sound administrators, who she regarded as vital contributors to her proposed programme of 'efficient and cost-effective management'. I term this new breed of mandarin 'managerially-oriented, can-doers'. The chapter concludes by arguing that, during the 1980s, a cultural change occurred in Whitehall. This was reflected in a shift in the role of the mandarinate: their duties narrowed with an increasing emphasis upon efficiently operating the machinery of government. The net effect was that the previous emphasis on the role of senior officials, as policy-makers and formulators, noticeably waned.

Chapter 7 examines how Mrs Thatcher's increased intervention in the appointments procedure resulted in the personalisation, rather than the politicisation, of the senior Civil Service. The Prime Ministerial role in top appointments changed from being passive and approving, to pro-active and critical. Personalisation was reinforced by the longevity of the Thatcher Government: after eleven years in office Mrs Thatcher had a working experience of the majority of senior officials in central government. As such, she commanded a greater 'inside' knowledge than previous Prime Ministers. This personalisation, on occasions, meant a less rational approach in senior appointments. Catching the Prime Minister's eye, in a positive manner of course, became increasingly important. Further, because catching the Prime Minister's eye became one of the most effective means of securing preference to the highest grades, this strengthened the 'centre effect' in senior appointments; serving in the Cabinet Office, Treasury or Prime Minister's Office became an even more important step on the road to rapid promotion.

Chapter 8 more thoroughly explores the notion of the 'centre effect'. Evidence is presented which confirms the view that to succeed in Whitehall in the 1980s, it was vital that officials were noticed by the Prime Minister in a positive light. To achieve this one needed a successful tour of duty at the centre. Two hypotheses are put forward, as to how officials impressed Mrs Thatcher. First, it is suggested that officials at the centre became socialised into the *en vogue* working practices which permeated through Whitehall in the 1980s. Such practices emphasised being positive, pro-active and having sound administrative techniques. Officials who displayed such traits attracted the attention of Margaret Thatcher and their cards were marked for future promotion. However, there is a second, more subtle, but potentially more powerfully, version of this hypothesis which posits a reconstruction effect. In this interpretation, the high-flyers sent to the centre can be regarded as strategic operators who recognised the potential length of the Conservative's incumbency in Government. Thus, in order to enhance their chances of future promotion, they reconstructed themselves to fit the *en vogue* work practices. The combined evidence of the quantitative and qualitative analyses indicate both that a centre effect occurred in the 1980s and that the more powerful explanation of this phenomenon was the notion of reconstruction.

Chapter 9 presents a series of case studies of individuals affected by Margaret Thatcher's increased intervention in the appointments procedure. These portray a number of *vignettes* depicting the various guises of Sir Humphrey. To do this, officials whose careers Margaret Thatcher affected are divided into a number of categories: managerially-oriented, can-doers; those who politicised *themselves* while in office; those who had become disillusioned by the Civil Service, knowing that Margaret Thatcher had effectively black-balled them; and 'traditional' Deputy Secretaries who did not feel comfortable with the newly-emerging generation of pro-active implementors and so their careers never scaled the heights they might have done in another Whitehall era. Finally, a category of officials who followed a 'normal' Whitehall career path and who attained a Permanent Secretaryship in spite of, not because of, Margaret Thatcher is introduced. This category is important because it indicates that any Thatcher effect on the higher Civil Service was far from universal.

Chapter 10 turns to the Major era and examines the dramatic increase in Civil Service reform since 1990. In particular, the rapid growth of agencies, shifts towards privatisation through market testing and the pressures placed on public servants following the introduction of the Citizen's Charter. Against this background, John Major's approach to senior appointments is examined, in order to assess whether there was any change in the type of senior official which John Major appointed in the 1990s. Finally, I look at a number of individual appointments, most notably that of Michael Bichard, who crossed the Rubicon from Chief Executive to Permanent Secretary. The chapter concludes by arguing that, officially, the Major Government was committed to the traditional principles upon which the modern-day Civil Service was founded. However, this commitment rings hollow in light of the continued haemorrhaging of sub-units of Whitehall departments into Next Steps Agencies, along with the increasing privatisation of central government work, following the 1991 White Paper 'Competing for Quality'. Civil Service reform has proved to be one of the most radical policy areas during the Major Administration and this has presented serious implications for the governments of the next millennium.

The final chapter argues that the existence, or otherwise, of politicisation in the Civil Service is a matter of subjective judgement. The Blair-led Labour Party seems to be content to inherit, wholesale, the Civil Service bequeathed it after eighteen years of Conservative rule. They broadly appear unperturbed by the claims of some that they will inherit what Peter Hennessy calls a 'Bluehall'. However, the Civil Service of the 1990s is a vastly different organisation from the Civil Service of 1979. As such, I conclude by placing, in a wider context, the last eighteen years of dynamic, structural and personnel evolution which has swept the corridors of Whitehall. It is suggested that, in the light of the personalisation of appointments and the introduction of Next Steps and privatisation, a paradox now exists: at a time when the public profile of the mandarinate has never been higher, by the turn of the century, top civil servants may have been contracted-out to full-time gardening-duty in the Shires of South East England.

1

Did the 'Vicar of Bray' Reside at SW1 in the 1980s? What the Commentators Thought

'The Vicar of Bray', a well-known song of unknown authorship, dating from the eighteenth Century. The subject is a time-serving parson, who boasts that he has accommodated himself to the religious views of the reigns of Charles, James, William, Anne, and George and that 'whatsoever king may reign' he will remain Vicar of Bray. Various suggestions have been made as to who this Vicar was. Haydn (Dictionary of Dates) quotes Fuller as stating that Symon Symonds, vicar of Bray, Berkshire, in the reigns of Henry VIII, Edward VI, Mary, and Elizabeth, was twice a Papist and twice a Protestant. When charged with being a time-server, he is said to have replied: 'Not so, neither, for if I changed my religion, I am sure I kept true to my principle, which is to live and die the vicar of Bray'. (Oxford Companion to English Literature, 1985)

IN A RECENT ARTICLE on the changes in the Civil Service since 1979, Terence Heiser, a now retired Permanent Secretary at the Department of Environment, drew an analogy between the senior Civil Service and the mythical character, portrayed in the eighteenth Century song, the 'Vicar of Bray'. Heiser was attempting to distinguish between the notion of 'energy and goodwill', which he regarded as essential requirements of a senior mandarin and 'commitment', which he believed to be problematic because it had the potential to undermine an official's impartiality. Heiser's article concluded:

Hostile critics of the Civil Service might quote from the 'Vicar of Bray':

"And this is the law, I will maintain
Unto my dying day, Sir
That whatever King may reign,
I will be the vicar of Bray, Sir."

But the vicar of Bray did change sides and unlike the modern civil
servant, did not seek to be neutral. (Heiser 1994, p. 22)

The Vicar of Bray was a religious chameleon who, in order to
advance himself, willingly transferred his allegiance to whichever
sovereign ruled the nation. This chapter examines the views of
those critics and commentators, throughout the 1980s and 1990s,
who questioned whether or not a modern-day 'Vicar of Bray' could
be found in the corridors of SW1.

A review of the literature on the Civil Service in the 1980s
suggests that Margaret Thatcher increasingly intervened in the
senior appointments procedure. Commentators developed separate arguments. The first, simplistic view was that she appointed
officials who were Conservative Party sympathisers. As the decade
progressed, this interpretation was rejected by most as too crude.
It was replaced by the more subtle notion that Margaret Thatcher
wished to see 'can-doers' and sound administrators as her senior
civil servants. This chapter will survey the literature dealing with
these two notions of politicisation, establishing that the existing
evidence on this subject is superficial. Commentators have been too
willing to rely on hearsay and rhetoric, whilst failing to undertake a
systematic analysis of the 1980s, in order to substantiate the various
claims that the higher Civil Service became politicised.

Increased Intervention in the Appointments Procedure

Ridley (1983b), Fry (1985b), Theakston (1992) and Drewry and
Butcher (1991) have all argued that Margaret Thatcher took
a far greater interest in the appointments procedure than her
predecessors. This view is also echoed in the media accounts
of experienced journalists such as Hennessy (1989), Harris (1990)
and Young (1989). Commentators were attracted to the idea that
Mrs Thatcher concentrated on individual appointments, because
it reflected the widely-held view that she was not interested in
changing institutions.[1] Instead, her preoccupation was with people.
Young (1989, p. 162) argued: 'these first few months . . . the ground
began to be laid for the colonising of Whitehall with departmental

leaders whom the Prime Minister approved of'. Similarly, Ridley (1983b, p. 40) commented that: 'a new type of official is required. Perhaps the energetic pursuit of such policies even requires commitment – "conviction civil servants" as well as "conviction politicians".'

These accounts persuaded the Royal Institute of Public Administration (RIPA) to set-up a working party to examine the possibility of prime ministerial interference in senior appointments. Its findings suggested that Mrs Thatcher had indeed taken an increased interest in the appointment of senior mandarins, but that this had had no overall effect. The structure and work of the Civil Service remained unchanged (RIPA, 1987). However, their conclusions did little to check the ever-burgeoning number of claims that the Civil Service had become increasingly politicised. Two putative hypotheses emerged, which were not mutually exclusive, of the politicisation of Whitehall during the 1980s.

Politicisation Mark I – The Appointment of Conservative Sympathisers

During the first half of the decade, political commentators argued that the higher Civil Service had become politicised through the use of the senior appointments selection procedure, as Mrs Thatcher intervened at Grades 1/1a and 2.[2] The general view was that she promoted or appointed individuals who, if not members of the Conservative Party,[3] were at least sympathetic to the Party's policies and, in particular, to the neo-liberal, monetarist policies of the 1980s. There were a number of prominent proponents of this position. Ridley and Doig (1986) suggested that the political polarisation of the early 1980s called into question whether or not officials could collaborate in policy-making without a degree of commitment to the Conservative Government's radical political views and values. In a similar vein, Jessop (1988, pp. 87, 146, 177) contended:

> In particular, the state has been Thatcherised through Civil Service reorganisation and politically motivated promotion to key official posts . . . Unity was secured through a series of other more or less irreversible developments, [including] politically motivated appointments in the Civil Service and the quasi-state organisations . . . The step-by-step recomposition of the top Civil Service to promote people who are 'one-of-us', has helped consolidate the political gains of the 'Thatcher revolution'.

In a different vein, Garrett (1980) argued that Mrs Thatcher had a gut-feeling that Whitehall was essentially obstructive to radical policies. During her time in Parliament, the Fulton Committee had been established. Thus, she witnessed, first hand, the manner in which top mandarins were able to water-down the radical thrust of that Report. When, eleven years later, the opportunity presented itself, Margaret Thatcher introduced broad political change at the highest level in appointments and promotions. The retirement of a significant number of senior mandarins during the early 1980s,[4] facilitated this process. In 1981, Lord Bancroft, having been effectively dismissed by Mrs Thatcher, claimed there were: 'clear indicators of the Thatcher Government's determination to assert political control over the service' (Bancroft quoted in Fry 1984, p. 327) Similarly, Kavanagh and Seldon (1989, p. 209) noted that she appeared to intervene more directly than previous Prime Ministers in the promotion of Permanent Secretaries: 'preferring less senior and "obvious" candidates, apparently on the grounds that they were impatient with the status quo and defeatist'. Madgwick (1991, p. 207), also supported this view:

> She came to like some sharp bright officials; indeed, a handful became quite close to her, and she depended on them. In this sense she 'politicised' some of her 10 Downing Street officials. Some of these *favoured* officials went on to rapid high promotion; others stayed, becoming almost too close for further movement within the service.

Indeed, John Silkin, Shadow Leader of the House of Commons 1980–3, suggested that: 'Mrs Thatcher had tampered with the traditional political neutrality of the Civil Service and pledged that a Labour Government would subject top officials to a 'test of impartiality' (*The Times*, 4 November 1982).

Few civil servants supported the notion that officials were appointed to senior positions as a direct result of their 'sympathetic' political views. However, Clive Ponting (1986, p. 222), one of the more controversial figures to emerge from Whitehall during the 1980s, believed: 'She has not been content like many of her predecessors to accept the recommendations of the mandarins, but has instead looked for candidates she believes are sympathetic to her general aims'. Finally, the journalist Hugo Young (1989, pp. 162, 332) argued in his biography of Mrs Thatcher: 'the Whitehall culture was beginning to change . . . and was now in the hands of some senior people, each of whom could justly be described as "one of us".'

Despite the fact that, by the mid-1980s, the overt politicisation view was widely regarded as being out-dated and redundant, a few continued to champion it in the 1990s. For example, Bernard Crick, writing in May 1992, argued that:

> Mrs Thatcher's early populist assault on the higher Civil Service . . . Far from depoliticising it . . . politicised it to an appalling degree. Far from trimming the power of the mandarins, rather she put 'our sort of people' into key posts. (*The Guardian*, 7 May 1992)

Politicisation Mark II – Emphasis on a 'Management-Efficiency' Ethos

By 1985, most commentators adopted a different stance and one which presented a more subtle interpretation. This view of politicisation proved far more popular than the earlier, rather crude, notion. It was suggested that intervention in the appointments procedure occurred to promote a certain type of individual to the most senior ranks. Peters (1986, p. 41) outlined this position, arguing that the aim was to: 'push those she [Mrs Thatcher] believes to be dynamic, cost conscious and managerially inclined to top posts'.

The essence of this argument was that there had been an attempt to introduce a 'management/can-do' culture into Whitehall, through the accelerated promotion and outside appointment of certain individuals. Thus, McDonald (1992, p. 88) rejected any notions of overt politicisation:

> Yet for most people, as the decade wore on and as Mrs Thatcher's position within her own party began to weaken, the credibility of the politicisation charge began to fade as well . . . The fact is that the evidence for alleged politicisation was slight, inevitably based on rumour. Promotion has clearly not depended on the individual's ideological commitment during the Thatcher Governments any more than it did in the preceding years. No one's promotion has been held back or accelerated because of their political views. A certain style has been relevant. Civil servants who demonstrate the ability to take decisions and follow them through were more likely to succeed under the Thatcher Governments than those who consider all the difficulties and obstacles to such an extent that action and decision

do not take place. The emphasis is on subsequent implementation. Senior civil servants in the past would have considered that their work was completed once the minister had taken a decision, but they are now expected to ensure that something happens once the decision has been taken.

Much of the literature in this second category was inspired by the views of John Hoskyns,[5] in the aftermath of his departure from Mrs Thatcher's 'Policy Unit'. Hoskyns had become disillusioned by the slow pace of reform in the machinery of government and argued that essential changes were necessary to the framework of Whitehall.

At the time of Hoskyns's resignation from Whitehall, commentators began to notice the importance Mrs Thatcher placed, both on relationships with individual businessmen and academics from the 'monetarist/supply-side school' and the way in which the Policy Unit was operating. On this basis, they surmised that new appointments and promotions in the Service were being determined by a desire to promote a 'management-efficiency ethos'. This view firmly rejected the notion that any overt politicisation had occurred:

> There is no hard evidence that appointments have been based on the candidate's support for or commitment to particular political ideologies or objectives . . . The signs have been that gutsy young men who were not born to rule and did not go to public school are far more to her taste than the suave smoother-over of Whitehall legend. (Simpson 1989, p. 7)

Although Simpson did not substantiate this observation, he did conclude that:

> Allegations of this kind do not seem to have been made under previous governments. Even if such allegations are unjustified, some civil servants clearly believe that they are justified. That, in itself, is a cause for concern. The impression of 'political' appointments has been created. (Simpson 1989, p. 7)

Ridley (1983a, p. 195) illustrated the thoughts of this group, by rejecting the notion of overt politicisation. Instead, he contended:

> Mrs Thatcher's interventions are probably not party-political in the sense that such politicisation is found on the continent. She is more

likely to favour those she believes will be forceful in implementing her policies . . . It seems to be personality she judges and personal contacts also seem to play a role. She has her favourites and cannot get on with others.

Connell adopted a more general approach, concluding it was not about appointing political sympathisers, but rather selecting the *goodies* over the *baddies*; those who were willing to display an enthusiasm for the government's programme:

> What special qualities these goodies have is a nice point. 'Is he one of us?' is a favourite prime ministerial question, about everyone from a journalist to a backbench MP. But the signs are, with the civil service, that it is not political conviction so much as professional style and tough-minded enthusiasm that win her approval. (*The Sunday Times*, 11 July 1982).

Fry (1984, p. 330) broadened the debate, citing the dismissal of Lord Soames, the abolition of the Civil Service Department, the introduction of the Management Information System for Ministers and the Financial Management Initiative of 1982, as necessary steps to:

> Make the Civil Service as much like a business organisation as possible, and the dictates of sound money indicated the desirability of ending the division at the centre and formally restoring Treasury predominance.

A year later, Fry developed his own version of 'capture theory'; a theory previously used in the United States by economists and politicians to highlight the 'take-over' of independent regulatory commissions by the economic interests which they were supposed to regulate. He argued that the Civil Service had formed an institutionalised outlook, based on working with successive administrations and that 'governments were ill-equipped to govern'. Hence, the Civil Service felt the task of government should be performed by 'permanent politicians', i.e. themselves. They therefore reacted when Mrs Thatcher appeared to upset the existing status quo:

> The career civil service having 'captured', if in part by default, higher ground than constitutional theory allowed, did not seem to be always

gracious about conceding it to a Thatcher Government which, like its more co-operative predecessors was equipped mainly with slogans. (Fry 1985a, p. 547)

In this view, by altering the ethos of the Civil Service and effecting a culture change at the highest levels in Whitehall, Mrs Thatcher aimed to ensure that 'capture' became a redundant practice of a previous era. Such a change in culture was to be brought about by the appointment of positive, efficient managers at the most senior levels in Whitehall, in the hope that, their approach to public service would permeate the lesser grades. This was certainly the view Greenaway (1988, p. 43) adopted: 'More emphasis is placed upon entrepreneurial abilities and upon drive, initiative and managerial skills: there is correspondingly less demand for the "well-rounded" individual'. Here, Greenaway stressed Mrs Thatcher's desire to find implementors, doers, not those who wanted to spend the lion's share of their working day questioning the rudiments of her government's policies. Indeed, the general view of this set of commentators was that style, rather than political belief, was important. They argued that the style which appealed to Margaret Thatcher was a 'can-do' approach.

Meanwhile, Barberis's (1996a p. 140) longitudinal study of Permanent Secretaries of the twentieth century noted that there has been a change in the characteristics of Permanent Secretaries appointed during the 1980s:

> Intellectual rigour remains essential, even if the policy role with which in the past it was often associated is no longer quite so dominant. It is less dominant because the role of Permanent Secretaries has changed and because management has become increasingly important. This calls for technical qualities. It demands a more deliberate, systematic approach. This includes a broad familiarity with techniques such as accounting, operational monitoring and strategic planning.

Hennessy (1989, p. 116) also emphasised Mrs Thatcher's preference for officials well-versed in modern management techniques, noting that: 'the ethos of the senior Civil Service would be changed from a policy-making to a managerial culture when it became plain that the route to the top would be open to those who got most out of people and cash'. More recently, Hennessy (*The Guardian*, 18 January 1993) observed that:

There are relics like the concept of the 'good chap' when it comes to appointments, but a different type of person has arisen: the post-war generation of civil servants retired and there is an element of the entrepreneurial servant.[6]

One of the few civil servants to have served the Thatcher Governments, and who later published his recollections, was Leo Pliatzky, a senior Treasury official. Pliatzky (1989, p. 164) rejected the notion that Mrs Thatcher made overtly political appointments, instead arguing that she chose candidates for promotion with whom she had had contact:

> Margaret Thatcher takes a closer interest and has more say in the general run of these appointments than did her predecessors. Her choices are likely to be candidates personally known to her, which means that it is an advantage to have served a spell in No. 10 or the Cabinet Office, but she does come across other officials from the Treasury and other Departments. The private political affiliations or sympathies, if any, of candidates for appointments are not known or inquired about. They are not asked if they agree with the government's policies but are expected to deliver them.

It was implicit in Pliatzky's observation that those officials who worked close to her, and whom she later selected for promotion to the senior grades, were the type whose interests lay in doing the job asked of them, rather than in questioning the rationale behind a particular policy to be implemented. Terence Heiser (1994, p. 23), another senior civil servant to have publicly commented on the effects of Mrs Thatcher, concluded:

> If there has been a change in the composition of senior civil servants in the eighties, it may have been more in the type of individual selected from within the ranks for promotion in a world of greater visibility and pressure for rapid action – a tendency to choose what Mr. Waldegrave, the Minister for the Civil Service, has called 'a certain kind of personality on the Eysenck scale'.

Heiser believed that a more pro-active type of senior civil servant had been appointed to the most senior grades in Whitehall and that this trend, once established, was set to continue.

By the end of the Thatcher administration, commentators argued that a 'Thatcher effect' had occurred within the upper echelons of Whitehall. They believed she had implanted a 'management-efficiency ethos' at the highest levels in Whitehall, through the promotion and appointment of a certain type of individual. Since Mrs Thatcher left office there has also been considerable retrospective analysis of her involvement in the Civil Service appointments procedure. Kavanagh (1990, p. 252) felt that: 'Mrs Thatcher has been more concerned to reward senior civil servants who are "doers" – good at implementing policy, concerned with good management and value for money – rather than appoint more policy advisers'. While Theakston (1990a, p. 47) argued: 'she does not appear to have applied a partisan litmus test when making top appointments, but to have preferred a decisive and energetic "can-do" style'. Similarly, Drewry and Butcher (1991, p. 216) declared that:

> There is little overt evidence that the Thatcher government . . . is trying consciously to subvert the traditional neutrality of the Civil Service . . . At the same time, we also accept that absolute neutrality has probably become an unrealistic aspiration in an age of increasingly polarised party politics.

Dowding (1995, p. 124) develops this notion by arguing that Mrs Thatcher was drawn to officials who looked to solve problems at the policy formulation stage rather than find them. This was reinforced by Campbell and Wilson (1995, p. 296) who argue that, in the 1980s, the subordination of officials to politicians was greater than at any recent time.

One can conclude from the retrospective accounts of commentators that civil servants had to be committed and display enthusiasm for the Thatcher Government's programme, implying a 'hands-on, can-do' approach. This ties in with the findings of the most systematic attempt, to date, to assess Mrs Thatcher's effect on the Civil Service; the 1987 RIPA Report. Their investigation into the senior appointments procedure rejected outright any notion of 'overt' politicisation, but concluded that: 'the appointment process has become more personalised, in the sense that, the top level "catching the eye" of the Prime Minister (in a favourable or unfavourable manner) may now be more important than in the past' (RIPA 1987, p. 43)

Finally, Savoie (1994, p. 251), using the benefit of hindsight, advanced a slightly different interpretation. He argued that Mrs Thatcher made more use of the appointments procedure than her predecessors, not only to promote 'can-doers', but also to appoint more outsiders into the senior ranks of Whitehall. However, he did question whether or not, a new breed of mandarinate had emerged by the end of the decade:

> Thatcher sought to control the appointment process more closely than previous prime ministers had done, and to tap private sector expertise. She had ample opportunities to shape the senior levels of the British civil service since eleven of the twenty-three most important positions at the permanent-secretary level became vacant through 'natural' retirement between 1981 and 1983 alone. She also sought to add more 'grit' to the civil service by appointing 'doers' rather than thinkers. Thatcher carefully studied the list of potential candidates that the Cabinet Office put forward, and she rejected some. Whether the people she approved for appointment were markedly different from previous office holders, or from those who would be chosen by a different prime minister is, however, questionable.

Seeking Out a Modern Day 'Vicar of Bray'

Despite the fact that, even in the 1990s, the notion persists in both academic and media circles that some form of politicisation of the Civil Service occurred under Mrs Thatcher, the assertions lack detailed analysis. What is more, after eighteen years of Conservative Government the debate has been further widened. One needs to address the notion of whether or not the Civil Service can remain neutral and impartial, when a growing number of officials have only ever worked for and with Conservative politicians.[7] Hennessy labels this problem 'thought colonisation'.

The aim of this book is to unpack the whole notion of the politicisation of the senior Civil Service. It has been over six years since Margaret Thatcher left office, yet the evidence in this area has remained anecdotal and under-conceptionalised. Presenting a quantitative study of the 1980s will help to establish the extent to which accelerated promotion to the highest grades or appointment from outside Whitehall occurred. This analysis is then complemented by a qualitative survey of the views of the politicians and civil servants who were directly involved in the senior appointments procedure. The intention is to add substance to the assertions and anecdotal evidence which often pass for analysis in this field, and to answer more adequately the question: 'Did the modern day vicar of Bray appear in the ranks of the higher Civil Service during the 1980s?'

The first step is to put this systematic survey in its context. Thus chapter 2 examines the broader context of the Conservative Administration's reform of the Civil Service during the 1980s, and chapter 3 identifies the constitutional position of the Prime Minister, in relation to senior appointments in the higher Civil Service.

2

Evolution Not Revolution: the Reforms of the 1980s

'We are the masters at the moment and not only for the moment, but for a very long time to come'. Sir H. Shawcross speaking to the House of Commons during the third reading of the Trade Disputes and Trade Union Bill, 2 April 1946. (Cited in Butler and Butler 1994, p. 269)

An Evolution, Not a Revolution: the Switch from Effectiveness to Efficiency

A GENERAL CONSENSUS exists that in the 1980s Margaret Thatcher displayed a greater interest in the appointment of top officials in Whitehall than any other twentieth-century Prime Minister. In order to understand why she adopted such a high profile, an examination of her broad approach to the reform of the Civil Service is required. During her eleven years in office the appointment of a new breed of officials paralleled wider macro reforms of the Civil Service – what the Government called its 'grand strategy'.[1]

This chapter examines the increased dissatisfaction, after 1960, with the structure and operating practices of Whitehall, the attempts at reform by various governments before 1979 and the programme of restructuring implemented in the 1980s. The Thatcher Government's approach can be linked to previous reforms, but they also differ, particularly in the degree of political will which underpinned change.

From the 1960s, a common theme can be traced in the attempts at reshaping the operating procedures of Whitehall: an emphasis on what has been termed the 'three e's' – efficiency, economy and effectiveness. As such, the Thatcher reforms, which attempted to elevate 'efficiency' above the two other elements, should be regarded more as an evolution, than a revolution. A switch in emphasis from 'effectiveness' in the Heath and Callaghan years to 'efficiency' in the Thatcher era took place. Further, the higher profile Mrs Thatcher adopted in the appointment's procedures was linked to her grander scheme for Civil Service reform.

The Roots of Dissatisfaction: The Cult of the 'Amateur'

By the beginning of the 1960s, a common theme took root that there was a growing malaise in British public institutions, in what, increasingly, became a period of national re-examination. This was symbolised by the then Conservative Government which was perceived as being increasingly out of touch with the people it purported to represent; Party and Government had been rocked by the Profumo Scandal, the 'Night of the Long Knives' and shaken by the elevation of Alec Douglas-Home to Prime Minister. It was an administration which, it was widely held, was devoid of any new ideas after thirteen years in office. This increased national dissatisfaction did not bypass Whitehall, an institution which had never been overly receptive to outside criticism. The 'amateurish' status of the Civil Service came under sustained attack. Commentators believed Whitehall was failing to keep abreast with the pace of change, in what was becoming an increasingly complex and technologically advanced society.[2] Indeed, this problem was endemic in many of Britain's public institutions and was part of the underlying rationale for what became known as the 'white heat of technology' programme, introduced in 1964 by Harold Wilson and his newly elected Labour Government.

The first overt signal from the Macmillan Government that Whitehall was starting to fall behind in the tasks demanded of it came in 1961 with the publication of the Plowden Report. A Committee had been established in 1959, under the direction of Sir Edwin Plowden, to examine government control of public expenditure. The main thrust of the Committee's findings emphasised that the Civil Service devoted too much time to policy advice, at the expense of effective management control (a theme which was to become very familiar in Whitehall circles during the 1980s).

Fulton: Limits, Success, Failure and the Lessons Learnt

It was during the Wilson Government of 1964 that the flow of criticism of the functions and operating procedures of Whitehall

increased. Wilson was a renowned opponent of the social exclusiveness of civil servants and their amateur status. He was constantly
distracted in his work by a belief that any attempts at radical
change implemented by his Government would be undermined
in the corridors of Whitehall.

In February 1966, in an effort to counter Whitehall's amateur
status, Wilson announced to the House of Commons the establishment of a Departmental Committee of Inquiry into the Civil Service,
to be chaired by the then Vice-Chancellor of Sussex University,
Lord Fulton. From the outset, there were limits placed on the
committee's remit. In particular, it was made clear there would
be no investigation into the actual structures of the British central
system of government. As Wilson announced when setting up the
committee:

> The Government's willingness to consider changes in the Civil
> Service does not imply any intention on its part to alter the basic
> relationship between Ministers and Civil Servants. (House of Com-
> mons Debates 1966, p. 210)

In addition, the fact that the committee included four civil servants
meant that a constraint on truly radical change was in-built.

In June 1968, after two years of gathering evidence, the Fulton
Report was published. It made twenty-two recommendations. What
is most striking about the Report is the disparity between the
scathing findings of the Committee and the conservatism of its recommendations. The Report argued that the service was still imbued
with the nineteenth-century philosophy of the Northcote–Trevelyan
Report, that of amateurism. Whitehall was, therefore, unable to
consistently deal with many of the tasks demanded of it in the
second half of the twentieth century. It was critical of
the class system of Whitehall, in particular arguing that the work
of the 'specialist' was greatly under-valued. It was also scathing of
the Civil Service ethos:

> Too few civil servants are skilled managers . . . [administrators]
> tend to think of themselves as advisers on policy to people
> above them, rather than as managers of the administrative machine
> below them . . . Civil servants are moved too frequently between
> unrelated jobs, often with scant regard to personal preference or
> aptitude . . . There is not enough contact between the Service and
> the rest of the community. (Cmnd 3638: 1968)

The recommendations of the Report testify to the constraining influence of the mandarins on the committee. It proposed that the administrative class should continue, but be grouped into two categories: those specialising in economic or financial spheres and those involved in social administration. As far as recruitment was concerned, there was no requirement for a degree relevant to the job. Instead, a Civil Service College was to be established to improve training, but which would be under the control, and influence, of Whitehall. To oversee these changes a Civil Service Department was to be set-up, again staffed by civil servants and operating within the existing Whitehall system. Writing twenty years later, the ex-civil servant Clive Ponting (1986, p. 194) pinpointed the shortcomings of Fulton:

> The way in which Fulton was implemented, or in practice not implemented, is a superb example of the top civil servant's ability, whilst paying lip service to the concept of the Fulton Report, to subtly redefine questions in ways favourable to the administrators.

From its conception, Fulton was flawed. It lacked effective political clout from the Cabinet and, as such, it was open to manipulation by the insiders of Whitehall. However, a decade later the Fulton Report proved to be important to the Thatcher Government, in terms of the lessons it offered. Fulton had highlighted the imbalance in Whitehall between policy-makers and effective economic managers. As Drewry and Butcher (1991, p. 195) argued, the key theme of the Report was the promotion of efficiency:

> the higher Civil Service in particular tended to think of themselves as 'advisers on policy to people above them, rather than as managers of the administrative machine below them'. Fulton has been described as the 'high-water mark of managerialism', and as being imbued with a 'business-managerial philosophy'.

This theme resonated in the Thatcher reforms. The Fulton experience taught Mrs Thatcher the importance of having the right personnel in key positions, to ensure support for reforms and the need to apply strong political leverage, when undertaking any effective reform of the institutions and practices of Whitehall.

Heath Adopts The 'Effectiveness' Format

When the Conservatives, under Edward Heath, surprised many

by winning the June 1970 election, a new phase in reforming the 'instruments of government' commenced. In October 1970 a White Paper was published, entitled *The Reorganisation of Central Government*.[3] The establishment of the Central Policy Review Staff [CPRS], effectively a US-style 'think-tank', was the prime manifestation of this paper. For Heath, the rationale behind the CPRS was borne out of his experience in the Shadow Cabinet:

> he had been very struck that it was possible for the Shadow Cabinet to consider a strategy as a whole, to take a slightly longer-term view of things. But as soon as they became a Government, it was impossible to do that. And he had set-up the Think-Tank in order to remedy that. (Hennessy 1989, p. 221)

The White Paper was also responsible for establishing the Department of the Environment and the Department of Trade and Industry. It supported a system of accountable management and this was later reflected in the introduction of new arrangements for the scrutiny of policy formulation and implementation – the Programme Analysis and Review (PAR). PAR sought to assess the effectiveness (one of the three 'e's') of current departmental programmes and assess alternative options. Although PAR was dropped by the Callaghan Government in the late 1970s, its importance was in the signals it sent out – that the Heath Government was committed to maximising the effectiveness of the output of Whitehall. This was a theme which was to continue to run throughout that decade; it was supplanted in the Thatcher era by a greater desire for efficiency in Whitehall.

The Callaghan Years: Whitehall Overcomes its Critics

Due to the inflationary pressures facing the Callaghan Government, the Cabinet (no doubt persuaded by forceful arguments from such high profile Treasury officials as Leo Pliatzky) were persuaded to adhere to what had become a standard, Treasury, anti-inflationary tool, Cash Limits. This was to have obvious ramifications for Whitehall. In 1976 and 1977, the House of Common's Expenditure Committee, under the Labour MP Michael English, conducted a major investigation into the Civil Service. At this stage, Whitehall, with 747,000 employees, employed more personnel than at any time in the post-war period. This prompted the Callaghan Government to seek an economy drive, aimed both at shedding employees and saving money. The Committee's findings resulted in the cutting of 15,000 jobs and an estimated saving of £140 million by 1979. However, the report, which formally praised Fulton, lacked any penetrative analysis and, as one critic concluded:

> All the available evidence suggests that there had been virtually no significant change at all in the period since 1968 and that the old-style Civil Service dominated by the administrative amateur still flourished. (Ponting 1986, p. 196)

Fulton to Thatcher

During the period between Fulton and Thatcher, successive governments conducted their own reviews into the operating procedures of the Civil Service. Each new initiative adopted many of the *solutions* of its predecessor, but civil servants would normally be involved on the relevant committee. Thus, a pattern of reform was established in which the dynamic conservatism of Whitehall was always able to de-radicalise each committees' final recommendations. The major theme of reform in this era was the search for greater effectiveness and a desire to achieve targets set for Whitehall. A notable switch away from this occurred in the 1980s when efficiency became the hallmark of the Thatcher era. Yet, the 1970s was an important period in Whitehall reorganisation, not so much in terms of the tangible results achieved, but in the lessons it provided for the Thatcher Government. In 1979, her Government was elected with a mandate promising to reduce the role of the state and cut public expenditure. Drewry and Butcher summed up this change of emphasis:

> The developments of the 1980s are primarily concerned with efficiency, with the major focus on costs, rather than with the more elusive concept of effectiveness. There has been a shift of emphasis from what one civil servant has termed 'grand schemes' like PAR to ones which are predominantly management exercises. This shift reflects the changed context of civil service reform. (Drewry and Butcher 1991, p. 212)

The Reforms of the Thatcher Government

Mrs Thatcher can be regarded as the first post-war 'outsider' to rule Whitehall. Unlike her more recent predecessors, she had not previously been a civil servant and both her background and temperament produced a style which did not fit comfortably with the established working patterns of the Civil Service. Her party was elected on a Manifesto which promised to:

> reduce public expenditure and the role of the state, the government's policy towards the public sector was to make substantial economies by reducing waste, bureaucracy and 'over-government'. (*The Times Guide to the House of Commons*, 1979, pp. 282–94)

The Manifesto was grounded in New Right thinking, arguing the need for the more efficient management (read reduction) of the state. Thus, the Thatcher Government, driven by a strong anti-statist instinct, implemented a series of Whitehall reforms which have been widely referred to as New Public Management (NPM). Greer has categorised the features of NPM:

- a shift to disaggregation in public services organisation;
- a preference for limited term contract employment of senior staff over traditional career tenure; wholly monetised incentives rather than the traditional structure of control in the public sector through a mix of non-monetary factors (ethos, status, culture) and uniform fixed salaries; top managerial 'freedom to manage' over a network of constraints (notably by central personnel agencies) on action by line management;
- a divorce of provision from production (or delivery) in public service;
- an emphasis on cost cutting;
- a shift from policy management with the focus primarily on efficiency and cost of service delivery – leading to an emphasis on quantifiable methods of performance and investment appraisal and efficiency criteria; and
- a shift from process to outputs in controls and accountability mechanisms. (Greer 1994, p. 8)

It can be argued that NPM, encapsulated in the themes of cost awareness and management control, was an example of strategic learning by the Conservative Government based on the lessons of the previous decade – an era which had witnessed the introduction of cash-limits and a squeeze on departmental budgets. To this the Government added its own political goals:

> the regeneration of the economy through the reduction of the public sector and the exposure of the residual to competitive forces.

The successive Thatcher governments and undoubtedly the Prime Minister herself have therefore been interested in 'managing the Civil Service' as an adjunct to managing the state. (Gray, Jenkins, Flynn and Rutherford 1991, p. 46)

For Thatcher, the rationale behind reform was the perceived lack of managerial skills in the higher Civil Service; officials spent too long on policy-making and too little time on efficient management. The 1980s was a watershed for Whitehall; emphasis was placed on the introduction of business managers rather than policy-makers. This was compounded by the introduction of the Next Steps reforms in 1988; the establishment of agencies, with accountable Chief Executives, providing a service along similar lines to a business operating in the private sector. Next Steps was not a radical departure from earlier attempts at reform; rather, it was a reaction to, and consolidation of, past ad hoc attempts at change.

The Thatcher reforms demonstrate both continuity, with previous attempts at reform, and change, by introducing a new political agenda. From Raynerism to Next Steps, the Government was continually modifying the management system of Whitehall. For Mrs Thatcher, an important element of improving the efficiency of the Civil Service was the need to introduce a certain 'type' of individual to the highest tiers in Whitehall. It was hoped this would allow new operating procedures to permeate throughout the rest of the Service. As she commented:

> I took a close interest in senior appointments in the Civil Service . . . because they could affect the morale and efficiency of whole departments . . . I was enormously impressed by the ability and energy of the members of my private office at No. 10 . . . Those who came were some of the very brightest young men and women in the Civil Service . . . I wanted to see people of the highest calibre, with lively minds and a commitment to good administration, promoted to hold the senior posts in the departments. (Thatcher 1993, p. 46)

This is a crucial element in the political legacy which the Thatcher government bequeathed its successor.

The Seeds of a 'Grand Strategy' – Raynerism

Two years prior to the 1979 election, a former civil servant, Leslie Chapman, published *Your Disobedient Servant*,[4] which was largely an account of inefficiency in the Property Services Agency. The book brought the subject of bureaucratic waste onto the political agenda. Mrs Thatcher adopted a number of themes from Chapman's book when formulating her broader strategy for *rolling-back-the-state*. She proposed a cut in the number of officials and public employees, in order to reduce public expenditure (in May 1979 the total size of the Civil Service was 732,000).[5] Her programme also aimed to promote efficiency and to aid her in this she appointed Derek Rayner, the joint managing director of Marks & Spencer, as a part-time, unpaid adviser. He was allocated a small Efficiency Unit in the Cabinet Office in order to conduct a series of in-depth 'scrutinies' into various aspects of departmental government work. One member of the Efficiency Unit was Clive Priestley. In an interview, he described to me the composition of the unit:

> On the 8 May 1979 I was working in the Civil Service Department (which was subsequently abolished in 1981). I was there as a Grade 5 official and I was summoned over to see Sir John Hunt, Sir Ian Bancroft, Sir John Herbecq and Sir Derek Rayner and was offered the post of Sir Derek Rayner's Chief of Staff. He was to be the Prime Minister's Adviser on Efficiency and Waste. His little unit comprised a Chief of Staff, an Under Secretary, that was me. We inherited an Economic Adviser from Harold Lever because we took over his rooms in the Cabinet Office and with it a man called David Allen, on secondment from the Treasury. We also had one personal secretary and one Executive Officer. That was called the Rayner Unit, subsequently the Efficiency Unit. When the CSD was abolished in 1981, most of it was transferred to the Treasury which is what we had been fighting for, for two years, but a small rump of the department was established as the Management and Personnel Office. The Efficiency Unit was located temporarily in that office and part of my job, as official Head of the Efficiency Unit, was to take on the management of what was called the Management and Efficiency Group. This group had a number of Assistant Secretaries in it. (Priestley interviewed, 14 November 1994)

The Efficiency Unit's objectives were clear; they were to undertake a series of scrutinies and provide:

> critical examination, to a tightly controlled timetable, . . . of a particular policy, activity or a specific aspect of organisation in central government, with a view to reducing the cost of administration

and increasing efficiency and effectiveness, especially by cutting out unnecessary work. (Allen 1981, pp. 10–16)

Rayner appointed civil servants, rather than outside consultants, to carry out the efficiency studies. John Cassels argues this was an important, but correct, decision:

> I think Rayner was very shrewd in having them [scrutinies] done by civil servants, because he understood perfectly well that if you get civil servants to do them it was infinitely preferable to getting in consultants. He relied on departments and people acting on his behalf, i.e. Clive Priestley and his minions, to be sure that they did choose ambitious people, and then these ambitious people did their studies. Although, in form, the whole thing was frightfully constitutional, everyone knew that if Rayner supported the outcome of the report, Margaret Thatcher would also and so someone had better do something about it. My own view of that was that it did get some changes done, but there was a huge element of fraud about it as well. (Cassels interviewed, 20 December 1994)

When questioned on what he meant by a 'huge element of fraud', Cassels replied that the scrutinies became an invitation for people to 'show-off' and to be rather sweeping in what they recommended. However, he also stressed the importance of the message:

> There was no magic here: civil servants are good people who, given their head can do just as good a job as anyone – perhaps even better. The fact that the scrutiny officers were part of the culture, made it far harder to resist their recommendations, or to argue that they just did not understand the issues properly. (Cassels interviewed, 20 December 1994)

Cassels makes a very important point here. It is implicit in his comment that the strategy Rayner felt most appropriate for successfully delivering results was one of divide-and-rule. Rayner actively fostered a culture within the Civil Service of different units competing against one another. This was a lesson Margaret Thatcher drew upon when she oversaw the introduction of the FMI and Next Steps.

When the scrutineers were sent out to the various departments, they were detailed to ask three simple questions of each department examined; What is it for? What does it cost? What value does it add? By December 1982, when Rayner had decided to return full-time to Marks & Spencer, 130 scrutinies had been conducted which had produced £170 million savings, with £39 million once-and-for-all savings and a further £104 million of possible economies identified. In terms of personnel, the targeted figure for cuts had been surpassed, the number of Whitehall posts being reduced by 108,000.[6]

Later, as Hennessy noted, Rayner conceded the Unit would have had only a marginal impact if it had not been for: 'the unique political imperative created by Mrs Thatcher, as support for the initiative was not extensive among other ministers or at the highest echelons of the Civil Service' (Hennessy 1989, p. 595). He continued: 'The Rayner experience was similar to the Fulton reforms in that both demonstrated how vital is the patronage of the Prime Minister: Wilson lost interest; Thatcher did not'.

Yet, despite this political clout and the seemingly impressive statistical results, the scrutinies were not a total success. Clive Ponting was less than thrilled by Raynerism, but, ironically, was later awarded an OBE for his scrutiny of the MoD. He argued that, similar to previous attempts at reform, Whitehall had absorbed Raynerism. He felt Rayner had underestimated the ability of Whitehall to 'fudge' implementing reports it believed were detrimental to the Service. He argued:

> The classic Whitehall response follows a fairly predictable sequence. The department will generally welcome a report, argue that a detailed study is required, and then set up a committee report on possible implementation of the proposed changes. Those responsible for the existing, criticised system will be well represented on this committee and psychologically opposed to major changes. After a few months a report is produced saying that some, but not all, of the proposed changes should be workable but need further study. A number of sub-committees are convened to look at all these detailed areas, there are difficulties about implementation and possibly more studies are needed. After a couple of years, everything has been so reduced to questions of detail that the general problem has been largely forgotten. A few minor changes can be implemented as the 'first steps' towards the full reform package. Gradually the whole process grinds into the sand of bureaucratic inertia and little, if anything, is achieved. (Ponting 1986, p. 214)

Ponting's view, though arguably jaundiced, touches on the limitations of the scrutinies. This was confirmed by a 1985 Efficiency Report which concluded that the scrutinies were not the unparalleled success at first thought:

only half the planned savings had been made and even then they had taken twice as long as expected. Officials have been actively opposed to carrying out the studies, and the so-called action-plans have usually only been little more than a time scale for taking decisions in the future with no commitment to change anything. Whitehall has seen the whole process as one of 'damage limitation', implementing as little as possible but just enough to avoid the accusation of outright obstruction. (*The Guardian*, 1 November 1985)

Furthermore, others questioned the universal application of Raynerism across the whole of Whitehall. In particular, some felt it an unnecessary exercise to carry out scrutinies in smaller, policy-oriented departments. Thus, Donald Maitland, a Permanent Secretary at the Department of Energy, then one of the smallest departments in Whitehall, argued that:

Pressure was being exerted from the centre to reduce costs and increase efficiency. A Chain of Command Review and the scrutinies conducted by Sir Derek Rayner and his team were important instruments for reform. However, central initiatives which could produce substantial benefits in large departments with numerous executive functions were not necessarily suitable for small policy-oriented departments. These might in any case have their own ideas for improvement. (Maitland 1996, p. 242)

However, Clive Priestley defends both Rayner and the scrutinies, believing they were a justifiable exercise. He argued that Rayner specifically turned his back on a 'cosmic solution', unlike Fulton or Chapman's *Your Disobedient Servant*. Instead, Rayner felt that, firstly, the 'scrutinies' would provide evidence, be it positive or negative, about administration. They would indicate what bright young officials were capable of, given a time limited remit of ninety days to:

go into something, turn it upside down and come up with a solid practical report and recommendations. The first round provided the Cabinet, in October 1979, with the incontrovertible evidence from a series of parables, that changes needed to be made. Second, he wanted a permanent cultural change. That depends absolutely on two things – people and systems. (In part, the 'people' are a system too. One thing we never felt we succeeded in, was a general message to staff that they were valued. Provide high moral through good conditions, reasonable pay and a sense of value for doing important work. There was quite a lot of scepticism, if not resistance, up to June 1982. The 'systems' side has gone off in kangaroo bounds as it has turned out). General Galtieri was the turning point, making the Prime Minister's personal authority unassailable. (Priestley interviewed, 14 November 1994)

In addition, Priestley did not underestimate the importance of the support the scrutinies received from Margaret Thatcher. He claimed this was a vital element in guaranteeing full-scale, Whitehall, observance. Indeed, he commented on how she hosted two evening parties for the scrutineers, in order to foster team spirit and let the rest of Whitehall know she was serious about change:

> The critical fact was that Margaret Thatcher was genuinely interested in these matters and was prepared to stick at them. One of the signals she tried to send to the Service was that she *did* mean this. She had two parties for the scrutineers during 1980. This was her playing the system at its own game. The second party was held to show that she really was serious about reform. The point about those parties was very much about her sending a signal to Whitehall about her strong attachment to the whole reform process. (Priestley interviewed, 14 November 1994)

Undoubtedly, the scrutinies did make a number of major economic savings, whilst also introducing a more cost-conscious atmosphere to Whitehall. However, the fact remained that the scrutinies' broader goals were not achieved. Officials, at the highest level in Whitehall were unwilling to embrace the findings. Raynerism facilitated a climate for further change, but, in terms of logistics, it fell short of its own goals. Its failure was in its scope; it had no mandate to examine the individuals who were to be in charge of implementing the scrutinies' findings. Even Priestley accepted that on its own, Raynerism was not enough. He commented:

> She appointed, in Rayner and Ibbs, a high quality, small staff which was intended to be the oyster that brought her ideas. One of the ideas that Ibbs obviously brought to her was that: 'It was not working. We have quite a lot of good things going, we are making a lot of savings, economies are coming along quite well, but we are not getting the necessary systemic change. Let us have a scrutiny of Raynerism, if you like.' On these grounds, one could never conclude that she sat

somewhere and dreamed that all up herself, because she did not. (Priestley interviewed, 14 November 1994)

It was obvious to all those who had been involved in this first stage of reform that something greater than Raynerism was needed.

The Financial Management Initiative

In 1982, the Government launched the Financial Management Initiative (FMI). The initiative was conceived by Michael Heseltine, whilst he was Minister in the Department of Environment (DoE). Three years earlier, Heseltine had introduced a Management Information System for Ministers (MINIS) at the DoE, which aimed to inform him of 'who did what, why and at what cost'. MINIS was accompanied by Joubert – an organisational structure that apportioned the DoE into 120 'cost centres', each with an annual budget to cover running and staff costs. This enabled the minister to compare actual expenditure with planned expenditure and conduct systematic budget reviews. Heseltine argued MINIS improved both the efficiency and the effectiveness of the DoE and, subsequently, he introduced it to the Ministry of Defence, when head of that department. Yet, Whitehall gave Heseltine's initiatives an indifferent reception and other ministers displayed little interest in introducing similar information systems to their own departments. Heseltine (1987, pp. 16–20) later testified to this:

> on one memorable occasion, I was asked by the Prime Minister to give my colleagues an account of how MINIS was helping the DoE to put its house in order. My fellow Cabinet Ministers sat in rows while I explained my brainchild, each with his sceptical Permanent Secretary behind him muttering objections, or so I suspected. Any politician knows when he is losing his audience's attention, and I knew well enough. When I had done, there were few takers and absolutely no enthusiasts.

However, the one key department which did support Heseltine's scheme was the Treasury. The Treasury and Civil Service Committee, in its 1982 *Report on Efficiency and Effectiveness in the Civil Service*, was:

> highly critical of the absence of any clear orientation towards the achievement of efficiency and effectiveness at the higher levels of

the Civil Service, and of the limited attempts to set operational objectives, measure outputs and results, and thus to guide the proper use of resources. (Drewry and Butcher 1991, p. 204)

The Committee recommended that an equivalent of MINIS should be introduced to all departments. This formed the basis of the Government's 1982 White Paper announcing the FMI.[7] The aim was to extend MINIS and Joubert to all government departments. Thus, the paper called for wholesale reorganisation and a new style of management, based on devolved authority and accountable management. The aim was to:

promote in each department an organisation and system in which managers at all levels have:
(a) a clear view of their objectives and means to assess and, wherever possible, measure outputs or performance in relation to those objectives;
(b) well defined responsibility for making the best use of their resources, including a critical scrutiny of output and value for money; and
(c) the information (particularly about costs), the training and the access to expert advice that they need to exercise their responsibilities effectively. (HC 1982b: 5,21)

Thirty-one government departments were required to assess their operating procedures and develop techniques to improve financial management. They were not required to adopt a standard approach. Each department came up with their own variation of MINIS, the DoE blueprint. For example, the Department of Energy introduced DEMIS, the Department of Trade and Industry produced ARM, the Ministry of Agriculture, Fisheries and Food had MINIM and the Lord Chancellor's Department adopted LOCIS. A small central body was established to oversee and guide the progress of these initiatives; originally known as the Financial Management Unit, it was later replaced by the Joint Management Unit (JMU). A process of decentralised, budgetary control was also introduced. Departments were divided into 'cost centres' and managers were introduced, who were accountable for budgets allocated.

The Cassels Report: A Need for a New Breed of Skilled Manager?

These macro reforms – new management information centres, a

decentralised style of budgetary control and increased accountability – were all targets of the FMI. Yet, this alone was not
enough:

> without a new breed of skilled manager. Consequently, FMI is being
> complemented by a set of improvements in personnel management,
> based in part on the Cassels Report of 1983, including improved
> career management and training for those with potential to rise to
> senior positions.[8] (Drewry and Butcher 1991, p. 206)

The implication was obvious; Mrs Thatcher was not comfortable
with initiating reform schemes in Whitehall, whilst paying no attention to the officials directly involved in their execution. Drawing on
the experiences of both Fulton and Rayner, she instigated a review
of the personnel side of management. Alongside the introduction
of the FMI, a review by the Management and Personnel Office was
set up to examine personnel work within the Civil Service. The
review was co-ordinated by John Cassels, the department's Second
Permanent Secretary, and the report he published was regarded as
a blueprint for the future conduct of personnel management in
Whitehall. The review's brief was to examine all areas of personnel
work, ranging from recruitment, redundancy, staff movements and
career management, in order to identify new methods with which
to improve individual performance targets. The Report drew on
evidence from nine major departments and its conclusions were
sweeping:

- staff to be appointed to jobs and not grades;
- increased job transfers with industrial and commercial managers;
- merit pay awards to reward individual effort and initiative;
- line managers to be allocated more responsibility and authority
  over personnel matters; and
- inefficient staff to be dealt with more swiftly.

Many commentators regarded the report as the beginning of the end
for the traditional appointments procedure. *The Times* (26 November
1986) commented that:

> High-flying civil servants . . . are to be given performance related
> increments to prevent them being tempted to jobs in the private
> sector. The change . . . is in line with the Government's philosophy
> that pay should be related to profit, performance and productivity.

Civil Service unions argued that this represented a further shift towards the widespread privatisation of duties in Whitehall. The Levene appointment in 1984, soon after the report was released, certainly inflamed the situation: Michael Heseltine appointed Peter Levene, the Chairman of United Scientific Holdings, as Chairman of Defence Procurement in the MoD. Pyper (1991, p. 115) argues that:

> this was the most significant and controversial example of a growing number of secondments to the top levels of the Civil Service, which challenged the traditional appointment procedures overseen by the Civil Service Commission . . . Levene had been appointed with a salary of £95,000, twice the normal rate for this post, without reference to the Commission.

Although individuals were occasionally seconded to Whitehall from outside, a number of the appointments made following the Report prompted some interested parties to suggest that a form of 'creeping politicisation' was occurring. However, these appointments, supervised by the Senior Appointments Selection Committee, were supported by the House of Commons Select Committee on the Treasury and Civil Service[9] and the Royal Institute of Public Administration (1987, p. 61). They found no irregularity in the functioning of the appointments procedure:

> only about two per cent of the members of the Senior Open Structure are 'outsiders' temporarily brought in to fill particular vacancies. Whitehall is too cautious in this respect. More could be done centrally to liaise with business, universities and the rest of the public sector to seek out talent. More Civil Service posts should be publicly advertised, and applications for them encouraged from the existing civil service and from outside Whitehall.

In an interview with John Cassels, I asked whether there had been a vital need for personnel change in light of the structural reforms Whitehall was undergoing at that time. Also, whether his report aimed to introduce a cultural change in the Civil Services operating procedures? Cassels replied that, at the time, the work he was involved in was very much an attempt to modernise the approach towards personnel management in the Civil Service. That included the ability to understand what the FMI was about and how to implement it. The phrase he used to describe his project was 'to produce a more professional Civil Service'. He argued that for a long time the Civil Service had been extremely professional about the handling of parliamentary business which had enhanced the effectiveness of ministers. However, Cassels felt where the Civil Service had been less effective was in being professional about the subjects it dealt with.

I asked whether or not by 1983, following a series of structural changes since Fulton, personnel was out of step with the newly developed machinery of Whitehall? He believed that was the case, arguing that:

> I am one of those who feel the Civil Service wasn't as good as it thought it was. It was really alarming how poor they were and quite a lot of things they should have been better at. Above all, they were professional at the politics of it but unprofessional at the realities of it and especially uninterested at implementation. The Civil Service is bad at implementation and always has been, because clever chaps can think up policies all the time, but find it dreary to apply them. We have never been good at doing that. We are always making mistakes. Look at the National Curriculum, that is a Civil Service shortcoming, as much as anything else. It is the politicians who have taken the blame for it, but it was just badly done. (Cassels interviewed, 20 December 1994)

Cassels then went on to argue that the Civil Service was top heavy with policy-makers and lacked 'hands-on' implementation. He also noted that there had been an earlier, failed, attempt at personnel reform which had occurred under the guise of the Civil Service Department.

> Setting up the Civil Service Department had been a formalised attempt at that, but it turned out to be a complete fiasco. Rather surprisingly as well. I had nothing to do with it, but at the time the CSD was set up, I thought 'thank goodness, personnel work could be done so sketchily and badly by the Treasury, and it was about time this problem was addressed'. By the time I came on the scene, the CSD had come to look as though it were a vested interest, looking after the material welfare and privileges of civil servants and not being about an efficient, well-trained, professional Civil Service. That is how it seemed and that is how I guess it looked to Mrs Thatcher. (Cassels interviewed, 20 December 1994)

I also questioned Cassels about the selection of the nine departments to be examined. In particular, why the central and highly influential departments of the Cabinet Office, the Treasury and the Prime Minister's Office were excluded from those chosen? The implication here was whether or not there was a political agenda involved in the choice of the nine departments selected for examination and why these three core departments had been omitted. Cassels replied:

> I thought they would be pretty hard nuts to crack, but that it wasn't particularly important to tackle those hard nuts. One was interested in big departments, with larger personnel problems. I thought it was more important to get on with the big departments, which had a job of implementation and doing things. I said, at the very start, I think the Civil Service is bad at implementing things. It can easily pick up policies but is bad at implementing things. If they [the Cabinet Office and Treasury] had wanted to resist it, they would not have managed it. Anything Rayner wanted, he could get. Everyone knew that. Now, why I mentioned this was because of the dangers of that and one says 'have these been transferred higher up to the way people have been appointed at the top'. I don't think so. I think the way that appointments were made, while Thatcher was there, was within the bounds of what an ambitious, active and wilful Prime Minister could properly do. I don't think she ever stepped over the line. (Cassels interviewed, 20 December 1994)

Whether or not the Cassels Report was responsible for legitimising a new era in Civil Service appointments through the introduction of a new breed of official, it certainly aroused suspicions that the traditional patterns of promotion were not necessarily any longer the norm. Indeed, a serving official in the Senior Civil Service Group, accepted that:

> In the 1980s, the Civil Service placed much more emphasis on personnel development, actively seeking individuals with the ability to manage change. There had been a shift away from, what in the early 1960s would have been termed policy-makers, high intellectual types, to those with good interpersonal skills, competent runners of organisations, able to manage staff. People still needed high intellectual qualities but they do also need the managerial and interpersonal skills. Therefore, the individual sought after, is one capable of managing change and running a staff.

The FMI: a Stepping Stone for Next Steps?

Despite the two-pronged attack involving both institutional reforms in Whitehall and a review of the personnel responsible for the implementation of reform, the question has to be asked: was FMI only the foundation for further grandiose reform schemes? Not surprisingly, the official line was that the FMI was a welcome breakthrough in reform, even a watershed. The Comptroller and Auditor General felt that:

> departments consider that the visible benefits of their FMI systems have included greater cost-consciousness at all levels of management and the MDR of budgeting cites many examples of administrative cost savings arising from management action inspired by the improved information and the constraint on resources imposed by a tightly drawn budget. (HC, 1986: 588)

Outside commentators also praised the FMI and the earlier scrutinies as a success: 'the first eight years of Raynerism represented . . . a formidable achievement in absolute terms as well as in comparison to anything that had gone before' (Hennessy 1989, p. 619). Even the Permanent Secretaries displayed signs of enthusiasm for the reforms. Hennessy (1989, p. 619) recalls a conversation with one of the most influential mandarins of the era. On the topic of the FMI, this Permanent Secretary declared:

> I never realised what an effort it would be turning this tanker around. But over the past year it has become clear that it [the FMI] will endure. If there was a change of government, we would still want to do it for our own purpose.

Despite this, there were those who were less willing to praise the initiatives. Metcalfe and Richards (1987, p. 131), who undertook one of the most detailed studies into the reforms of this period, argued that long-term, effective, management reform was not just a matter of introducing new operational techniques and systems. Reform of Whitehall also had to take account of a deeply entrenched culture:

> the, often unspoken, set of assumptions about their role within which senior civil servants think and act. [A culture] . . . where writing a well constructed ministerial brief on a topical subject

or steering a Bill through Parliament has a higher value . . . than implementing a new policy or improving the administration of an existing policy.

The Civil Service unions argued it was contradictory to ask managers to be fully accountable for their spending, whilst allowing them little or no control over determining what the size of the budgets should be. They argued that the FMI's downfall, in relation to the demands of the government, was:

> the allocation of real money to managers . . . But giving them real money would, of course, mean giving them real power down the line – the last thing that the central departments, or, for that matter, departmental-level managements, would contemplate. So we are left with the usual half-baked Civil Service compromise. Civil Service managers have all the rigours and disadvantages of developed power, without being allowed to exercise the power. (Bulletin 1985, p. 17)

Whether or not it can be argued that the FMI stands on its own as a step forward in Civil Service reform, it certainly broke new ground. It encouraged a greater cost-consciousness by individual departments and, with it, the greater economies which the Government demanded. It also provided officials with a clearer view of policy objectives. The Cassels Report had attempted to address the issue of personnel changes in relation to these reforms. FMI signalled the first moves towards a programme of decentralisation for Whitehall, which were later to reach fruition in the Next Steps reforms. As Barney Hayhoe, the then Minister for the Civil Service, concluded, the FMI meant:

> a push to greater decentralisation and delegation down the line . . . will represent a highly significant change in the culture of the Civil Service . . . Recruitment, training, promotion, prospects and practice will all be affected. (HC 1982a: 918)

The efficiency scrutinies, MINIS, Joubert and the FMI can be regarded as the heirs of Fulton based on the principle of economy. FMI was not a period of revolution for Whitehall, but of piecemeal change. A shift away from the previous emphasis on effectiveness. The culmination of these changes provided the foundations for the Government's largest scheme of reform – the 'Next Steps'.

Building on the Past – the Next Steps

The Next Steps Report was compiled under the guidance of Sir Robin Ibbs and involved the interviewing of over 150 ministers and senior civil servants. The Report was seen as a further development of the FMI, but on a far grander scale. Yet, its roots can be traced back to Fulton, where the idea of separate executive units had been discussed but never implemented (Cmnd 3638: 1968). The main objective of the Next Steps was that the central Civil Service should be reduced in size to: 'a relatively small core engaged in the function of serving ministers and managing departments, who will be the 'sponsors' of particular government policies and services' (Jenkins, Caines and Jackson 1988, para 44). All other services performed by Whitehall were to be hived off in the form of executive agencies, operating along similar lines to that of a company in the private sector.

The Evolution of Next Steps

In November 1986, Ibbs instructed three members of the Efficiency Unit – Kate Jenkins, Karen Caines and Andrew Jackson, to work on a project to:

- assess the progress achieved in improving management in the Civil Service;
- identify what measures have been successful in changing attitudes and practices;
- identify the institutional, administrative, political and attitudinal obstacles to better management and efficiency that still remain; and
- report to the Prime Minister on what further measures should be taken.

The team conducted a series of interviews with ministers, top civil servants, central and local government officers and members of the private sector[10] to gather information on various means of improving efficiency.

By the beginning of 1987, a report was presented to the Prime Minister, which, due to its sensitive nature, was kept secret until after the June election of that year. The Report's two main themes emphasised the limited effectiveness of post-1979 attempts at Whitehall reform and the need for major constitutional and managerial reform.

The Findings of the Report

The Report was highly critical of the time many top civil servants devoted to policy formulation to the detriment of effective and efficient management. It argued that senior Civil Service management: 'is dominated by people whose skills are in policy formulation and who have relatively little experience of managing or working where services are actually being delivered' (Jenkins, Caines and Jackson 1988, para. 4). The Report also questioned the existence of a unified Civil Service as an effective framework in which to conduct government business:

> the Civil Service is too big and too diverse to manage as a single entity. With 600,000 employees it is an enormous organisation compared with any private sector company and most public sector organisations. A single organisation of this size which attempts to provide a detailed structure within which to carry out functions as diverse as driver licensing, fisheries protection, the catching of drug smugglers and the processing of Parliamentary Questions is bound to develop in a way which fits no single operation effectively. (Jenkins, Caines and Jackson 1988, para. 10)

The Report recommended that, where appropriate, agencies be established to undertake the executive functions of government:

> The aim should be to establish a quite different way of conducting the business of government. The central Civil Service should consist of a relatively small core engaged in the function of servicing ministers and managing departments, who will be the 'sponsors' of particular government policies and services. Responding to these departments will be a range of agencies employing their own staff, who may or may not have the status of Crown Servants, with clearly defined responsibilities between the Secretary of State and the Permanent Secretary on the one hand and the Chairman or Chief Executive of the agencies on the other. Both departments and their agencies should have a more open and simplified structure. (Jenkins, Caines and Jackson 1988, para. 44)

Given that the Report's authors estimated that over 95 per cent of the work of the Civil Service centred on the delivery of government services, their findings implied a fundamental challenge to the existing framework of Whitehall.

Implementation – The Report Catches On

On 18 February 1988, Mrs Thatcher announced to the House of Commons the Government's reaction to the Next Steps Report. She argued that the Government had ruled out any possibility of constitutional changes in relation to ministerial responsibility and were adamant that the Treasury would maintain overall control of budgets, manpower and income bargaining. The Prime Minister also announced the appointment of Peter Kemp, then Deputy Secretary in the Treasury (and an individual who had spent 15 years in the Treasury), to the post of Second Permanent Secretary in the Office of the Minister of the Civil Service. It appeared that any hint of radical change in Whitehall would, once again, be appropriated by dominant, conservative Treasury forces. Writing in *The Independent*, Clive Priestley offered an unenthusiastic response to the Government's reaction:

> the report shows that even after seven years of Prime Minister-led reform, 'management' has not yet caught on generally in the echelons of the Civil Service. The distinction between 'policy' and 'management', although not unique to Whitehall, has a peculiar strength there. Ministers' lack of interest in management is echoed by many Parliamentarians, much of the media and, alas, much of the public. (Priestley 1988)

Surprisingly, despite these signs, Next Steps rapidly caught on in Whitehall. Peter Kemp proved he was by no means a 'Treasury mole' and, under his guidance, with strong backing by the Prime Minister, change began to take shape. On 1 August 1988, the first Agency was set-up, the Vehicle Inspectorate. By the end of 1990, twenty six Agencies had been established, involving 60,800 officials, comprising more than 11 per cent of the Civil Service. By April 1996, these figures had risen to 109 executive Agencies, involving over 350,100 civil servants, comprising 71 per cent of the Civil Service. In an attempt to ensure that the dynamism of the reforms was not quelled, a sub-committee of the Commons Treasury and Civil Service Committee was established and has subsequently met regularly to inquire into the progress of the Next Steps Programme. The new agencies, once established, guaranteed that the programme of reform, in contrast to its predecessors, was not likely to falter. The National Audit Office, after completing an investigation into the project in May 1989, concluded that:

Generally, the National Audit Office consider that the Project Team (Jenkins, Caines and Jackson 1988) have carried out their role in relation to the launching of the Next Steps initiative in an energetic, well-organised and effective way. Generally, too, departments have responded to the initiative and set-up arrangements and policy and resources frameworks in a sensible way. Clearly, though, much will depend on how their relationships with the new Agencies evolve in future. (HC 410: 13–14)

Altering the Framework and Operational Patterns of Whitehall

Unlike previous attempts at Whitehall reform, Next Steps clearly produced more than a simple, cosmetic change to the face of Whitehall. In an interview with a retired Civil Service Commissioner, he concluded that:

If you are looking at the structure of the senior Civil Service, I don't think you can ignore the introduction of Agencies. They have very much affected the nature of the senior people advising ministers. I would say that is one of the most significant changes to the Civil Service, since perhaps the Northcote–Trevelyan reforms. It seems unfortunate to me that it has been done without Parliamentary legislation. But if you are talking about the type of people now involved at the highest levels in the agencies, I think you will find a great deal of them come from the private sector. So you have got this infusion of people from outside.

There is still some way to go before all the goals of Next Steps are realised, yet, as Clive Priestley informed me, the changes of the 1980s are firmly established and still shaping the Civil Service of the 1990s:

The astonishing thing is the pace of reform has not slackened. The machinery is still there. The FMI has taken strong root and is now expressing itself in terms of what was thought of elsewhere at least 25 years ago. The Efficiency Unit is still in place and John Major has introduced the Citizen's Charter Unit and the Market Testing Unit. Systemic reform in the personnel of the Civil Service is now, of course, expressed through the 1993 *Oughton Report* and the 1994/95 White Papers *Continuity and Change*. Meanwhile, *The Citizen's Charter* is Major's personal thing and is very much in line with Raynerism. This is unique, in that you have continuity from one Prime Minister to another, in the reform of institutions and systems of government. So, although the style is different, the substance is the same. (Priestley interviewed, 14 November 1994)

The reforms have produced tangible effects both for the Civil Service and the functioning of British Government as a whole. Chapman (1992, p. 4) pinpoints the most notable consequence of the reforms; the threat of decentralisation which he argues is a product of increased managerial autonomy:

> The lesson seems to be that the British Civil Service, as a distinct institution of the public service, identifiable primarily through an authoritative and/or legal definition, no longer exists. If others claim that it does, can they reasonably point to unifying characteristics to sustain their claim? How can such an institution be so identified if it has flexible methods of selection of staff; or has different staff grading and pay structures; or different conditions of service for staff employed in a large number of independent or quasi-independent departments and agencies? In some cases, pay is not even dependent on moneys voted by Parliament. Moreover, throughout the system, if system it is, there is positive encouragement of staff to identify with their independent units rather than with the service as a whole; and there is encouragement, too, for staff to discard their anonymity and exercise management enterprise and initiative on their own account.

Metcalfe (1993, pp. 363–4) further develops this theme, arguing that five key issues have arisen from Next Steps. First, it is hard to envisage that the development of the agencies can continue to evolve within the existing framework of ministerial accountability. At present, a grey area exists in defining the responsibilities of a Chief Executive and those of the Permanent Secretaries in relevant departments. Indeed, this view was backed up in an interview with an official from the ECGD:

> So much has now gone out to Executive Agencies and they have largely an executive job to do. We have lost those days when you had the key policy-makers also running the big executive functions, within a large department. That opens some new questions about the role of the Permanent Secretaries and higher civil servants in what is left of the policy making departments, as distinct from the Executive

Agencies. The Executive Agencies will presumably roll on under a new administration.

Second, it is debatable whether the traditional pattern of 'joint-problem solving' between departments can continue. Metcalfe argues that increased managerial autonomy may encourage agencies to 'sub-optimise'. These are problems of both accountability and co-ordination. There is also a question as to whether:

> agencies are specifically intended to implant a business culture or whether they simply represent a divisionalisation of existing departments in order to achieve the benefits of specialisation that accrue from decentralisation? (Metcalfe 1993, p. 364)

This raises the further question as to the degree to which the existing Civil Service Code is under attack. An official from the Department of Energy made this very point:

> I think the current reforms are extremely worrying. I think there is a danger of destroying the existing code and with it the Civil Service ethos. You are going to have to separate departments, you are going to have people with an alien culture, which raises questions of accountability and also, I think, standards. Whether it has gone too far or not, I am not sure.

There is also a problem of attaining a balance between centralisation and decentralisation. With the Next Steps reforms, this tension occurs between decentralised management within the agencies and the maintenance of tight central monetary control imposed by the Treasury. Finally, the question arises: is there one standard 'model' agency? A 'business management model' is not necessarily always the most appropriate model for certain agencies. There is an enormous diversity between agencies; for example in size alone the Wilton Park Conference Centre has a staff of thirty, whilst the Social Security Benefits Agency has over 65,000 employees (Hogwood 1993, p. 5).

However, despite the fact that the Next Steps reforms are still far from complete, they have produced a sea-change in the structure and operating procedures of Whitehall. While Fulton was tamed by the dynamic conservatism of the Civil Service, the 1980s reforms and in particular, Next Steps, have radically altered attitudes within the service. As Metcalfe (1993, p. 352) concludes:

Management methods, concepts, models, and values have been accepted as an integral part of the way the business of government is conducted. Whether they are the right management concepts is open to debate, but then acceptance goes much deeper than almost anyone thought possible in 1979. It is difficult to imagine these reforms being reversed . . . Without suggesting that a total transformation has occurred or that the changes have been completely successful. It is increasingly clear that a fundamental shift has been made which will have a permanent influence on the functioning of British government.

A New Agenda for Change

The increased interest Margaret Thatcher (1993, p. 46) accepts she paid in the appointment of top officials in the Civil Service can be regarded as a direct corollary of the NPM reforms Whitehall underwent during the 1980s. Intrinsic to the success of NPM was the need for a new breed of official to counter the omnipotent, dynamic conservatism civil servants had displayed in de-radicalising all previous attempts at reform.

If one traces the various attempts at Civil Service reforms, which governments have undertaken from Fulton through to the Next Steps, a common theme resonates throughout: the emphasis on what has been termed the '3e's' – efficiency, effectiveness and economy. The Thatcher reforms elevated efficiency above economy and effectiveness. However, the 1980s reforms should be regarded as a period of dynamic evolution in Whitehall, not revolution. Most importantly, previous reforms taught Mrs Thatcher a series of strategic lessons, which helped ensure her own approach would not encounter the same resistance as in the past.

The most common theme from Fulton to Thatcher was that officials devoted too much time to policy advice, at the expense of effective management control. An imbalance existed between policy-makers and effective economic managers. The Fulton experience taught Mrs Thatcher the need to: install the right personnel in key positions; ensure support for her reforms; and maintain strong political support for the changes. As Kate Jenkins, one of the members of the Efficiency Unit and co-author of *Improving Management in Government: The Next Steps* (1988), informed me:

I think she [Mrs Thatcher] gave us political backing and that was very important. She was essentially *our* Minister . . . It was

undoubtedly the case that everyone we interviewed knew we had the
Prime Minister's backing. (Jenkins interviewed, 2 October 1996)

Up to the 1980s, officials had consistently been able to appropriate
any attempts at reform and re-style the agenda to suit their own
terms. Mrs Thatcher addressed this problem by introducing a new
approach to implementing change. She avoided direct confrontation
with the Civil Service, instead applying the principal of 'divide-and-
rule'. She set departments against each other, with each competing
to carry out her changes. This created rivalry and, in so doing,
ensured that the initial dynamism of reform was neither lost nor
undermined. Hence, although a number of parallels can be drawn
with the attempts at reform from Fulton to Callaghan, the 1980s
differed largely in the more strategic methods used to implement
change. The net effect of this for Whitehall in the 1990s is that the
agenda for reform has radically altered: 'In future the questions will
be about what forms of public management are appropriate rather
than whether management, as such, is relevant to government'
(Metcalfe 1993, p. 352).

3

Appointments to the Highest Grades in the Civil Service – Drawing the Curtain Open

For in the case of nutrition and health, just as in the case of education, the gentleman in Whitehall really does know better what is good for the people than the people know themselves. (Jay 1947, p. 258)

Top Appointments in Whitehall – a Procedure Cloaked in Secrecy

IN 1987, the Royal Institute of Public Administration published a report on its own investigation into top promotions and appointments in the higher Civil Service.[1] In its introductory passage, the Report stated that:

> The group criticises the excessively 'private' nature of the procedures for appointing and promoting senior civil servants – the secrecy which enshrouds them and the absence of any external monitoring or evaluating capacity. (RIPA 1987: i)

Constitutionally, it is known that the Prime Minister, on the advice of the Head of the Home Civil Service, approves all appointments to the top two grades in the higher Civil Service. Presently, it is the Head of the Home Civil Service, in the recent past also the Cabinet Secretary, who makes the final appointment, having listened to the views of the Senior Appointments Selection Committee (SASC) and the minister of the relevant department in which the appointment is to be made. One of the fundamental problems for the political scientist examining these procedures is the secrecy in which they are shrouded. Even RIPA's own report into top appointments, which received the unofficial blessing of the then Cabinet Secretary Robert Armstrong, conceded that:

> Apart from brief references to the need for the Prime Minister's approval and the existence of SASC, procedures at the top of the service are shrouded in secrecy: Only those directly involved in the process know exactly how and why decisions are taken. Consequently, the account that follows of the operation of the SASC system describes only in general terms our understanding of current senior promotion practices. (RIPA 1987, p. 25)

Their Report devotes only thirteen pages to these procedures and accepts that some of the information is based on speculation. Elsewhere, writing on this subject is sketchy and, in some cases, misinformed. The most eminent, general works on the modern British Civil Service – Drewry and Butcher's *The Civil Service Today* (second edn 1991), Hennessy's *Whitehall* (1989), Theakston's *The Civil Service since 1945* (1995) and Campbell and Wilson's *The End of Whitehall* (1995), either say nothing or devote only brief passages to SASC. None have provided a detailed account of the processes at work in appointments to the highest two grades in Whitehall. The problem has been the limited, official information available and the reluctance of those who have been involved to accurately detail what actually occurs.

This chapter is devoted to the top appointments procedure and is divided into two sections. Part One is an authorised account of the procedures which are put into operation when a post falls vacant at either Grades 1 or 2. This can be read as the 'official view' of the top appointments procedure.[2] Part Two makes use of information from interviews with a number of senior officials who, during the 1980s and 1990s, were involved in the appointments procedure. The aim is to piece together what actually occurs in what remains a highly secretive area of Whitehall proceedings.

Present-day procedures reflect the Government's decisions on the recommendations of the Efficiency Unit report on *Career Management and Succession Planning* (the Oughton Report, 1993), the White Paper *The Civil Service: Continuity and Change* (1994), the Treasury and Civil Service Committee's *Fifth Report: The Role of the Civil Service* (1993–94) and the second White Paper *The Civil Service: Taking Forward Continuity And Change* (1995). These recommendations have produced an increased professionalisation in the system of personnel management in Whitehall. However, the procedure for top appointments has not changed a great deal since the early 1980s. The main actors involved in these top appointments are still the Prime Minister, the Head of the Home Civil Service, the Senior Appointments Selection Committee, the Civil Service Commissioners and the Office of Public Service (previously the Management and Personnel Office). This chapter examines the role and functions of these bodies and presents a chronology of the procedures involved when a vacancy occurs at Grades 1/1a in the Home Civil Service.

Part One: The Authorised Version

Chatting Behind Closed Doors – The Senior Appointments Selection Committee

In 1968, Fulton proposed that a committee should be established to assist the Head of the Home Civil Service in his duty to appoint officials to the top two grades in the higher Civil Service. Although Fulton's proposal was not implemented in the manner in which the Report had recommended, a Civil Service Memorandum to the House of Commons Expenditure Committee in 1976 indicated that:

> In July 1968, with the Prime Minister's approval, a committee consisting of a number of senior officials, including senior professional civil servants was set up to assist the official Head of the Home Civil Service in making his recommendations to the Prime Minister for the filling of home Civil Service vacancies at Deputy Secretary level and above. The committee has met monthly since. (HC 1976–77, 535, II, p. 2, para 7)

This committee was called the Senior Appointments Selection Committee (SASC). In Autumn 1996, the composition of SASC was:

> *The Chairman* – Robin Butler, Secretary of the Cabinet and Head of the Home Civil Service.
> *The Body* – Four or five of the most senior Permanent Secretaries in Whitehall. Membership of the Committee is not *ex officio*, but based on the personal qualities of the individual and his/her standing within the Whitehall community. An individual normally stays on the committee until his retirement. Terence Burns

– Permanent Secretary, HM Treasury, Anthony Battishill – Permanent Secretary, Inland Revenue, Richard Wilson – Permanent Secretary, Home Office, Richard Mottram, Permanent Secretary at the MoD.

An Outsider – Sir Michael Angus – Chairman, Whitbread plc.

A Woman – Valerie Strachan, Chairman, Board of Customs and Excise.

The First Civil Service Commissioner – Sir Michael Bett. Once SASC has decided whether a particular post should be filled through open competition, rather than by internal selection, the Commissioner's role is to oversee open competition for senior posts. The post is held by the equivalent of a Grade 1 official who, following the Government White Paper *The Civil Service: Taking Forward Continuity and Change* (1995), will in future probably be appointed from outside the Civil Service.

The Secretary – Mr Brian Fox, Head of the Senior Civil Service Group, Cabinet Office/OPS and Senior Secretary to SASC.

The Relevant Permanent Secretary – The Permanent Secretary of the department in which the vacancy has arisen will attend (but only temporarily), as well as the Permanent Secretaries of other candidates who are being considered for promotion.

SASC is chaired by the Head of the Civil Service and the individuals who sit on SASC do so at his invitation. Their official role is to give advice. The Permanent Secretary of the department in which the vacancy is to be filled will also be invited to join the Committee, if he or she is not already a member. SASC acts solely in an advisory capacity to the Head of the Home Civil Service. The Cabinet Office/Office of Public Service supplies a secretary to SASC, normally a Grade 3 official.

When examining a vacant post SASC have to decide whether it should go to 'open competition', or whether it should be made from within the department. Subsequently they:

> look strategically at the senior staffing position across the Service in the light of discussions which take place with the Heads of Departments and the Principal Establishment Officers. They examine the succession plans for the most senior posts and the adequacy of succession and career development management arrangements. When a vacancy arises, and on the basis of the succession planning material, SASC considers the relative merits of civil servants for promotion to posts at Grade 1 and 2 level and advises the Head

of the Home Civil Service on the candidates to be recommended under the procedures described above. They are guided by a detailed description of the job to be done, a specification of the qualifications, skills and experience required for the post, and an analysis of the candidates including their annual appraisal record of performance and achievement. (TCSC 1994, p. 12)

Keeping the Door Ajar – The Civil Service Commissioners

The origins of the Civil Service Commission (CSC) date back to the Northcote–Trevelyan Report. The Commission was established to:

> prevent political patronage moving in a reverse-flow into the Civil Service . . . It has operated on the basis of Order in Council ever since, and answers to the Queen, not the Prime Minister, as an institutionalised guarantor of merit and probity against the corrupting forces of political favouritism and patronage. (Hennessy 1989, p. 371)

The Commission's *raison d'être* is to maintain the principles of open and fair competition, with selection to the Civil Service being based on merit. In its own internal brochure, the Commission states:

> The Commissioners are appointed under the Royal Prerogative, not under statute, as part of the Executive. They derive their powers from the Civil Service, and Diplomatic Service, Orders in Council, 1991. The Orders promulgate the government's general policy in respect of entry to the two Services – no appointments may be made unless selection has been carried out 'on merit on the basis of fair and open competition'. All appointments are made by Ministers, or on their behalf. In respect of certain defined grades the Orders provide that the Commissioners' approval is a precondition of appointment; the Commissioners base their approval on the knowledge that in each case selection has been conducted in accordance with the policy. The Commissioners act independently of Ministers when giving or withholding approval in individual cases, and are personally answerable for the decisions they reach. The Commissioners report annually on their work to the Queen, not to Parliament, and their report is published. (Internal; Civil Service Commissioners 1993, p. 1)

The First Commissioner sits on SASC, in order to ensure that this principle is maintained. The CSC's chief weapon is the 'certificate of qualification', which is required by all individuals in the senior Civil Service and which only the Commission can grant. In the 1980s, this resulted in a number of conflicts between ministers and the Commission.

In 1991, two new Orders in Council were made, one for the Home Civil Service and one for the Diplomatic Service. The Orders cover areas of responsibility involving 95 per cent of recruitment to the Service. At the same time, the Civil Service Commission was relocated to the Office of the Civil Service Commissioners and, under Next Steps, the Recruitment and Assessment Service (RAS) was created. The role of the Civil Service Commission is being reconstituted. Up to January 1995 its role was to:

> oversee the open competitions for senior posts once SASC has decided that a particular post should be filled through open competition rather than by internal selection . . . The OPS/Cabinet Office works closely with CSC on recruitment policy, including that of senior appointments. But the Civil Service Commissioners are independent, and if a post goes to open competition the CSC oversee that competition, including chairing a selection board, and makes a recommendation. That recommendation will invariably be accepted by SASC and by Ministers.[3]

However, in the light of the Government White Paper *The Civil Service: Taking Forward Continuity and Change* (1995) it has been given new functions. In future the CSC will replace the Cabinet Secretary as an independent 'court' of appeal for any civil servant wishing to report an alleged breach of the Civil Service Code, or who wants to speak on an issue of conscience. To facilitate this, in future the First Civil Service Commissioner will be appointed from outside the Service.

The influence of the First Civil Service Commissioner has also been increased:

> the First Civil Service Commissioner will, in future, attend the Senior Appointments Selection Committee . . . (He or she) will be able . . . to comment directly to the Minister concerned or to the Prime Minister on the choice between open competition and internal appointment. In the Commissioner's Annual Report, he or she will be able to set out the balance between open competition and internal appointment in filling senior civil servant vacancies, comment as necessary on the development of senior selection processes, and

draw attention to any ministerial decision which, should it ever arise, appeared to him or her to depart from the principle of selection on merit. (Cmnd 2748: 1995, p. 7)

In addition, the Commissioner's remit has been broadened. In future, they will be responsible for:

> the interpretation of the principles of fair and open competition on merit for all Civil Service recruitment – not, as now, only for senior appointments . . . The Commissioners will also be responsible for approving all appointments from outside the Civil Service to the new Senior Civil Service.[4] (Cmnd 2748: 1995, p. 7)

Succession and Career Plans: What is Involved?

Since 1968, when the Fulton Report called for an expanded and unified central management body for the Civil Service, there have been five incarnations of such a body – The Civil Service Department (CSD) 1968–81, the Management and Personnel Office (MPO) 1981–7, the Office of the Minister for the Civil Service (OMCS) 1987–92, the Office of Public Service and Science (OPSS) 1992–5 and, presently, the Office of Public Service (OPS). The most recent body, the OPS, is part of the Cabinet Office and brings together:

> the responsibilities of the former Office of the Minister for the Civil Service, including the Next Steps programme, with the units responsible for the Citizen's Charter, Efficiency and Market Testing. Its principle, relevant aims are 'to raise the standards of public services, including the privatised utilities, and to make them answer better to the wishes of their users' and 'to improve the effectiveness and efficiency of central government'. (TCSC 1994, p. lxxxviii)

The Senior and Public Appointments Group is located within the OPS. It has responsibility for co-ordinating the annual 'career plans' and 'succession plans' made by each department for specific posts and individuals. These plans were first introduced in 1983 on the recommendation of the MPO. From the outset:

> succession plans were regarded by the MPO as a valuable management tool, indicating a 'short list' of people who, after an annual review of their promotion potential, would be thought qualified or suited to future vacancies. (McDonald 1992, p. 93)

At present, the Head of the Senior and Public Appointment Group (a serving Grade 3 official) reports to SASC on the details of these plans and also acts as Secretary to the Committee. This group is at the centre of personnel planning for the Senior Civil Service.

In theory, 'succession plans' aim to identify potential successors to particular posts, in order that they can receive, in advance, the proper training and experience. The 1993 Oughton Report, *Career Management and Succession Planning Study*, presented a detailed account of what was involved in the making of 'succession plans':

> Each year, departments conduct a succession planning exercise to assess the future staffing needs of each department at its senior levels and the supply of people to meet these needs. They identify staff with potential for further promotion, check people are being developed to enable them to fill likely future jobs effectively, and identify people who might benefit from a move either within a department or between departments, or to some outside organisations. For this purpose, departments are asked to assess staff already in Grades 2 and 3 and staff in the feeder grades, and map out their human resource development plans, making available information to the Cabinet Office (OPS) each Autumn.

This process involves the following arrangements:

(a) *Promotability*
    The promotability of all staff in Grades 2, 3, 4 and 5 is assessed each year. Some people can be assessed as 'promotable within a year' or 'very likely later to be promotable' or 'not listed'. Staff in grades 4 and 5 are listed if they are considered 'promotable now or within a year'.
(b) *Longer term potential*
    Departments are asked each year to identify their high potential achievers in Grades 2, 3, 4, 5, 6 and 7 who are likely to merit early advancement and timely development opportunities to fit them for such advancement.
(c) *Succession plans*
    In addition to succession plans for any of their posts which any department may make, every autumn, departments are required to produce and send to OPS succession plans for all Grade 2 posts, for Grade Principal Establishment Officer (PEO) or Principal Finance Officer (PFO) posts, for other Grade 3 posts, with significant resource management responsibilities,

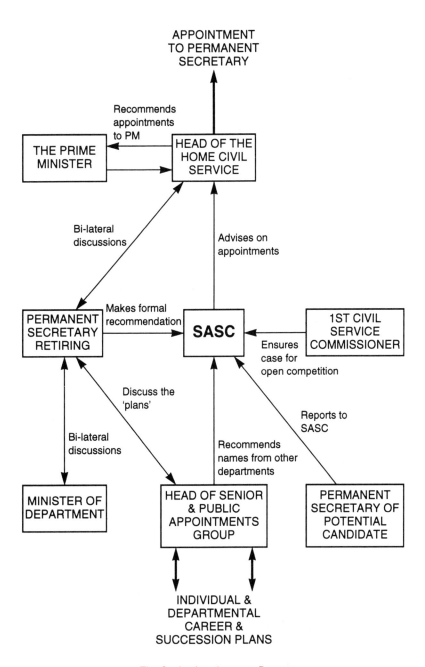

The Senior Appointments Process

or which are likely to be difficult to fill, and for Agency Chief Executive and senior Agency posts at Grade 3 level and above. Departments are required to identify an emergency successor, next normal successors, and, more generally, later successors. While the plans are no more than possible future options, and do not represent a settled or irrevocable decision – they are merely management's current intentions or options – where departments judge this appropriate, there should be a shared understanding between the department and the individuals concerned about both the plans and the main areas of development necessary to fit an individual for possible or likely future postings. Succession plans may, of course, also identify the option of running an open or limited competition for a future vacancy or seeking someone on secondment.

(d) *Bilateral discussions*

Following receipt of the succession plans the senior Secretary of SASC (Head of the Senior Civil Service Group) each winter visits each PEO and Permanent Secretary. The aim is to discuss succession plans and other issues about the management of staff in the Senior Open Structure, including from Grade 7 level upwards proposals for interdepartmental movement for development or for structural reasons, or to give someone a new challenge.

The extent of disclosure of the contents of any of these future plans is at the discretion of each Head of Department, subject to the general guidance on openness contained in the appraisal guidance and the presumption under this and equal opportunities law that procedures and criteria should be transparent and well understood by all concerned as possible. (Efficiency Unit 1993, pp. 114–15)

In 1993, all departments undertook formal succession plans for: every job at Grades 1 and 2; all key jobs at Grade 3; about 50 per cent of jobs at Grades 4–5; and only 15 per cent of jobs at Grade 6. For that year there were no succession plans held for Grade 7.[5]

To complement the 'succession plans', each department is expected to make 'career plans'. These apply to all officials mentioned in the 'succession plans', unless that official is aged 55 or over. These also include any official at principal level or above who has been identified as a 'high-flyer'. The rationale behind the career plans is to: 'note the individual's past experience, areas of work for which he or she is particularly suited and take a forward look at postings and training needs' (RIPA: 1987, p. 30). Following the annual 'milk round', normally conducted between December and March, the Senior Civil Service Group will co-ordinate the information presented in both the 'succession plans' and the 'career plans'.

When a post falls vacant at the top two grades, the major actors who are involved in the selection process are the Head of the Home Civil Service, SASC, the OPS, the CSC and the Prime Minister. The diagram below portrays the relationship between these various bodies:

'Sir Humphrey is Leaving, What is to be Done?'

This section presents a chronology of the sequence of events which occur when a post falls vacant at Grades 1/1a in the Home Civil Service:

Stage One - The Permanent Secretary retiring will discuss his succession in detail with the Head of the Home Civil Service, after which the Permanent Secretary will then make a formal submission to the Senior Appointments Selection Committee. He will specify: what he regards are the qualities required for the vacant job; the challenges in the future; the needs of the senior team; and whom he believes would be well-suited to the post. The Permanent Secretary will take account of the 'succession plans', which are updated once a year (normally in March). He will then discuss with an official from the Cabinet Office/OPS, the succession plans for the Senior Civil Service, who may also suggest some additional names from outside the department. These are individuals who have been identified as high-flyers in departmental succession and career plans. On this basis, using career and succession plans, the Permanent Secretary will then compile a list of names of those individuals he feels are suitable for the vacant post. The list varies in length, depending on the post to be filled. The norm is between three and eight names, but typically six or seven names are presented.

Stage Two – SASC review and discuss the individuals on the list. At this stage the retiring Permanent Secretary has already consulted with his minister on any preferences he has and any input he wishes to make. In particular, attention is paid to whether or not the minister has a strong aversion to working with any individual. However, the Minister's views are only a consideration and, even if he is strongly opposed to working with a certain individual on the list, it does not mean that that person's name is necessarily deleted. SASC also receive a full curriculum vitae on the relevant individuals and their annual 'assessment and personal qualities reports'. They will conduct a series of discussions about the individuals. If any problems come to light concerning a person on the list, the Head of the Home Civil Service will undertake a series of bilateral talks with the relevant actors in order to smooth out the whole process. He will then return to SASC, with the problem normally resolved.

Stage Three – Following the SASC consultation stage, the Head of the Home Civil Service will then determine his final recommendation to be presented to the Prime Minister. It is the recommendation of the Head of the Civil Service and his alone. All the other outlets – SASC, Permanent Secretaries, the Civil Service Commission, the OPS and Ministers – are there only in an advisory capacity. The Cabinet Secretary will send a written submission to the Prime Minister, providing qualifications and details (but not the career and succession plans), of normally two or three suitable candidates for the vacant post. He will also make a recommendation. It is only at this stage that the views of the Prime Minister are officially sought.

Stage Four – If necessary, the Prime Minister and the Cabinet Secretary will have an informal discussion on the various choices. At this stage, the candidate for the post is chosen. The Prime Minister's role is to approve or reject the recommendation of the Head of the Home Civil Service. This is a peculiarly British process: the Head of the Home Civil Service cannot make an appointment without the approval of the Prime Minister, but the Prime Minister cannot approve an appointment which has not be presented to him/her by the Head of the Home Civil Service. They therefore need each other.

The chronology of events described above represents the official version provided by the Office of Public Service of the process involved when a post falls vacant. They regard these procedures as a well-oiled, efficient and a fair means of ensuring that the *crème de la crème* of senior officials are selected for the highest grades in Whitehall. In an interview, one of their officials argued that:

> In the early 1980s, the succession plans were not as professional as they are now. The present system would stand up to strategic planning of any large, successful, private sector company like Marks & Spencer.

However, the procedures outlined above do not mirror the views of the individuals I interviewed. Thus, Part Two deals with their perception of the 'reality' of the top appointments procedure, examining what occurs in practice when a post falls vacant.

Part Two: The Top Appointments Procedure in Practice

SASC . . . is the institutionalised embodiment of the 'old boy network'. Shared assumptions and values are very important, if not indeed critical, to its activities. Those who believe in it see it as the only way of doing an essential job – by sceptics, as completely anomalous in a modern personnel management system and a modern democracy. Operating at the centre of Whitehall, behind closed doors, its membership until recently unpublished, unsullied – unlike the Civil Service Commissioners – by any non-official member, SASC is a powerful symbol of the traditional Civil Service. SASC also reflects the confidence of the Civil Service as a profession in its own judgements about its own future and about the national interest, and about the congruence between the two. Its formal meetings are now supplemented by informal lunches hosted by the Head of the Civil Service. (Plowden 1994, p. 41)

Reality Departs from Theory

The above quote from William Plowden, an ex-government official turned academic and Whitehall watcher, encapsulates the environment in which SASC, actually operates. Whitehall is a tightly-knit community, especially as one goes further up the bureaucratic ladder. The reality of top appointments is that, behind closed doors, a degree of subtle influence takes place, in order to try to ensure that any individual who is appointed to one of the top two grades does not *upset* the rest of that community. Therefore, when analysing the village community 'in action', one must distinguish theory from practice. Officially, when a senior vacancy falls open, the machinery for top appointments is triggered and the Prime Minister's input is limited to the final stage of negotiations. However, official theory rarely reflects practice. Indeed, if it did, then the commentators who believed Margaret Thatcher took an over-active role in the top appointments procedure would have had little evidence to support their arguments. The key to understanding top appointments is to appreciate the relationship between the Prime Minister and the Cabinet Secretary.

Unpacking the Top Appointments Procedure: The Relationship between the Cabinet Secretary and the Prime Minister

Two vital elements in the senior appointments procedure are the character of the Prime Minister and the relationship she or he has with the Head of the Home Civil Service. These two factors directly bear upon the top appointments process and the way in which it functions. For example, the two scenarios described below highlight the importance of this relationship and the differences that can arise:

Scenario One: If a Prime Minister adopted a passive attitude towards the top appointments procedure, believing it to be the domain of the Civil Service and thus, regarded the Prime Minister's function simply as a rubber stamp, then SASC would be the dominant actor in the process. It would be in their jurisdiction to determine the short list of individuals whom they believed most suited to the vacant senior post. They would then send their Chairman, the Head of the Home Civil Service, to consult the Prime Minister, with his recommendation as to the best equipped candidate and simply allow the Prime Minister to officially approve that recommendation. The Chairman would then return to the corridors of Whitehall to formalise the appointment.

Scenario Two: If the Prime Minister felt it was his or her responsibility to take a direct, pro-active role in the process and it was clear that the Prime Minister had a strong preference for a particular individual, or type of individual, then the whole process would take on a distinctly different character. First, when SASC sat down to discuss the short list of six or seven names, derived from the recommendations of the retiring Permanent Secretary and the Head of the Senior Civil Service Group, the Cabinet Secretary would remove the name of any person on that list of whom the Prime Minister disapproved. Thus, despite the fact that at this stage, theoretically, the Prime Minister has no input into the process, he or she has already had a indirect, but very tangible, effect. Of course, such indirect influence is dependent on the Cabinet Secretary knowing the thoughts and views of the Prime Minister he serves. However, this can be taken as read. By its very nature their association is close, based on a day-to-day experience of working in direct contact with each other. The officials I interviewed were all adamant that the Cabinet Secretary would be aware of the Prime Minister's line of thought, through their many daily conversations. An official from the Office of Public Service clearly makes the point:

> Prior to this stage, the views [directly] of the Prime Minister are not gauged, but obviously in working closely with the Prime Minister, the Head of the Civil Service will be aware of any general views his master may hold.

The relationship between these two central actors altered following the 'retirement' of Sir Ian Bancroft in November 1981, after which the post of Cabinet Secretary and Head of the Civil Service were combined. This placed the new Head of the Civil Service in the contradictory position of being the agent for his organisation, whilst also undertaking a role as the Government's spokesperson in Whitehall. By fusing the two jobs the most senior official in Whitehall has been put in the unenviable position of serving what, at times, can prove to be two conflicting masters. However, as Plowden (1994, p. 110) observes:

> Ultimately, the Cabinet Secretary is the servant of Ministers. He is the quintessential insider. He is, in particular, also the government's chief trouble-shooter, the man who fixes the machine to help them steer out of difficulty. As champion of the Civil Service, he is bound to find himself, at the very least, inhibited. His Cabinet Secretary's hat is a couple of sizes bigger than his Head of the Civil Service hat, and can easily hide it from view.

The second, vital difference in the top appointments procedure, in the case of a pro-active Prime Minister, concerns the stage at which the Cabinet Secretary seeks his Prime Minister's approval for the appointment of an individual from the short list of two or three names. The passive Prime Minister would regard it as his or her function to rubber stamp the recommendation of the Cabinet Secretary. The pro-active Prime Minister may, in some circumstances, reject outright all three names on the short list; and instead provide a preferred list of individuals. The Cabinet Secretary would then have to return to SASC for further discussions and a mutually acceptable compromise candidate would be sought. To date, no Prime Minister or Cabinet Secretary has 'officially' gone on record, declaring that an impasse in discussions has been reached, whereby the parties involved could not find an acceptable candidate. However, since this process was first inaugurated, there have been a number of occasions when the system's wheels have needed a large amount of 'lubricating' in order to ensure that the whole process has not gone off the rails, possibly resulting in a constitutional crisis.

These two different scenarios represent two opposing poles concerning the roles of the major actors involved in the top appointments procedure. However, having interviewed a number of key officials involved in this process, it appears that these characterisations do not misrepresent the reality. For example, certainly in his second term in office, Harold Wilson was renowned for his paranoia over Whitehall as an institution, which he believed to be hostile to his Government's programme. Nevertheless, he failed to influence the make-up of the personnel at the highest levels. In 1974, it was generally felt he would take a close interest in senior appointments, but, as Clive Priestley commented: 'What one recollects at the time is that Harold Wilson lost interest in Civil Service management' (Priestley interviewed, 14 November 1994). He adopted a passive attitude toward the top appointments procedure. This could be partly explained by the fact that Wilson was an ex-civil servant who was regarded by some as a Permanent Secretary manqué. However, the overriding explanation of Wilson's passivity was his reluctance to 'take-on' the Civil Service.

His successor, James Callaghan, paid closer attention to senior appointments, as the evidence he gave to the TCSC indicates:

> I took considerable interest in this, perhaps because I have known a lot of people in the Civil Service in my official capacity . . . The degree of interest would depend on my knowledge of the persons involved. If I did not know them I would be willing to accept the advice of people who did know them . . . If somebody was put up to me to become Under Secretary in the Ministry of Agriculture and I had no idea about the three people who had been put up I would choose the one recommended which had already gone through the permanent secretary in the department and a small group of permanent secretaries who knew these people together with the Civil Service Department . . . I do not think I ever overruled them. If they were aware of my interest and knowledge I think they were a little reluctant to make a recommendation; they would put the facts in front of me and ask 'What do you think?' I cannot say I ever overruled them. I do not think that happened. (Treasury and Civil Service Committee 1986, q.725–728)

During his political career, Callaghan had served in the three 'great' Departments of State: the Treasury, the Home Office and the Foreign Office. Thus, when being consulted on a vacancy as Prime Minister, he would have often known the individuals concerned, from one of the departments in which he had worked. This gave him a deeper pool of knowledge than Wilson upon which to draw and was reflected in his greater input into the senior appointments process. He was, however, instinctively conservative and one witnessed this in the degree to which he accepted the recommendations presented to him.

In the case of Mrs Thatcher, evidence suggests she took a much closer interest than her nearest predecessors in the appointments procedure. In her own memoirs (Thatcher 1993, pp. 48–9) she argues that there was little point in trying to change the existing bureaucratic structures, as they were too deeply entrenched. Instead, her attention centred on the encouragement of certain types of individual within Whitehall. Mrs Thatcher's own approach is dealt with in detail in chapter 6, so at this stage I will not dwell on her role. However, if one were to take the two opposing polar 'types' of Prime Minister described earlier, then Harold Wilson would be located close to the 'passive' pole, James Callaghan would be situated somewhere near the centre and Margaret Thatcher close to the 'pro-active' pole.

Interviews conducted with mandarins who have been directly involved at the centre of the top appointments process, stress the importance of the relationship between the Cabinet Secretary and the Prime Minister. Their comments, in many cases made unwittingly, augment the general perception that Whitehall, particularly at the highest grades, is a very insular, closed community, shut away from the public glare. In addition, the appointments procedure, despite the recent innovation of introducing an outsider on to the board of SASC, still reinforces this isolation from the outside world.

When I questioned Peter Kemp on this subject he painted a clear picture of the cosy world in which an official is selected for a top post. In an interview, I suggested to him that, theoretically, the Prime Minister only had an input in the appointments procedure, once the Cabinet Secretary had compiled the short-list of two or three names and that the Prime Minister simply said 'yes' or 'no'. Yet, this was not reflected in the actual practices of Whitehall:

Of course, I was never a member of SASC, but I am sure formally speaking that this is what is meant to happen. But the way the top of government works in practice, given the way No. 10 and the Cabinet Office are connected by corridors, the fact that people talk together an awful lot, and the fact that the last two Cabinet Secretaries, Robert Armstrong and Robin Butler, have both been Principal Private Secretaries to the Prime Minister they served, means that, not surprisingly, the whole process becomes very much personalised. You can imagine that they get to the end of an agenda, get out the whisky and, while having a quiet drink, the Prime Minister may say: 'By the way Robin, I see so and so's post is soon to be vacated, X is a nice guy, has worked for me in the Cabinet Office, I wouldn't mind that sort of name coming forward'. Of course, this sort of exchange would take place over very many different matters, not just senior appointments. (Kemp interviewed, 17 November 1994)

The implications of Kemp's comments are obvious; these are informal negotiations held 'behind closed door'. He confirmed that the reality did not necessary reflect the 'official' Whitehall version which argued that the whole process is a clear, well-regimented, fair and effective means of selecting a candidate. Instead, the implication is that a great deal of activity goes on behind the scenes, where the machinery's wheels are being thoroughly oiled. This, in itself, reinforces the notion of Whitehall as a very close-knit, village like, community:

> A very closed society. There is nothing dishonest about this, it just means that everything on paper, all the systems, have to be seen in a wider environment, of what is actually said and done. (Kemp interviewed, 17 November 1994)

Kemp's description of the manner in which the Prime Minister and Cabinet Secretary are able to get together over a late night drink, in order to attain a candidate they both find mutually acceptable for a vacant post, is revealing. When I questioned Peter Middleton, a serving member of SASC during the 1980s, on this same subject, he also emphasised the overriding role both the Cabinet Secretary and the Prime Minister can play in appointments. However, Middleton placed a more formal gloss on the procedures involved:

> SASC is a committee of senior Permanent Secretaries, or at least it was in my time. SASC changes its characteristics. It has now got a non-executive on the board. What SASC did, was to consider

senior appointments, that is Grades 1 and 2. It went through a succession planning process, to pick out the people for posts. It did the usual business of asking itself who would do the job if someone fell under a bus? Who, ideally, would you have in the fullness of time? It considered whether they thought Heads of Departments had performed properly. Whether you want to retire someone early, or suggest they should be. Whether they were getting on with their minister. Whether there were problems of that sort. It developed a plan for vacancies, ahead of time, so it could be properly discussed. Treasury appointments were always a little bit different, because Prime Ministers, being First Lords of the Treasury, felt they had more of a direct interest in the Treasury, than in most other departments. The system is always the same; you go to SASC. Most Permanent Secretaries wouldn't go to SASC without having discussed the issue with their own minister first. SASC then goes through it and produces a list. What you normally do is go for three, with a front runner. Sometimes two, with a front runner. Sometimes four, with a front runner. It just depends on what the field for that job was. Then the Head of the Civil Service, it just happens to be the Cabinet Secretary, would go to see the minister and say 'I think this, that and the other'.

Middleton then described the role the Cabinet Secretary, as Chairman of SASC, on the rare occasion in which the Prime Minister had difficulties with the individuals on the list:

As Chairman of SASC, the Cabinet Secretary would not add names to the list of individuals to be discussed. However, what he would do, if he couldn't agree a name with the Prime Minister, would be to return to SASC in order to come up with a suitable alternative. This very, very, rarely happened. Sometimes you had an individual picked who you were not expecting to be picked. In which case there was nothing you could do about it. However, SASC wouldn't have put the individual forward in the first place, if they felt the individual was a poor candidate for the post. By and large, we didn't just give a list of names because we thought we ought to give a list. We picked people we thought could actually do the job. Sometimes, though it didn't usually happen, you got a completely different name back from the ministerial process. Sometimes they were good ideas and sometimes they were not. This would continue to go back and forward. At the end of the day, of course, the Prime Minister and the Cabinet Secretary could pick who they wanted.

> But in my experience they were always very, very reluctant to pick someone whom the system said was not up to the job. That included Margaret Thatcher. Indeed if anything, she was very keen on 'up to the jobness' herself. (Middleton interviewed, 16 November 1994)

Middleton is unequivocal in his comment that the Prime Minister and Cabinet Secretary could, if they wished, circumvent the whole 'formal' appointments procedure and 'pick who they wanted'. Again, this reflects the close, fraternal atmosphere in which decisions in Whitehall are taken. However, it is hard to conceive of a situation in which the Prime Minister and Cabinet Secretary would completely override SASC's recommendations. One must remember that the Cabinet Secretary is also Head of the Civil Servie and, even when wearing his Cabinet Secretary hat, he remains Whitehall's broker. He will therefore not wish to appoint a candidate whom his organisation opposes. As the OPS official points out:

> The Head of the Home Civil Service is certainly aware of the importance of not making a poor choice appointment, on the grounds that individuals have to work together as a team and, as such, it would be foolish to make a selection that would create tension or conflict.

What one has to emphasise, given the closely-knit environment of the Whitehall village, is that the Cabinet Secretary's role, in relation to SASC and the Prime Minister, is to ensure that the machinery is kept well-oiled and running smoothly. Thus, the emphasis is on putting together a team which can function together effectively. To facilitate this, the Prime Minister's views, on both individuals and forthcoming vacancies, would be informally circulated to key actors, long before the official SASC procedures are triggered. More importantly, the Cabinet Secretary would be fully aware of the Prime Minister's line of thought, through numerous informal conversations, well before he approached the Prime Minister with any formal recommendations. The informality of the system is highlighted by an interview with a Treasury official who informed me that it was impossible to stick to the 'strict letter of the law'. He tacitly accepted that the formalised procedures for top appointments could be legitimately set aside for the sake of harmony and the maintenance of a smooth-running ship. In defending such a system, a retired Civil Service Commissioner argued:

> I would be very surprised if the Secretary to the Cabinet didn't go to the Prime Minister and say: 'Here are three names who we think

are suitable. We would recommend X, and as for Y and Z, we have other plans for them'. If you have a Permanent Secretary, he or she has got to be able to work with the minister. It is no good ignoring the personal element in all this. So if the Prime Minister, or the Minister who was being consulted, said: 'I am not having you', I am afraid that is final. I don't think that minister's preferences ought to win at levels below that, but certainly at that level. You have to see your Minister two to three times a day, if he can't bear you, it is just not going to work.

It comes as no surprise that a Civil Service Commissioner is willing to defend what can, at times, be a flawed system. It was his job to protect such a system.

An Outsider Keeping the Door Shut?

The introduction of the outsiders, Michael Angus and Michael Bett, to the SASC Board will probably have no tangible effect. If anything, it is a further example of the Civil Service paying lip-service to the ideals of more open government, while ensuring that the procedures are still kept tightly within their own domain. As Peter Kemp explained:

Michael Angus and now Michael Bett have been brought in as the outsiders on SASC. There are two points. First, whether the cultures they come from – Unilever and British Telecom respectively – are sufficiently different to the senior Civil Service to bring about a new and distinctive view about the sort of people who ought to be appointed or promoted; and second, whether as outsiders they will get very far in such a closed circle. You might say that these appointments are actually an illusion, one looking two ways: to the outside world, they can say – 'Look, we have these outsiders on the Board'; to the insider – 'Well look, it doesn't really matter, it is only old Angus and Bett. We know they won't rock the boat'. (Kemp interviewed, 17 November 1994)

The Top Appointments System – A Flawed Exercise?

Having compared the 'official theory' with what the mandarins and other commentators regard as the actual reality of events, one can conclude that the system of senior appointments is flawed.

The work of SASC, the Civil Service Commission, the Senior Civil Service Group and all the strategic planning which has gone before it, can potentially be nullified by an over-bearing Prime Minister and a deferential Cabinet Secretary. These two individuals can sit down together, with one or two other officials drawn from the mandarinate and, in a couple of hours, over a glass of whisky, determine the appointment of an official to one of the highest posts in the British bureaucracy. This leads one to question the legitimacy of such a system and, in turn, the cost-effectiveness of all the time, money and manpower spent on personnel planning.

It is worth asking if the making of career and strategic plans are ineffective exercises, as, in some cases, they may have no bearing on the end result of a senior appointment? There are two important points to be made here. Firstly, the senior appointments system would only be rendered impotent, if an overly-dominant, pro-active Prime Minister manipulates the system. To date, this has not happened. Even a domineering Prime Minister would think long and hard before risking the type of constitutional crisis which might result from such an intervention. Secondly, much of the strategic planning, involving succession and career plans, is not made with the sole intention of producing a first-rate Permanent Secretary or Deputy Secretary. Rather, it aims to ensure that, as with any large organisation, the system of personnel management exhibits coherence and logic. Indeed, Frank Cooper argued:

> Many in industry and commerce would regularly admit that personnel management in the Civil Service is much better than it is in their own organisations. This is not surprising because there are a vast number of people working in personnel management in the Civil Service. But I think the Civil Service is very highly regarded by the private sector, as a model for good personnel practices. In the private sector it is usually the case that, when somebody from outside is taking up a new job in another concern, four or five of his own chums will follow from the previous company. Whereas, in the Civil Service, everything is very carefully recorded. Everything is carefully regulated. People are looked at every year and it is the job of every head of department to look right down his department and see the younger ones coming up. (Cooper interviewed, 20 December 1994)

Thus, the comments in the latter part of this chapter are not levelled at the Civil Service's approach towards personnel planning below the level of Grade 2. Instead, it is an indictment of the 'club-like' atmosphere which is fostered when one reaches the 'Gods' in the Whitehall hierarchy. Indeed, the strategic planning which goes on below Grade 2 has a crucial bearing on the officials who find themselves in a position to be considered for promotion to the top two grades in the Civil Service. At the formative stages of an official's career, the individual is targeted as being potentially of the calibre for a future Permanent Secretary. This is a result of the accepted Whitehall practice of sending officials to the 'Centre' to gain experience.

The Centre – A Stage upon which to Perform

It is a commonly accepted practice in Whitehall's strategic, person- nel planning to send lesser officials, normal in Grades 5, 6 and 7, to the Centre of Whitehall in order to gain some form of experience. This is the routine exercise whereby 'high-flying' officials are iden- tified and provided with the opportunity to perform at the heart of government. The Centre itself comprises the Cabinet Office, the Treasury and the Prime Minister's Office. An ex-Cabinet Secretary offers an historical overview of this Whitehall exercise:

> From the 1960s on, it had become widely established across the ser- vice that there were significant benefits to the individuals concerned, to their departments and to the country, if the careers of 'flyers' – those in Grades 5 and 7 who were recognised as having potential to rise to the highest levels in the service – included periods in 10 Downing Street or the Cabinet Office – which are largely manned by relatively short-term imports from other departments – or in the Treasury.

The OPS official provides the rationale for such an exercise:

> It is essential for those individuals who might possibly go on to serve at the top to gain knowledge of how to handle 'heavy weight' political individuals. They can then gain experience of how to offer such individuals professional advice etc. It is also important for these individuals to gain knowledge of how the 'Centre' operates. This will help them [if they achieve Deputy Secretary or Permanent Secretary status] to be competent in guiding their own minister through the Whitehall minefield, to give advice in Cabinet meetings or how to

work the Treasury. In being placed at the Centre, an official becomes well known throughout the whole system. He or she will establish networks and rapport's with various individuals and will become 'visible' within the Whitehall village. This helps later, when advising [in the capacity of Permanent Secretary] your minister or helping him, as the official will know the system and understand how it operates. It is in effect, a 'testing ground', in that, just as an official can shine in the period he or she spends at the Centre, there is also the opportunity to fail spectacularly. It is therefore very much a period where one's career is either made or broken.

Obviously, there is a logic to such a system. It would not be rational to appoint an individual to the level of Permanent Secretary, in, for example, the Department of Trade and Industry, if that person had spent his or her whole career in an obscure position in the Department of Education and had no prior knowledge of how the Centre operates. There are, however, three criticisms to be made of such an exercise: first, such a system means the promotional prospects of the traditional Whitehall 'generalist' remain much brighter than those of 'specialists' who, by their very nature, often find themselves for long periods of their Whitehall career in obscure positions. Thus, the advancement of the generalist, of the kind criticised by 'Fulton', continues to be sustained. Second, despite being sent to the Centre for a year or two experience, due to the normal competition between Whitehall departments, each department continues to covet its most able officials, guarding them against incursions from outside. Third, such a system remains self-perpetuating. As Plowden (1994, p. 44) observed:

> Spells in the Cabinet Office or as a Minister's private secretary are useful crash courses in the working of the top of government. But it is hard to think of types of experience better suited to transmitting and reinforcing accepted ways of doing things.

Cynics would argue that the process enables the system to inculcate young officials in the ways of the 'fraternal club' of the mandarinate, in preparation for their potential future there. Indeed, as John Sparrow, an economic adviser seconded to Whitehall in the 1980s, confirmed:

> A civil servant who is bright and is on his way to the top goes there [the Centre] as that is part of the way to top. I think under any Prime

Minister, the Civil Service picked those people sufficiently well, for most of them to go on and get either to, or very near to, the top. I think that process continues. Part of those individuals' success story would be the fact that they get to meet, to hob-nob with, not only the Prime Minister, but possibly visiting Heads of State, certainly the rest of Cabinet and certainly the whole of the top echelon of the Civil Service as it stands, at the time of being an aspirant. But then again, I think that is normal, has remained unchanged and is part of the process of developing your eventual elite. (Sparrow interviewed, 15 November 1994)

As Richards (1992) concludes, there is a problem with this: 'Learning through doing, under supervision, is an approach to training which has many merits, but where discontinuities with the past are more important than continuities, it will not do.'

The Top Appointments System: By Whitehall, for Whitehall and of Whitehall

In this chapter, I have presented an 'official' description, recounted by a senior OPS official, of how an individual is appointed to the highest grades in the Civil Service. I then analysed the views of retired senior officials to piece together how the system operates in practice. In the post-Fulton era, it is clear that the system for appointing senior officials has operated in a secret and unobtrusive manner, because the actors involved have been willing to stick to the rules of the game. This reflects the fraternal, club-like atmosphere which is nurtured at the highest levels within the mandarinate. The rules, of course, have been drawn up by Whitehall, for Whitehall. Therefore, the system operates in a manner which suits the needs of the elite, while also perpetuating it. The process works smoothly and with no hiccoughs, as long as the one 'outsider' involved in the proceedings, the Prime Minister, sticks to the unspoken rules. However, when a Prime Minister is appointed who adopts a more pro-active approach, then problems can arise. The Cabinet Secretary's work is cut out to ensure that to outward appearances, the machinery operates smoothly. For a Whitehall observer, discontent among the lower ranks is a tell-tale sign of trouble. Those individuals who, in the normal course of events, would expect to reach the exalted, bureaucratic heights of Permanent Secretary or Deputy Secretary, suddenly find that individuals of a younger age and a different outlook have leap-frogged over them. Worse still are the occasions when an outsider is brought in to fill what others may have regarded as *their* next post. It is then that civil servants break ranks, the veil of secrecy is lowered and the Whitehall observer is afforded the opportunity to gauge what has gone on. Of course, Margaret Thatcher was a Prime Minister who opted for a more pro-active approach towards the top appointments procedure and so the veil slipped.

4

Quantifying a Thatcher Effect

Measuring a Thatcher Effect

O NE OF THE REPERCUSSIONS of the 1968 Fulton Report was the introduction of the SASC procedures for senior Whitehall appointments. Until now, these procedures have remained largely cloaked in secrecy. It is widely known that appointments at Grade 1 (Permanent Secretary), Grade 1a (Second Permanent Secretary) and Grade 2 (Deputy Secretary), together with any transfers between these grades, requires the approval of the Prime Minister.[1] However, despite the abundant literature concerning Mrs Thatcher's approach to the appointments procedure, there has been no systematic analysis of her role, or that of any other Prime Minister, in the actual processes. The arcane nature of British central government has placed obvious restrictions on such an analysis. This probably explains why most observers have contented themselves with anecdotal and hearsay evidence. Yet, for political scientists, such evidence, though intriguing, is inconclusive. In order to further the debate, a quantitative analysis has an obvious utility.

A number of useful surveys have been conducted, analysing the demographic nature of the mandarinate in the twentieth century. They present a detailed picture of the type of official who served at the highest grades in Whitehall. However, none directly deal with the question of putative accelerated promotion in the 1980s. This chapter will present an overview of these existing surveys, as they do provide useful comparative information. Subsequently, I proffer my own systematic analysis of accelerated promotion during the 1980s.

A Portrait of a Mandarin

Existing statistical surveys of the senior grades in the Civil Service usually offer only broad demographic surveys of the mandarinate in the twentieth century, analysing shifts in age, gender, class, educational background and length of tenure in office. However, these surveys do provide a useful, comparative bench-mark against which to consider my data.

There have only been a limited number of systematic surveys of the social and educational backgrounds and career patterns of the mandarinate. Kelsall's (1955) study comprehensively examined the higher Civil Service from 1870 to 1950. Harris and Garcia (1966) analysed the social and educational backgrounds of the mandarinate from 1900–63. Theakston and Fry (1989) extended the Harris and Garcia study to include Permanent Secretaries appointed up to 1986. Sheriff (1976) presented a detailed analysis of all Grade 1, 2 & 3 officials serving in Whitehall in 1971, paying particular attention to the promotional paths these officials followed. The most recent survey by Barberis (1996a) involved a longitudinal study of Permanent Secretaries from the mid-nineteenth century to the present day. There have also been two major studies of the educational and social origins of British elites: Rubenstein's (1986), *Education and the Social Origins of British Elites* and Greenaway's (1988), *The Political Education of the Civil Service Mandarin Elite*.

None of these surveys attempts to systematically address the question: did any official receive accelerated promotion, prior to, or during the 1980s? Of all the surveys carried out, the most relevant to my own research is that conducted by Theakston and Fry (1989), although even here they only analysed Grade 1 officials.[2] Their survey, which examines the 304 Permanent Secretaries appointed between 1900 and 1986, indicated that the average age of appointment to Grade 1 was 51.7 years. During this period, only two women were promoted to Grade 1: Dame Evelyn Sharp in the Ministry of Housing and Local Government, 1955–66; and Dame Mary Smieton in the Ministry of Education, 1959–63.[3] As far as education is concerned, 60 per cent attended public school: although in the later half of the century there was a fall in the number of individuals attending 'Clarendon schools',[4] with a converse rise in the number who attended maintained, direct-grant or grant-aided schools.

These figures confirm that the majority of officials came from the upper-middle and lower-middle classes. Overall, 83.9 per cent of this group attended a university and, contrary to expectation, as the century progressed the figures for Oxbridge rose, rather than fell. Thus, between 1965 and 1986, 75 per cent had attended one or other of these two universities. As regards the length of tenure of Permanent Secretaries, the numbers who had served for less than 15 years before their appointment to Grade 1 fell from 46.7 per cent between 1900 and 1919 to only 2.5 per cent in the period 1965–86. Conversely, the percentage who had served for more than 26 years before their appointment rose from 28.1 per cent to 72.5 per cent. Over the whole period, Theakston and Fry only recorded 17 cases of outside appointments to Grade 1 and, significantly, none occurred in the post-war period. They also noted the importance of officials spending time serving in a minister's private office or gaining experience in one of the central departments: 'It is an important first step in the building of a mandarin's career, occurring usually when the individual concerned is in his late twenties or early thirties' (Theakston and Fry 1989, p. 139). The average age of appointments to Grade 1 rose from 49.7 years between the period 1900–19 to 53.9 years in the 1965–86 period. Not surprisingly, in the same two comparable periods, the average length of tenure of service at Grade 1 fell from 9.9 years to 4.8 years. No official appointed since 1966 has served for more than 12 years as a Permanent Secretary.[5] Theakston and Fry (1989, p. 145) concluded that:

> The higher Civil Service . . . still seems to exhibit a considerable degree of social homogeneity, though perhaps less so than 50 years ago . . . Nearly all the chiefs of the Civil Service are to be ranked with the upper and upper-middle classes by the mode of life which they practice and the society which they keep, though many of them did not by origin belong to those classes.

The Theakston and Fry study identified the high degree of social exclusiveness of the mandarinate in the twentieth century. It reflects an all-male, middle and upper class elite, which is self-perpetuating, thriving in such institutions as the 'clubs' of London. As Harris and Garcia (1966, p. 43) noted in their earlier study:

> Participation in the activities of a leading club enables a [Permanent] Secretary to meet informally and in pleasant surroundings civil servants from other departments, businessmen and professional people and to obtain insights into problems facing government ministries. Frequently, advance information is made available informally and, of course, contacts and friendships thus pleasantly established may prove to be useful in negotiations undertaken at a later date.

Barberis's (1996a, p. 140) demographic analysis of all Permanent Secretaries from the mid-nineteenth century to the present day includes a check-list of the qualities he regarded as necessary to become a Permanent Secretary:

> There are personal, intellectual and technical attributes. At the personal level all permanent secretaries must be resilient, mentally and physically. They must be good team players, yet able when necessary to rise above the tide of consensus. This includes the ability to work with ministers of any hue or persuasion though without sacrificing their own integrity or that of the office of permanent secretary. An equable temperament will help, though a bit of *'fizz'* is sometimes needed to push things through or to knock heads together. Charisma is a further asset, or at any rate a leadership style that inspires others. Intellectually, permanent secretaries must be able quickly to assimilate and analyse vast amounts of material; to seize upon the central issues and see the way forward. They must be good at problem-solving. They must also be sound in judgement – quick to spot trouble while maintaining a sense of proportion.

If one links the qualities described above, with Theakston and Fry's demographic analysis of Permanent Secretaries, it is possible to create something similar to a Galtonian composite photograph of the Sir Humphreys who graced the corridors of Whitehall for the majority of the twentieth century. Throughout the remainder of this book, I refer to such a character, as a 'traditional type of Permanent Secretary'. However, my own research has a different focus; I am concerned with the accelerated promotion of officials to the top two grades in Whitehall since 1979. Unfortunately, other surveys have not traced the promotional paths of the mandarinate in previous administrations. I have therefore undertaken my own comparative survey, contrasting the appointments of the Labour Government of 1974–9 with those of Mrs Thatcher's Administration.

A Systematic Analysis of Politicisation
under Margaret Thatcher

Any attempt to systematically analyse the potential politicisation of the higher Civil Service during the 1980s involves two initial stages: a demographic comparison and the identification of cases of accelerated promotion. The first, and obvious, step is to undertake a demographic comparison of first-time appointments to the levels of Permanent Secretary or Deputy Permanent Secretary during the Labour Governments of 1974–9 and the Thatcher Government of 1979–90. This will identify any disparity in the demographic make-up of the officials appointed during the two separate administrations. It is then necessary to identify any cases where there is *prima facie* evidence of interference in the 1980s – that is cases in which accelerated promotion occurred. Here, the analysis concentrated on those cases where the appointment of an individual to Grade 1/a or Grade 2 involved a rise of two or more grades. Such a rise is faster than the Whitehall norm, where traditionally promotion has been determined, in part, by the length of service and 'Buggins's turn'. I also examined all outside appointments to these grades in order to ascertain whether or not Mrs Thatcher introduced a number of 'outsiders' to assist her and her Government in their programme of change for Britain.

The method employed involved a number of stages:

- Compiling a list of all the departments in Whitehall and of any structural changes in the Government between 1974 and 1990.

- Identifying all the Permanent Secretaries (Grade 1), Second Permanent Secretaries (Grade 1a) and Deputy Secretaries (Grade 2) who held posts in those departments between 1974 and 1990 using the *Civil Service Year Book* (see Appendix B).

- Comparing the social backgrounds of first-time appointees to Grades 1/1a and 2, during the Labour and Conservative Governments, considering age, gender, schooling and higher education records.

- Examining each individual appointment/promotion to Grade 1 and 1a, noting cases of accelerated promotion, that is, promotion by two or more grades, and all outside appointments.

Any political scientist who has used government statistics will realise that a certain degree of error is involved.[6] It therefore comes as no surprise to find that if one examines comparable academic analyses of Civil Service statistics the figures vary.[7] In compiling my statistics, I used the CSS and *The Civil Service Yearbook*. Therefore, like others, I have had to accept that my statistics contain an inevitable, structural element of error.

Another problematic area in utilising Civil Service statistics concerns the date on which an individual is appointed. It is not always possible to ascertain the year in which an actual appointment is made. More significantly, this is compounded in the election years of 1974 and 1979 and in 1990, when Mrs Thatcher ceased to be Prime Minister; in these years it is impossible to determine precisely which Prime Minister was responsible for which appointment. The final date on which the Government statistics are annually compiled is April 1. I had to accept this as the final date on which appointments were made for each particular year. Again, this causes error and inaccuracy.[8]

However, overall, the results only contain a limited degree of error which is unlikely to have a significant bearing on the final analysis.

Results and Analysis

Table 4.1a   Number of officials serving at Grades 1/1a and 2 (1974–9)

	1974	1975	1976	1977	1978	1979
Grade 1/1a	41	42	44	44	42	42
Grade 2	149	145	157	156	156	158

Table 4.1b   Number of officials serving at Grades 1/1a and 2 (1980–90)

	1980	1981	1982	1983	1984	1985	1986	1987	1988	1989	1990
Grade 1/1a	42	41	40	37	40	39	38	39	44	38	37
Grade 2	158	150	143	133	136	141	134	136	135	126	140

During the two periods, the numbers serving in the mandarinate are almost constant. In 1974 there were 41 serving Permanent Secretaries and 149 Deputy Secretaries, whereas in 1990 the respective figures were 37 and 140; this, despite the fact that the 1980s was a decade in which there were dramatic reductions in the overall size of the Civil Service.[9] Clearly, the mandarinate was successful in resisting any attempts at downsizing within their own cadre.

Table 4.2a Number of promotions to Grades 1 / 1a and 2 (1974–9)

	1974	1975	1976	1977	1978	1979
Grade 1/1a	10	11	14	10	6	12
Grade 2	35	25	41	35	31	27

Note: The figures in this table are higher than comparable figures of other surveys. This is because other surveys have usually only included central government departments in their statistics. My survey has included all those defined in *The Civil Service Yearbook* as Grades 1, 1a or 2 officials. Thus, my set includes all officials serving in both Government Departments and 'other organisations'. A list of all the departments and organisations in my survey can be found in Appendix A.

However, my own statistics correlate with the statistical evidence of other surveys. For example, if one looks at 1983, the year with the highest number of promotions, the RIPA (1987, p. 45) survey indicates that there were 11 promotions to Grades 1/1a, while my own survey indicates that there were 16. Converseley, the year of fewest appointments in the RIPA study was 1981, with only 2 identified promotions. Likewise, 1982 was also the year of fewest promotions in my survey with only 5 being identified.

Table 4.2b Number of promotions to Grades 1 / 1a and 2 (1980–90)

	1980	1981	1982	1983	1984	1985	1986	1987	1988	1989	1990
Grade 1/1a	11	5	9	16	12	9	7	9	9	12	6
Grade 2	26	22	33	31	34	23	24	26	25	41	11

The number of promotions during the Labour Government of 1974–9 and the Conservative Government of 1979–90 were similar: the average yearly promotion to Grades 1/1a between 1974 and 1979 was 10.1 and for Grade 2 it was 31.7; in the Thatcher years at Grade 1/1a the average was 9.5 and for Grade 2 it was 27.1. This was hardly surprising, given that no major central government restructuring occurred between 1974 and 1990.

As such, unless either Government was responsible for a large number of early retirements (through disillusionment etc.), the natural process of personnel turnover would be likely to remain almost constant.

The year 1983 is interesting because of a higher than normal number of appointments and promotions. This reflects the fact that the post-war generation of officials had reached the age of sixty, the customary retirement age of civil servants. One can only speculate whether post-NPM, the age retirement remained at sixty.

Table 4.3a Number of first-time promotions to Grades 1 / 1a and 2
(1974–9)

	1974	1975	1976	1977	1978	1979
Grade 1/1a	6	10	11	9	5	9
Grade 2	26	.24	32	32	26	22

Table 4.3b Number of first-time promotions to Grades 1 / 1a and 2
(1980–90)

	1980	1981	1982	1983	1984	1985	1986	1987	1988	1989	1990
Grade 1/1a	9	4	8	13	11	8	6	8	4	7	6
Grade 2	19	18	30	25	27	19	21	21	22	27	6

By themselves, these statistics only indicate that there were a
similar number of first-time appointments made by both Governments. The 1980–90 group is composed of the Thatcher generation of senior appointees. It is in relation to this group that
accusations of politicisation were levelled. As such, it is of limited utility to analyse the horizontal appointments made to these
grades. What may prove more useful is a demographic analysis of
first-time, vertical appointees to Permanent Secretary and Deputy
Secretary.

If such an analysis indicated that the mandarinate of the 1980s
were composed of a different type of individual, it could imply that
an effect of some kind had occurred.

Table 4.4a Demographic profile of first-time appointees to Grade 1/1a

	1974–1979 Nos:[%]	1980–90 Nos:[%]
Average Age of Newly Appointed Official	54.5	53.8
The Number State Educated	6 [12%]	6 [7%]
The Number from Private School	44 [88%]	78 [93%]

The Number from University [excluding Oxbridge]	11 [22%]	25 [29%]
The Number from Oxbridge	34 [68%]	51 [61%]
The Number without University Education	5 [10%]	8 [10%]
The Number of Women	0 [–]	1 [1.1%]

Note: The total number of first-time appointees to this grade between 1974 and 1979 was 50; for the period 1980–90 it was 84.

Table 4.4b Demographic profile of first-time appointees to Grade 2

	1974–1979 Nos:[%]	1980–90 Nos:[%]
Average Age of Newly Appointed Official	52.9	52.2
The Number State Educated	16 [10%]	19 [8%]
The Number from Private School	146 [90%]	217 [92%]
The Number from University [excluding Oxbridge]	32 [20%]	64 [27%]
The Number from Oxbridge	109 [67%]	151 [64%]
The Number without University Education	21 [13%]	21 [9%]
The Number of Women	5 [0.6%]	4 [0.2%]

Note: The total number of first-time appointees to Grade 2 between 1974 and 1979 was 162; for the period 1980–90 it was 236.

Table 4.4 shows that the demographic make-up of first-time officials serving at Grades 1/1a and 2 in the Thatcher Government were similar to that of their predecessors who served the Labour Government. There was a small reduction in the age at which individuals were appointed to the mandarinate during the 1980s and a slight increase in the numbers who attended a 'red-brick' or 'plate-glass' university. Conversely, there was a drop in the numbers who received an Oxbridge education. Overall, the differences between these two cohorts were minimal. Thus, despite the rhetoric surrounding Margaret Thatcher's attempts to cultivate a more meritocratic society, this analysis suggests that, certainly when applied to the Civil Service, few in-roads were made. This is not surprising if one recognises the structural constraints involved in appointments and promotions in Whitehall. It would take over twenty years for a more 'meritocratic type' official[10] to work his or her way up the various ranks and bring about a change in the demographic make-up at the most senior grades. As the Prime Minister has no direct influence over appointments and promotions at more junior levels, any Thatcher effect would have been indirect. Her only direct means of advancing such a change would have been through the widespread introduction of outsiders to the highest grades. However, this was not the case.

There were nine cases of outside promotion to Grade 1/a: [see Appendix D]. Almost all these outside appointments were to specialist, technical posts, often in the Treasury or the Health Service. As such, it is not the case that Margaret Thatcher set about appointing a large number of outsiders to generalist Permanent Secretary posts.

The Case for Politicisation Remains Unproven

The demographic comparison revealed a high degree of homogeneity between officials promoted in the 1970s and their successors in the 1980s. However, this does not imply that all notions of politicisation by Mrs Thatcher can be rejected. The limited number of outside appointments indicated that she mainly approved insiders for promotion. Hence, the Civil Service continued to be the preserve of an all-male, Oxbridge educated, upper to middle classes elite.[11]

Nevertheless, the reduction in the age of officials at the time of their promotion to the mandarinate could prove significant. The inference here could be that there were a number of cases of accelerated promotion to the highest levels, involving younger officials who leap-frogged two or more grades. If this were the case, it would partially explain the fall in age of first-time appointees to Grades 1/1a and 2 during the 1980s. Here again, the statistics are not significant: there were three first-time appointees to Grades 1/1a during the 1974 Labour Government whose promotion represented a vertical shift of two grades. The comparable figure for the Thatcher period was four. Similarly, for Grade 2 officials, there were 11 cases of a rise of two grades between 1974 and 1979 and 15 cases between 1980 and 1990. At no stage did the case arise of an official being promoted more than two grades.

The analysis of accelerated promotion during both administrations indicates that there was no noticeable increase in the number of individuals who received rapid elevation to the highest grades under Mrs Thatcher; traditional patterns in the appointments procedure remained intact. However, as the review of the literature in chapter 1 indicated, a number of individuals have testified to the increased intervention in senior appointments by Mrs Thatcher. Such views were at odds with the findings of the quantitative analysis.

The results of the quantitative analysis in this chapter does not necessarily mean that a Thatcher effect can be rejected. What the analysis highlights is that the individuals appointed to the mandarinate during the 1980s were, consistently, career officials, insiders, who had generally followed a standard Whitehall promotional path to the top. This does not mean Mrs Thatcher did not introduce a new breed of official to the most senior grades. Potentially, she may have approved the appointment or promotion of only a certain type from within the range of individuals available for selection. Thus, the notion persists that she may have promoted individuals, already working in Whitehall, whom she knew to be politically sympathetic to the Conservative Party, or alternatively, whom she regarded as a 'managerially-oriented, can-doer'. Logistically, it is improbable either of these effects occurred at the Grade 2 level. It is unlikely that any Prime Minister, whose time is severely constrained by a very heavy workload, would concern him/herself with the large number of Grade 2 appointments which have to be approved.[12] Traditionally, the whole Whitehall personnel system has been geared to the moulding of officials to the highest grade. As Barberis (1996a, p. 141) noted, in his longitudinal analysis of Permanent Secretaries:

> Promotions to under secretary and certainly to deputy secretary level have been made by the bureaucracy with at least one eye upon the potential of the individual eventually to become a permanent secretary . . . Certain civil servants are marked out for potentially great things. They get the opportunities to succeed, or to fail. This marking out is not primarily a matter of personal favouritism, though both ministers and top civil servants have been instrumental in enhancing the prospects of those within whom they have worked . . .

Barberis (1996a, p. 141) presented further evidence that personnel planning in Whitehall revolved round the creation of high quality

Permanent Secretaries, when he quoted a Permanent Secretary as saying:

> You can afford to have some unsafe deputy secretaries but you can't have an unsafe permanent secretary. You can't afford to make mistakes as a permanent secretary . . . you've got to be much more rounded and much safer. None of your abilities may quite reach the heights of some deputy secretaries, but taken overall you must have a fairly high marking on most things. You must have a sort of 70 per cent rating across the board with perhaps the occasional dip down.

Grade 2 is an important and prestigious level within the Civil Service hierarchy, but its occupants pale, in significance, alongside departmental chiefs. Certainly, the level of Prime Ministerial scrutiny of Grade 1 appointments (where the numbers are far smaller and the post carries much more responsibility) is likely to be far greater than at the Grade 2 level.

The evidence suggests Mrs Thatcher had strong views on whom she regarded as the most suitable individual for promotion to Grade 1. Thus, in the majority of cases of appointments to Deputy Secretary she would have simply approved the appointment. However, at Grade 1 level it is conceivable that she forced through the appointment of individuals, not on the original SASC short list, on the grounds of one or other of the two notions of politicisation. Thus, it would be premature to conclude that, because the quantitative analysis suggested no effect occurred, Mrs Thatcher did not have an impact on the composition of the mandarinate in the 1980s. Certainly, the substantive evidence of politicians, civil servants and political commentators discussed next, contradict the results of the quantitative analysis.

5

Intervention in the Senior Appointments Procedure: Rhetoric, Reality and a Centre Effect?

D ESPITE THE EVIDENCE of the quantitative analysis suggesting there was no Thatcher effect on the higher Civil Service during the 1980s, a survey of the secondary literature in this area indicates otherwise. There are two parts to this chapter. Part One examines the more substantive evidence of both civil servants and political commentators concerning the two interpretations of politicisation. Here, the evidence refutes the notion that any form of overt politicisation occurred. Instead it is suggested that, particularly at Grade 1/1a level, Mrs Thatcher's increased interference aimed to effect a change in the composition of the most senior civil servants, with a view to seeing more positive, managerially oriented, can-doers appointed. The evidence suggests that she used the normal procedures of sending high-flyers to the centre to aid her in this task. In this way, she singled out those who displayed the type of characteristics she desired for all public servants. Part Two presents a compilation of the views of both Mrs Thatcher, as presented in her first autobiography *The Downing Street Years* and of her ministers, as expressed in their numerous memoirs. It also tentatively suggests that a form of socialisation occurred in the senior open structure; the inference here is that a generation of officials were socialised into Mrs Thatcher's way of doing things.

Part One: Intervention, Politicisation and the Centre – the Substantive Evidence

Peter Hennessy (1989, p. 635) argued that when Mrs Thatcher took office in June 1979:

With a few exceptions, [she] disliked the Permanent Secretaries she inherited and was keen to use her chance to replace them with a different breed as the post-war generation for whom [Lord] Bancroft's words, 'everything was achievable', retired in the early eighties in the same concentrated manner with which they had entered in the late forties.

This desire was reflected in her increased intervention in the appointments procedure.[1]

Overt Politicisation Rejected

As chapter 1 indicated, few political commentators or academics believed increased intervention was the result of Mrs Thatcher wishing to appoint Conservative Party sympathisers to the highest grades. Robert Armstrong, her longest serving Cabinet Secretary and the official responsible for making the final appointment at the highest level, is emphatic in his view that:

> She is not concerned with, and I can vouch for the fact that she does not seek to ascertain, the political views or sympathies [if any] of those who were recommended . . . She wants, as I want, to have the best person for the job. (RIPA 1987, p. 44)

Similarly, neither of the main opposition parties believed Mrs Thatcher had, in some insidious manner, attempted to overtly politicise the Civil Service. During a television interview in 1985, Neil Kinnock stated he would willingly accept the Civil Service inherited from the Conservatives. He indicated that if his Party had been elected they would not have retained Mrs Thatcher's special advisers, but, as regards Permanent Secretaries:

> We obviously have to examine the degree of enthusiasm and loyalty that they are prepared to demonstrate in support of a Labour Government and in the implementation of the policy of that Government. I'm prepared to work on that basis, the conventional basis, which has stood us in good stead in Britain. (Kinnock interviewed for *A Week in Politics*, Channel 4, 29 May 1985)

Although the Labour Party were not willing to accept, *per se*, every official appointed by Mrs Thatcher in the 1980s, the general conclusion was that:

The FDA and 'mainstream' opinion in the opposition parties both seemed sceptical about claims that the Civil Service has been politicised since 1979 and both opposed any moves towards openly party political appointments. (RIPA 1987, p. 49)

The Labour Party's acceptance of the higher Civil Service was welcomed by Robert Armstrong (1985) when he declared: 'He (Kinnock) can be sure that . . . the Civil Service would serve the Government of which he was the head with no less energy or loyalty, and goodwill than they had served the present government and its predecessors'.

Despite the secrecy which surrounded SASC during the 1980s, even then it was clear that Mrs Thatcher more regularly intervened in the appointments/promotion procedure to influence the appointment of Permanent Secretaries than her predecessors. However, the evidence here, confirms the view that there was little or no overt party politicisation of the senior Civil Service. As Barberis (1996a, p. 127) concluded:

Margaret Thatcher was more interventionist in the making of top appointments than were her predecessors. This was true. But associated implications of politicisation were unfounded – if by politicisation is meant the packing of top posts by officials known or assumed to share Conservative Party sympathisers.

Can-Doers and the Centre Effect

The notion that Mrs Thatcher appointed Conservative sympathisers was always too simplistic. In contrast, a more plausible assessment of the Thatcher approach to top appointments suggests that she appointed people with management experience or a 'can-do' reputation. Commentators such as Hennessy (1989), Savoie (1994) and Young (1989) cited the individual examples of Peter Middleton, Robin Butler, Peter Levene, Peter Kemp and Clive Whitmore as evidence of this type of appointment.[2] In addition, the literature in this area also emphasised the number of individuals, during the Thatcher era, who spent time serving in the Cabinet Office, the Treasury and the Prime Minister's Office, prior to their promotion to the highest grades. This pattern was especially noticeable in comparison with the period of Labour Government between 1974 and 1979.

Since 1968 it has been the policy of Civil Service personnel planning to send those individuals, already earmarked as 'high-flyers', to one of the central departments, in order to provide them with an opportunity to perform at the heart of British Government. Such a policy allows officials to gain knowledge of how to handle 'heavy-weight' political individuals, while also providing the Civil Service with the chance to assess how they *perform* in what can be regarded as a more intense and pressurised environment. There have been a number of surveys which have analysed this firmly established Whitehall procedure. Seldon (1990) used the testimonies from a series of interviews he conducted with Cabinet Office officials to unravel this process. Lee (1990) undertook a quantitative analysis of the officials who served in the Cabinet Office. Burnham and Jones (1993) built on the Lee survey, carrying out their own analysis of Cabinet Office officials, but also extended it to include the Prime Minister's Office. The results of the latter's analysis correspond with the findings of my quantitative analysis; the type of individual Mrs Thatcher appointed, particularly to the Prime Minister's Office, had similar demographic characteristics to the previous generations of mandarins. Having established that the Prime Minister's Office and the Cabinet Office were routes to the top, Burnham and Jones (1993, p. 314) concluded:

> Our findings contradict some other assumptions made about the staffing of Mrs Thatcher's office . . . [Her] stated preference for advisers from modest backgrounds is not borne out by the facts. PMO members were more likely to have been educated at the top private schools, belong to select clubs and bear aristocratic titles . . . and this was particularly true of appointments over which she had most say [the policy advisers and political staff].

An earlier survey by Theakston and Fry (1989, pp. 139–40) analysed the increasing number of Permanent Secretaries with experience in the central departments of Government. Their survey concluded that the modern generation of Permanent Secretaries:

> had experience of the Cabinet Office, reflecting the dramatic growth of staff of the Cabinet Office in the 1960s and 1970s. With the exception of the post of Secretary to the Cabinet Office itself, the staff of the Cabinet Office are typically seconded from their departments for a two-to-three year stint.

Finally, Barberis (1996a, pp. 135–7) concluded that a spell in either the Treasury or the Cabinet Office was a near vital step in an official's career development. He also drew an important distinction between the two departments:

> The Cabinet Office has tended to be served by future permanent secretaries who had made their mark in Whitehall – those already well on their way to the top. The Treasury, on the other hand, has also given more of an early boost to those who go on to head other departments, albeit only a minority of these people actually began their careers in the Treasury.
>
> The figures show that the further up the hierarchy civil servants progress, the more likely they are to have served in a central department . . . There is nevertheless a clear distinction between permanent secretaries and their peers. Over two-thirds had served in a central department prior to becoming a permanent secretary – at least among those recruited between 1937 and 1958. Most of them reached the top between the mid-1960s and the mid-1980s . . . It is worth noting that over 90 per cent of all who have become permanent secretaries since the mid-1960s, after a career spent in Whitehall, have served either in a private office or in a central department . . . All this suggests, if not a predestination to reach the top, then a deliberate nurturing of those within the elite corps, who are considered to have had potential.

On the basis of this information and the earlier evidence provided by commentators suggesting cases of individuals who were positive and managerially-oriented and were therefore selected for appointment to Grade 1/1a, the logical conclusion to draw is that Mrs Thatcher used the normal process of sending high-flyers to the centre to single out those individuals she regarded as future Permanent Secretaries. The suggestion here is that officials sent to the centre had more chance to catch her eye.[3] Thus, during the 1980s, she approved the appointment of civil servants who displayed the traits which she felt a senior civil servant ought to possess – the managers and the can-doers, at the expense of other, more traditional-type officials. This does not necessarily imply that Mrs Thatcher developed a conscious and rational approach, but that, while at the centre of Government, she subconsciously marked down those individuals she regarded as efficient and able civil servants.

This interpretation is strengthened by the comments of William

Pile, who served as her Permanent Secretary in the Department of Education. He noticed the speed at which Mrs Thatcher judged people:

> She made up her mind about people very quickly and didn't change it. She once said: 'I make up my mind about people in the first ten seconds and I very rarely change it' . . . When she made up her mind you were consigned either to a very short list of saints or a very long list of sinners and that was the difficulty, you couldn't work your passage from one side of the list to the other except in very exceptional circumstances. (Pile quoted in Young and Sloman 1986, p. 48)

To address the notion of a centre effect I developed Barberis's analysis to assess whether or not, during the Thatcher years, a higher proportion of officials who had served at the centre were selected as first-time appointees to Grade 1, than had been the case during the 1974–9 Labour Government. If a significantly higher proportion were appointed in the Thatcher years, this would suggest that she may have used the normal process of sending 'high-flyers' to the centre to single-out, possibly subconsciously, those she regarded as can-doers.

Quantifying a Centre Effect

The data-set I compiled to assess the centre effect was constructed along slightly different lines to my previous data-sets. Here, the aim was to identify the number of first-time appointees to Grade 1/1a, who, prior to their appointment to this level, had experience of working in one of the central departments. As such, I tested for this effect in Grades 2–6. If the results indicate that there was a substantial increase of Permanent Secretary appointees by Margaret Thatcher who had previously passed through the centre, this would suggest a centre effect of some sort had occurred. The departments examined in this data-set also vary from those in my original quantitative analysis, as a centre effect would not apply to such specialist departments as the Foreign and Commonwealth Office or the Lord Chancellor's Department, nor would they include appointments of individuals to Grade 1/1a in 'other organisations' as defined in *The Civil Service Yearbook*.[4] The departments I regarded as comprising the Centre were: the Treasury, the Cabinet Office and the Prime Minister's Office.

Table 5.1   First-time appointments to Grade 1/1a, with experience of the centre (1974–90)

	1974–79	1980–90
Cabinet Office	7	8
Treasury	8	15
Cabinet Office/Treasury	3	7
PPS to the Prime Minister	0	4
No Centre Experience	22	24
Total	40	58

Between 1974 and 1979, I identified 40 officials as first-time appointees to one of the mainstream departments at Grades 1/1a. Of those, 18 (45%) had experience of the centre prior to their promotion to Permanent Secretary. In contrast, between 1980 and 1990, 34 (59%) of the 58 officials who were first-time appointees to one of the mainstream departments at Grades 1/1a had experience of the centre, prior to their promotion to Permanent Secretary. Thus, there was a 14 per cent increase in the number of officials who, in the Thatcher period, passed through the centre, prior to their promotion to Grade 1/1a.

These results indicate that, during the 1980s, some form of centre effect occurred. In this period, two out of three officials promoted to Permanent Secretary had previous experience of a central department. This would suggest that, through relocation to the centre, their potential to catch the eye of the Prime Minister greatly increased. Thus, when the Cabinet Secretary approached Mrs Thatcher for approval of an appointment to Grade 1/1a, she would hold opinions about who she felt was the most suitable official. These opinions would be based on those individuals she had come across, which logic would suggest were those predominantly from the centre. Of course, this process could work in both a positive and a negative way. There may have been a number of cases of individuals who she came across of whom she did not approve and who, subsequently, were passed-over for promotion.

The other significant finding is the large number of Treasury officials who were appointed to the highest grade in the 1980s. It would appear that Mrs Thatcher was attracted to officials with Treasury experience, perhaps because she regarded such types as more efficient, cost-conscious managers. However, Treasury officials have limited experience in dealing with the implementation of policy and, so, the appointment of such a type has wider implications. Of course, the evidence here is speculative. A qualitative analysis of the views of those involved in the appointments procedure is necessary in order to confirm these findings.

Part Two: Qualitative Evidence of a Thatcher Effect

A relatively new source of material is available which offers fresh, qualitative evidence of a Thatcher effect. Margaret Thatcher and a number of her retired Cabinet colleagues have published their diaries and memoirs, providing an extensive and rich source of information depicting the Thatcher years. These memoirs include details of her Government's approach towards Civil Service reform. Part Two of this chapter sets out to substantiate the various themes which have arisen from the evidence so far compiled on a Thatcher effect, using information available from various memoirs. However, before assessing the testimonies of the politicians, one should examine the validity of the political memoir as a research tool.

Political Memoirs: Are they a Valid Source of Data?

Gamble (1994) assesses the usefulness and degree of reliability of political diaries and memoirs for political scientists. He focuses on the large number of memoirs published by ministers who served in the Thatcher Cabinets, although he also examines the Castle (1984) and Crossman (1975, 1976, 1977) Diaries, as well as the memoirs of Harold Macmillan (1966, 1967, 1969, 1971, 1972, 1973) and Harold Wilson (1974). Gamble argues that there are three basic types of memoir which can provide useful information for the political scientist: 'They can be classified according to the kind of insights they give into party politics; ethos and style; argument and doctrine; policy formulation and implementation' (Gamble 1994, p. 35).

Gamble cites Alan Clark's (Junior Minister at the Department of Trade, 1986–89) diary as an example of 'style and ethos', arguing that, while Clark's work tells us little about policy or how decisions are arrived at, it does: 'tell us a great deal about what Conservatives like Clark felt about the Thatcher years' (Gamble 1994, p. 37). In contrast, the memoirs of Nigel Lawson (Chancellor of the Exchequer, 1982–9) and Margaret Thatcher rarely offer subjective opinions of their period in office. Instead, they: 'present only their public selves. They appear as political agents seeking to carry through a specific political project' (Gamble 1994, p. 38).

The memoirs of Ian Gilmour (Lord Privy Seal, 1979–81) and Nicholas Ridley (Secretary of State at the Department of Trade and Industry 1989–90) are more valuable than Clark's diary because they provide a mixture of 'memoir, analysis, and polemic'. As such, Gamble categorises this type of memoir as 'political argument and doctrine' and argues that their true value is derived from the fact that:

> very different standpoints provide an interpretation of the ideological divisions within the Conservative Party, and an assessment of the intellectual and political rationale for the policies with which the Thatcher leadership was associated . . . These two books are valuable records of the reasons why Conservatives feel so differently about the Thatcher era. (Gamble 1994, p. 39)

Gamble's final category deals with 'policy formulation and implementation'. He cites the memoirs of Thatcher and Lawson as examples of this type. He argues that these two memoirs are of vital importance, not only because both individuals spent long periods at the hub of power in British politics, but also because of the authority with which they are able to speak of this period. Thus, their memoirs:

> are marked by the seriousness with which Lawson and Thatcher have attempted to document their account of the main events of their time in Government . . . Either Lawson's or Thatcher's memoirs would be a useful resource for political scientists on their own. But together they are even more valuable. It might have been expected that two such close political allies would have produced memoirs which largely confirmed each other . . . What makes the memoirs fascinating for the political scientist is that they offer quite different accounts of some of the key events in the Thatcher Government. (Gamble 1994, pp. 39–40)

In table 5.2 I use Gamble's three classifications to categorise the ministerial diaries which directly address the question of the role of the Civil Service in the 1980s.[5] As can be seen, the groups are not mutually exclusive.

Table 5.2   Classification of ministerial diaries

	Ethos & Style	Argument and Doctrine	Policy Formulation & Implementation
Carrington		YES	
Clark	YES		
Fowler		YES	
Gilmour		YES	
Heseltine		YES	YES
Lawson			YES
Parkinson	YES	YES	
Prior	YES	YES	
Pym		YES	YES
Ridley		YES	
Tebbit		YES	
Thatcher			YES

The crux of Gamble's argument is that the various accounts in ministers' diaries and memoirs indicate that much of politics revolves around the differing perceptions of political reality by the key actors involved. Thus, the aim of the second part of this chapter is to draw on the memoirs to qualify the evidence of the quantitative analysis. The first theme to address is the view Mrs Thatcher's ministers held of the Civil Service which served them in the 1980s. This is a necessary first step because if a minister was overtly hostile to the Civil Service, or felt alienated by a well-established, departmental culture he would, in all probability, tend to support, or at least display a sympathy towards, any attempt at reform.

The Ministers' View: An Institution Delivering the Goods

Surprisingly, in all the memoirs examined, not one minister openly criticised the Civil Service. In fact, most freely commend the work of their department and the diligence of the officials working for them. Thus Gilmour (1992, p. 227) believed that: 'with the possible exception of the French, the British Civil Service is almost certainly the best in the world'. Likewise, Carrington (Secretary of State at the Foreign Office 1979–82) argued that he:

> almost always found British civil servants, anyway in the highest reaches of the profession, to be models of what such men and women should be – intelligent, selfless, knowledgeable and fair-minded . . . They preserve both integrity and loyalty despite what must frequently be trying circumstances; and every Cabinet owes them a great deal. (Carrington 1988, p. 146)

These ministers were both regarded as 'wets', not noted for their sympathy or support for the aims of Thatcherism, thus their comments are hardly surprising. Yet, even Norman Tebbit (Chancellor of the Duchy of Lancaster, 1985–7) and Nicholas Ridley, both well renowned 'right-wingers', held similar views on Whitehall. Tebbit (1988, p. 182) maintained that: 'I found I had the benefit of officials of the highest integrity and ability. Once I had laid down policy they were tireless in finding ways to deliver what I wanted'. Similarly, Ridley (1991, p. 41) asserted: 'In my view, a good cabinet minister can always get what he or she wants out of the Civil Service'.

So, ministers from both wings of the Conservative Party appear to be satisfied with the workings of Whitehall throughout the 1980s. They unanimously supported a system in which an incoming government inherited permanent officials of a neutral, political hue. Norman Fowler (Secretary of State at the Department of Employment, 1987–90), whose memoirs, like those of Carrington, Gilmour, Ridley and Tebbit, can be categorised as involving 'argument and doctrine', concluded that:

> In countries like the United States, many senior public service appointments change with the administration, but the advantage of having a skilled and objective public service able to serve any elected government should not be underestimated. (Fowler 1991, p. 112)

Michael Heseltine (Secretary of State at the Ministry of Defence, 1983–6), whose own book *Where There's a Will* contains elements of both policy formulation and implementation and argument and doctrine, was the only minister whose views on Whitehall were more ambivalent. This is perhaps not surprising given he is a minister renowned as, if not a successful, at least an ardent reformer of bureaucratic operating procedures. His experience in the Department of the Environment and the Ministry of Defence led him to conclude that:

> the longer I spent in the office the more I was persuaded that members of the higher civil service are neither chosen nor trained to meet the exceptional demands of their jobs . . . Most civil servants do the job of policy-advising for which they are selected extremely well. But the talent to advise is very different from the talent to manage. Thinker-doers are in short supply. Thinker-advisers are the normal product of the system. (Heseltine 1987, p. 9)

Of course, Margaret Thatcher's views are not irrelevant here.

Margaret Thatcher's View: Whitehall – 'The Curate's Egg'

Margaret Thatcher was highly suspicious of many of the top officials she inherited from the previous administration. She was aware, during the 1979 change-over, that the Civil Service already knew a great deal about the new policy proposals of her Government – a result of the normal scrutiny by Whitehall of all major party manifestos at the time of a General Election. However, she questioned whether the Civil Service was truly capable of grasping the radical nature of her Government's blueprint for reform. Mrs Thatcher (1993, p. 18) observed: 'I quickly learnt, some civil servants would need more than a conscientious reading of our manifesto and a few speeches to truly grasp the changes we were intending to make'.

She was suspicious of her mandarinate, believing that many were not fully aware of, or else were not prepared to completely embrace, the nature of the programme to be introduced. Yet, having gained experience of working with Whitehall officials, she conceded that:

> the sheer professionalism of the British Civil Service, which allows governments to come and go with a minimum of efficiency, is

something other countries with different systems have every cause
to envy. (Thatcher 1993, p. 18)

Here, Mrs Thatcher is only referring to the structure in place to
expedite the transfer of power from one administration to the next.
Her observation does not conceal the fact she had reservations about
working closely and effectively with the top officials she inherited.
Thus, at the start of her first term in office, she paid a visit to all
Government departments. These brief departmental sojourns left
her unsure of the ability of Whitehall to effectively execute, what
she regarded as a radical programme of change.

She invited all the Permanent Secretaries to a dinner at Number
10 Downing Street in an attempt to address the many problems
she believed had to be resolved. Her stated aim was to create an
informal atmosphere in which her top officials would feel free to
air their opinions in confidence. But, as Mrs Thatcher (1993, p. 48)
noted, the whole scheme proved a disaster:

> I enjoy frank and open discussion, even a clash of temperaments
> and ideas, but such a menu of complaints and negative attitudes as
> was served up . . . was enough to dull any appetite I may have had
> for this kind of occasion. The dinner took place a few days before I
> announced the programme of Civil Service cuts to the Commons,
> and that was presumably the basis for complaints that ministers had
> damaged civil service 'morale'.

Yet this only scratches the surface of what, she felt, was a far deeper
problem:

> What lay still further behind this . . . was a desire for no change.
> But the idea that the Civil Service could be insulated from a
> reforming zeal that would transform Britain's public and private
> institutions over the next decade was a pipe-dream. (Thatcher 1993,
> p. 48)

For Mrs Thatcher there was no simple, solution to the problem.
Strategic lesson-drawing had highlighted the limited benefits to
be gained in attempting to change the structures and operating
procedures of Whitehall. They were too deeply entrenched to be
challenged effectively. Thus, her attention shifted to the individuals
working at the highest levels:

it became clear to me that it was only by encouraging or appointing individuals, rather than trying to change attitudes en bloc, that progress would be made. And that was to be the method employed. (Thatcher 1993, p. 49)

She aimed to induce a revolution from above, which would penetrate the lower tiers of Whitehall. She wanted her top lieutenants to engender into the lower ranks a whole new approach to going about their daily business. The emphasis was to be on efficiency, accountability and cost-cutting.

Mrs Thatcher's Attitude to the Higher Civil Service: Her Ministers' Perceptions

It is in the nature of British Government that most senior Cabinet Minister's cannot avoid striking-up a close working relationship with the Prime Minister of the day; the very essence of the job demands such proximity. Therefore, it is hardly surprising that a minister develops a detailed knowledge of the manner in which a Prime Minister operates in government. This was certainly the case during the Thatcher Administration. Many of her ministers document personal accounts of the manner in which they perceived Mrs Thatcher operated and the views she held. Thus, these memoirs are scattered with references to Mrs Thatcher's impression of Whitehall. Gilmour (1992, p. 227) painted a clear picture of what, he felt, his Prime Minister's attitude was:

> Mrs Thatcher . . . had no great admiration for the public servant in general – much preferring businessmen, sometimes rather dodgy ones – or for civil servants in particular, perhaps thinking that if they had been any good they would have been in the City making money. And she favoured people who provided her with solutions, even if they were not fully aware of the problems, over those whose knowledge pointed to difficulties. In consequence almost unanimous official advice against the Poll Tax counted for nothing. The Prime Minister wanted civil servants to implement dogma, not to expose its errors.

Gilmour's observations, if accurate, have a profound implication for the Service as a whole; it may involve the erosion of a core principal of the Civil Service – the willingness of senior civil servants to offer informed criticism of Government policy.

Gilmour certainly opposed what he saw as Margaret Thatcher's courting of a certain type of official and her disdain for many of the top officials she inherited. James Prior adopted a similar view. He cited the case of Donald Derx, a one-time high ranking official in his own Department of Employment. Prior observes that on a visit to the department, Mrs Thatcher became involved in an argument with a 'very dedicated civil servant'. The clash was over an issue concerning secondary industrial action. Prior noted that she knew neither the facts, nor the legal position, on this detail of policy. Derx ended the argument by bluntly inquiring: 'Prime Minister – do you really want to know the facts?' Prior (1986, p. 136) pointedly observed that afterwards Derx was consistently passed over for promotion, and concludes:

> It was a pity that she was not able to accept that by standing up to her, he was displaying qualities which a civil servant must have if he is to serve his Minister properly, and which she of all people used generally to accept.

Alan Clark was more forthright about the outcome of Derx's meeting with the Prime Minister. In his diaries he (1993, p. 22) declared that:

> The wretched Donald Derx apparently became impatient with [her] thought processes some time ago – early in the '79 Parliament before the old nostra had been undermined, and these changes confirmed by the electorate; and at their first meeting was emboldened to be 'cutting' in response. She marked his card on the spot, and he is going to take early retirement, having 'had it conveyed to him' that he will never make Permanent Secretary.

The attention Margaret Thatcher paid to individual officials was a common theme running through nearly all her ministers' memoirs. Like Prior, Cecil Parkinson (Secretary of State at the Department of Transport 1989–90) also referred a visit by Mrs Thatcher to the Department of Trade soon after the 1979 election, to examine, as he saw it, the work of those officials within that department. Parkinson noted (1992, p. 161) that she spent the first hour with senior civil servants, in which time:

> She asked each of them in turn to give a description of what they and the part of the department they were responsible for did and

what its immediate objectives were. After each had spoken I noticed that she was putting three dots under some names and a line under others. I came to the conclusion the line meant good and the three dots meant suspect.

Parkinson's observations appear to confirm that the aim of these brief departmental visits was to enable Mrs Thatcher to assess, at first-hand, the top personnel in Whitehall. Where an individual did not fit her personal requirements they were 'shifted out', to make way for a new 'type' of official. Parkinson (1992, p. 197) also confirmed the view that her interest was not in institutions, but in individuals: 'Although Mrs Thatcher had a deep distrust of the FCO as an institution, she had a very high regard for individual members of it, especially Anthony Acland'.

The emphasis on individuals is something Mrs Thatcher (1993, p. 49) confirmed in her own memoirs. However, Francis Pym (Secretary of State at the Foreign Office, 1982–3) developed a more subtle variant on this theme, concentrating upon those individuals with whom Mrs Thatcher surrounded herself – her own Downing Street staff. Pym (1984, p. 17) argued that, because of the sheer scale of government business, the Prime Minister was unable to dictate the policy of each department:

> her response has been to expand the Downing Street staff to include experts in every major area, thus establishing a government within a government. In most cases, people have been chosen who reinforce her point of view rather than challenge it, which produces a greater rigidity of outlook than that encountered in the Civil Service.

Pym argued that Margaret Thatcher was not confident that the introduction of a certain type of official to the highest grades in Whitehall would be enough. There was an urgent need to gather a personal staff round her, who worked daily with her and had the commitment and belief to support and carry out the urgent, radical policies she believed the country required. Certainly, the more infamous names associated with the Thatcher era, all of whom worked on her personal staff – Charles Powell, Bernard Ingham and Alan Walters – appear to confirm this view. If Mrs Thatcher believed she had the right individual in the right job, then her loyalty to that person was steadfast, often at the expense of political expediency. The political commentator Hugo Young identified a classic example of this involving her Chief Press Officer, Bernard Ingham:

In January 1985 Ingham cost the country rather a lot of money. Sterling appeared to be in free fall, and he gave a briefing to the Sunday Press which conveyed the impression that there would be no intervention to prop up the currency. It was put about that the Prime Minister, in conformity with her belief in market power, would not object to a 'one-dollar' pound. This was an unsophisticated effort, venturing into territory that Ingham probably did not understand, and he was harangued next day before a Treasury court consisting of Chancellor Lawson and his senior officials. It might have been a tricky moment for him. His words could plausibly be said to have cost the Bank of England several hundred million pounds in support for sterling. But he escaped scot free. He had taken the precaution of securing the Prime Minister's absolution, which effectively took the wind out of Lawson's indignation. A few days later, she was steering him round a drinks party in the Commons, saying 'This is Bernard. Bernard is the greatest'. (Young 1989, p. 445)

This event, so closely preceding the Westland affair, another incident which prompted many of Mrs Thatcher's close advisers to call for Ingham's resignation, highlights the loyalty she paid to *her* people. Her Cabinet ministers also testified to this loyalty. As Ridley (1991, p. 41) noted:

Margaret Thatcher's experiences must have left her with a certain animus against them [civil servants] in general – but she was loyal to them as individuals. She rightly saw civil servants as being in a very different category from ministers. Civil servants could not defend themselves from public attack, whereas politicians could. She was always fierce in her defence of her staff against Opposition attack.

Increased Interference – but was it Politicisation?

Minister's memoirs revealed that, in general, they regarded the Civil Service as a competently organised and well-run institution. They also confirmed the view that the Prime Minister took an increased interest in the appointment of top officials. They argued this was caused by her desire to effect a change in the ethos of Whitehall by the introduction of a new breed of official, rather than through an attempt to alter the firmly existing, firmly entrenched, structures. This inevitably leads to two questions: did minister's believe her increased interest led to some form of politicisation of the higher Civil Service?; what are Margaret Thatcher's own views on this issue?

'Overt Politicisation' – Lawson the Loner

Nigel Lawson's memoirs focused on the central role of the Treasury and he argued that, as a result of Mrs Thatcher's actions, this department regained ascendancy in Whitehall. Lawson felt she set out to surround herself with 'like-minded' individuals in posts of greatest importance. He argued that, in restoring the pre-eminence of the Treasury in Whitehall, it was Mrs Thatcher's aim:

> to create a bunker, staffed by appointees of whose exclusive personal loyalty she felt confident, into whom she could retreat – in the process distancing herself from her ministers and gradually losing touch with the real world outside. (Lawson 1992, p. 384)

However, Lawson also dealt with the ability of ministers to introduce the officials they wanted, against the preference of the Prime Minister. He contended that a minister strong enough and with a clear view of whom he desired to have working for him, could determine the final appointment of the highest officials within a department. He argued that this was the case, even if the minister's views were not supported by a Prime Minister, who was believed to undertake an active role in the appointments procedure. Lawson cited the June 1983 succession to Douglas Wass, then Permanent Secretary in the Treasury, as an occasion on which a minister determined an appointment against the views of Mrs Thatcher. Lawson acknowledged that all Permanent Secretary appointments had to be approved by the Prime Minister. However, he argued that the consensus in the Treasury was that neither of the Second Permanent Secretaries were up to the job and, thus, the choice lay between two Deputy Secretaries in the Department – David Hancock and Peter Middleton. Unfortunately, Mrs Thatcher did not concur with either her Ministers' or the Treasury's view on the subject, instead preferring Anthony Rawlinson for: 'whom she had a soft spot. He was not only the best looking . . . something that always cut a great deal of ice with her. He was also the one undoubted Tory of the three' (Lawson 1992, p. 267).[6] Yet Lawson maintained that Leon Brittan, Geoffrey Howe and he were able to force through Middleton's appointment. His observation that Mrs Thatcher's initial preference was for the only identifiable Tory suggested he gave credence to the notion that an official's political outlook held sway in the promotion stakes. He also suggested that, if opposed by a powerful coalition, in this case a united front of three eminent Cabinet Ministers, Mrs Thatcher's view might not necessarily prevail, despite the importance she supposedly placed on the appointment of top officials.

Although Lawson is the only Cabinet Minister of the Thatcher Government who appears to subscribe to the notion of 'overt politicisation', his comments should not be dismissed outright. Gamble (1994, p. 39) argued that Lawson's views are legitimised by the fact he was the longest serving Chancellor of this century and was, for most of the Thatcher years, right at the heart of her Government. He concluded that:

> Lawson is an intellectual [he worked as a financial journalist before entering politics] and he has an intellectual's curiosity about how government works and what the rationale for policy should be. What emerges from his book is a fascinating account of his time in government and of the Treasury in particular. (Gamble 1994, p. 40)

A 'Management-Efficiency Ethos' – Ridley and Carrington Detect the Signs

The two ministers who felt that Mrs Thatcher attempted to introduce a management culture into the highest echelons of Whitehall, Nicholas Ridley and Peter Carrington, both adopt in their memoirs what Gamble labels an 'argument and doctrine' theme. The fact that they came from different wings of the Conservative Party, yet concurred on the subject of Margaret Thatcher's approach to the Civil Service, adds credence to their views.

Ridley (1991, p. 44), one of Margaret Thatcher's closest allies in Cabinet, believed:

> Her relationship with the Civil Service was not easy . . . at least until she came upon civil servants who were both capable and loyal as individuals; these received her entire support and trust – but she was suspicious of the general body of civil servants. For

both groups the test was, 'Are you here to help or to hinder?' it seems to me a reasonable question for the Head of Government to ask, but perhaps she asked it to obviously.

Nicholas Ridley clearly felt that Mrs Thatcher sought out individuals who were capable of getting on with the job in hand. She wanted 'can-do' individuals, capable of implementing her agenda for change. Yet, the search for 'can-do', market-driven officials in itself creates problems. As the academic F. Ridley (1983b, p. 42) properly noted:

> One can make business efficiency the touchstone of the organisation of the state – but that is a political philosophy . . . associated with the market economy Right rather than with traditional Conservatism or the Left.

Likewise, Peter Carrington identified in Mrs Thatcher a desire to introduce individuals with business/managerial credentials because they would swiftly carry out what was requested of them. He emphasised her policy of openly introducing leading industrialists and businessmen into the corridors of Whitehall. Though his observations do not refer exclusively to the top layers of officialdom, he concluded that:

> It didn't work in the least well when put into effect after our return to power. In the first place, few businesses want to send their best brains away for any length of time. In the second place the businessmen who tried the experiment found, somewhat to their surprise, that the Civil Service they were intended to stimulate and broaden knew their jobs and understood the world a great deal better than they had been led to believe: and I suspect, at least as well as they did themselves. (Carrington 1988, p. 234)

The success or failure of introducing individuals from the business community into the Civil Service is not the issue here. What is of importance is Carrington's perception that Mrs Thatcher attempted to introduce a certain 'type' of individual to Whitehall – those concerned with good management and value for money. As Ridley (1983b, p. 42) noted, this, in itself, can be construed as a form of politicisation.

A 'Socialisation' Scenario? – Gilmour Falls between Two Camps

In his memoirs, Gilmour (1992, p. 227) emphasised that:

> Mrs Thatcher played a much greater part in the appointment of top civil servants than any of her predecessors. The charge that she politicised the Civil Service is over-stated; but the careers of those who crossed her seldom prospered, and that the enthusiastic championing of neo-liberal ideas was an aid to advancement.

Gilmour rejected the idea that any form of overt politicisation had occurred. He believed that Mrs Thatcher's increased interest in the appointment's procedure was not designed to infiltrate the top ranks of the higher Civil Service with a cohort of mandarins closely identifiable with the politics of the Conservative Government. Rather, he detected a more subtle type of politicisation, similar to that which Ridley and Carrington subscribed to – the appointment of individuals who were not sceptics when it came to 'neo-liberal' policies and 'laissez-faire' economics and who also displayed an interest in administrative techniques. Yet, there is another side to Gilmour's observations. The fact that the careers of those individuals who crossed her did not flourish indicated Margaret Thatcher's desire to surround herself with those she felt were of a similar 'mind-set'. She introduced mandarins who had passed the Hugo Young (1989, pp. 162, 332) test: 'Is he one of us?' This suggested Gilmour unwittingly evokes two different interpretations of politicisation. He acknowledged Mrs Thatcher's support for officials who were sympathetic to 'neo-liberal' policies and were effective 'can-do' individuals; yet, at the same time, he unwittingly points to a 'socialisation' effect. The suggestion here is that she preferred officials who had been at the centre and who had been socialised into the latest *en vogue* methods of conducting Government business.

Mrs Thatcher – the Private Office, a Route to Success

Mrs Thatcher's own position is most revealing; she accepted she had taken 'a close interest in senior appointments in the Civil Service from the first, because they could affect the morale and efficiency of whole departments'. She argued the importance of this strategy was because:

I was determined to change the mentality exemplified in the early 1970s by a remark attributed to the then Head of the Civil Service, that the best that the British could hope for was the 'orderly management of decline'. The country and the Civil Service itself was sold short by such attitudes. They also threatened a waste of scarce talent. (Thatcher 1993, p. 46)

Mrs Thatcher was more prepared than her predecessors to adopt an active role in the appointment's procedure. This, she felt, did not contradict the convention of a politically neutral Civil Service. She openly accepted the Pym observation that she surrounded herself with 'like-minded' people in her Downing Street Office:

I usually held personal interviews with the candidates for private secretary for my office. Those who came were some of the very brightest young men and women in the Civil Service . . . I wanted to see people of the same calibre, with lively minds and a commitment to good administration promoted to hold the senior posts in the departments. (Thatcher 1993, p. 46)

It was therefore logical that:

during my time in government, many of my former private secretaries went on to head departments. In all these decisions, however, ability, drive and enthusiasm were what mattered; political allegiance was not something I took into account. (Thatcher 1993, p. 46)

Margaret Thatcher categorically rejected the notion that any form of overt politicisation occurred during her period of office. Despite this, the description of her approach to appointments in the Private Office does nothing to allay the charge that a form of covert politicisation occurred. She conceded that individuals who had served under her in the Private Office often went on to become heads of other departments. This strengthened the notion that a form of 'socialisation' occurred; individuals who served in the Private Office were moulded into 'can-do' officials. They would graduate, having passed the 'one-of-us' test, and could expect a rapid promotional career path. Mrs Thatcher's memoirs suggest that she did have an effect on the higher Civil Service; she selected senior civil servants with certain qualities, skills and attitudes, who supported her Government's policies, or at least its approach towards problems. As F. Ridley (1983b, p. 43) concluded, a form of politicisation did occur:

> Intervention by politicians in promotion, even if it does not have a straight party-political character, tends to politicise the Civil Service and thus calls into question the constitutional convention that senior officials are the neutral servants of successive governments.

Political Memoirs – a Vital yet Partial Source of Material

In determining the usefulness of memoirs for the political scientist, Gamble (1994, p. 35) posed the questions: 'Do they offer more than self-serving, bland, highly selective, and retrospective accounts by politicians of their political careers? Do they provide fresh evidence about the events which they describe or are they merely plausible fictions?' The information extracted from the memoirs of Mrs Thatcher's ministers certainly provide new material concerning a possible Thatcher effect on the higher Civil Service. Thus, as a tool for research the memoirs more than justify themselves.

All the ministers who wrote memoirs believed that the Civil Service which served them was, generally, a well-run institution. More importantly, each minister felt Margaret Thatcher had taken an increased interest in the appointments procedure. Mrs Thatcher herself agreed with her ministers on this point. Interestingly, the memoirs also indicate that none of these ministers fully backed their Prime Minister's approach to reforming the Civil Service. However, they do testify to the loyalty she lavished on those officials she regarded as her allies in Government.

On the issue of 'politicisation', in its different forms, the ministers' views become more inconsistent. Nigel Lawson was the only minister whose comments suggested that some form of 'overt politicisation' occurred. Gamble (1994, p. 39) would argue that the views of Lawson cannot be discounted, for the simple reason that, for a long period, he was at the heart of the Thatcher Government. However, earlier evidence indicated that the notion of 'overt politicisation' is crude and over-simplified. The majority of political commentators and journalists reject outright the view that Mrs Thatcher set-out to appoint individuals sympathetic to the Party's policies. Mainstream opinion in all the opposition parties is also sceptical about any claims of overt politicisation. Thus, while political scientists should respect the comments of Lawson, they must be assessed in relation to strong evidence which refutes this interpretation of 'politicisation'. At the same time it should be recalled that Lawson became, for many, a maligned figure, following his acrimonious departure from Government. As Gamble (1994, p. 40) concluded:

> The book [Lawson's memoirs] is written as a defence of his record. After resigning in 1989 he found himself the object of vilification in the Tory press after having shortly before been one of their greatest heroes. He wanted to defend his record and he does it by setting out in great detail how policy evolved, and what the assumptions behind it were.

Two ministers, Carrington and Ridley, believed Mrs Thatcher's increased interest in the appointments procedure was a result of her desire to see those individuals with a managerial approach promoted. This supports the evidence of other commentators: Fry (1984, p. 330), Kavanagh (1990, p. 47), Drewry and Butcher (1991, p. 216). Yet, it is the observations of Gilmour and Thatcher which may prove most revealing. Gilmour, it could be argued, supported the 'managerially-oriented, can-do' scenario, yet attributed this to a possible 'socialisation' effect. Likewise, Mrs Thatcher accepted that she introduced a new breed of official to the highest grades of Whitehall, 'able to deal with the job in hand'. However, she also confirmed that a major route to the highest grades was through the centre. Gilmour and Thatcher's comments, substantiate the statistical evidence which highlighted the high number of officials who, prior to being appointed to Grades 1/1a had, at a previous stage in their career, served in either the Treasury, the Cabinet Office or the Prime Minister's Office. There are two possible explanations of this pattern: either individuals had been socialised into her way of thinking, cognitively becoming Thatcherites; or the centre could be regarded as a testing ground for officials lower-down the hierarchy who gained the reputation of can-do individuals. In an earlier article, I argued that:

> Mrs Thatcher was keen to see at first hand whether officials who had gained an efficient, able, 'getting on with the job' reputation, were in fact worthy of accelerated promotion. In transferring these individuals to the Treasury, Cabinet Office or the Prime Minister's Office she was able to gain a close working knowledge of how effectively they operated . . . Those who impressed gained accelerated

promotion to the highest ranks, the others were either held back or continued at the normal rate of progress. (Richards 1993, p. 25)

Unfortunately, Gamble does not point out that the political memoirs of ministers, by their very nature, are limited by their partiality. They present the views of Cabinet Ministers. To obtain a more balanced view, an examination of the experiences of all players involved is required. As such, we need the views of civil servants. However, very few officials who served in the 1980s wrote about their experience in office.[7] For this reason, I undertook a series of interviews with senior civil servants, mostly retired, all of whom had served in prominent positions in Whitehall during the 1980s. In particular, I wished to explore further the notion that there was a centre effect involving some form of socialisation.

6

The Mandarins Address a Thatcher Effect

For me her greatest single achievement, which made all these and other things possible, was her refusal to accept, or be daunted by, the prevailing air of defeatism which she confronted on taking office in 1979. (Ingham 1991, p. 229)

THIS CHAPTER USES information I compiled from a series of interviews with retired officials who served at the highest grades in Whitehall during the 1980s, to attain their views on a possible Thatcher effect on the higher Civil Service.[1] The focus is to identify whether or not Margaret Thatcher's involvement in the appointments process differed from that of her predecessors and, if so, what were the tangible effects for Whitehall. The interviews addressed a range of questions: Did Mrs Thatcher take an increased role in the top appointments procedure and, if so, why?; Did any overt politicisation occur?; Did she consciously attempt to appoint a new breed of official, one with specific managerial/can-do attributes?

The interviews were of great importance, as they provided both a counter-balance and an alternative perspective to views on the Civil Service presented by ministers in their memoirs. They demonstrated that the mandarins were unanimous in their view that Mrs Thatcher had taken a greater, active, interest in the appointments procedure, than her predecessors. In addition, all reject the notion that any form of overt politicisation occurred. However, their explanations of why she assumed a greater role in the process differ.

Mrs Thatcher and Top Appointments

Sir Robert Armstrong, the single Head of the Home Civil Service from 1983 to 1987, and the official solely responsible for making all appointments to the highest two grades in Whitehall during that period, has always emphasised that Mrs Thatcher paid keen attention to the appointments procedure. This was seen in the evidence he gave to the TCSC:

> Q   How much influence does the Prime Minister actually have over an appointment?
> A   The Prime Minister takes a very great interest in them and will discuss them all thoroughly.
> Q   Is she a dominant influence or does she simply concur in the recommendations you make?
> A   Sometimes she concurs, sometimes she wants to discuss them. Both things happen. (Evidence to the TCSC cited in RIPA 1987, p. 42)

In 1995, an ex-Cabinet Secretary substantiated this view in a communication to me, arguing rather reservedly that:

> It is difficult for me to compare Lady Thatcher's interest in the top appointments process with that of other Prime Ministers, since she was Prime Minister throughout my time as Head of the Home Civil Service. She certainly took a keen interest and my impression is that she gave more time to the consideration of these appointments than other Prime Ministers.

Unwittingly, this official touches on an important point here: if all Prime Ministers assumed a high profile role in the appointment of top officials, then a detailed, comparative analysis would be essential. Fortunately, the views of key insiders are unequivocal and, thus, a thorough comparison is unnecessary. Margaret Thatcher played a more active part in the appointments procedure than her predecessors. Certainly, James Callaghan, when interviewed by the TCSC, made it clear he was more willing than his successor to allow the Civil Service to guide him in appointments:

> the degree of interest would depend on my knowledge of the persons involved. If I did not know them I would be willing to accept the advice of people who did know them . . . If somebody was put up to me to become Under Secretary in the Ministry of

Agriculture and I had no idea about the three people who had
been put up I would choose the one recommended which had
already gone through the Permanent Secretary in the Department
and a small group of Permanent Secretaries who knew these people
together with the Civil Service Department . . . I do not think I ever
overruled them. (Cited in RIPA 1987, p. 42)

This view was confirmed by a number of officials. A Civil Service
Commissioner who played a central role in the appointments procedure noted that:

There was at one time a philosophy that really it was for the
Civil Service to find the right people and Callaghan was a Prime
Minister that obviously agreed with that. Mrs Thatcher had a
very considerable interest in individuals. She certainly exerted an
influence on this whole process.

Sir Frank Cooper (Permanent Under Secretary of State at the Ministry of Defence 1976–82) was one of a small number of officials who
sat on SASC and thus had first-hand knowledge of Mrs Thatcher's
involvement in the procedures. He argued that she:

adopted a more obvious interest than her predecessors. But no Prime
Minister treated, whatever recommendation was put to him, as if
it was simply a rubber stamp. If you ask did she have a higher
involvement than her predecessor, I am bound to say that James
Callaghan took a great interest, but he had a different outlook.
He thought the Civil Service should run the Civil Service and
implement ministerial decisions, whereas she definitely did not
think that. (Cooper interviewed, 20 December 1994)

Here, Cooper implied that Callaghan, as he earlier admitted, was
perfectly willing to allow Whitehall to guide him in the appointment
of top officials. Sir William Ryrie, a Second Permanent Secretary in
the Treasury 1980–82, stretched this point a stage further. He highlighted the degree of disparity in activeness, not just by Callaghan,
but between all modern Prime Ministers and Margaret Thatcher:

Unquestionably, she wanted to be involved in the appointment of
every Permanent Secretary and, to some extent, maybe not in
every case, in Deputy Secretary positions as well. She was far
more involved in that, than any previous Prime Minister . . . It

was a bit of a formality with previous Prime Ministers. (Ryrie interviewed, 19 June 1995)

Ryrie's point indicated that, whilst previous Prime Ministers undertook a passing interest in the appointments procedure, their role was more as a passive over-seer. This clearly contrasted with the Thatcher approach, which involved pro-active input at the Prime Ministerial stage, designed to have a tangible effect on the final appointment of an official.

Officials paid testimony to the fact Mrs Thatcher actively participated in the appointments procedure and thoroughly scrutinised any post that was soon to fall vacant. John Cassels, Second Permanent Secretary in the Management and Personnel Office 1981–83, was directly involved in personnel management in Whitehall. He concluded:

> I think that she probably took more interest than other Prime Ministers, with a result that a few of these appointments went one way rather than another and some certainly didn't go some particular way. (Cassels interviewed 20 December 1994)

A Deputy Secretary in the Department of Energy echoed similar sentiments:

> There is no doubt that, not only in relation to Energy, but departments elsewhere, she adopted a much higher profile. She wanted to be consulted intimately, certainly on appointments at Grade 1 and some Grade 2s and she often started out with a very pre-determined view.

In fact, all the senior officials I interviewed testified to Margaret Thatcher's higher profile in this process. What were the reasons for, and the consequences of, this increased interest? Was it a result of her desire to see Conservative Party sympathisers appointed?

Overt Politicisation – The Mandarins Reject the Premise

Every official I interviewed emphasised that Mrs Thatcher did not try to appoint individuals she regarded as openly sympathetic to Conservative Party policies. William Ryrie clearly stated: 'I don't think there was overt politicisation. She wasn't looking for people with a Conservative political view' (Ryrie interviewed, 19 June 1995). Likewise, an official directly involved in the appointments procedures during the 1980s believed he: 'knew of no case where somebody was picked, because he or she was a Conservative'. When I asked Peter Kemp, Second Permanent Secretary in the Cabinet Office 1988–92, if Mrs Thatcher set out to appoint politically sympathetic officials, he replied: 'That is absolute nonsense' (Kemp interviewed, 17 November 1994).

Not surprisingly, Bernard Ingham, Margaret Thatcher's Press Secretary from 1979–1990, was forthright in his rejection of this notion, and his response had a typical 'Ingham' resonance about it: 'I don't think she took a blind bit of interest in what their party affiliation was, otherwise she would not have appointed me. I have not actually been a member of any party since 1968' (Ingham interviewed, 22 December 1995). Ingham had previously been a polemical left-wing columnist, writing under the pseudonym of 'Albion', for the *Leeds Weekly Citizen* between 1964 and 1967. He was also a member of the Labour Party in the 1950s and 1960s. Indeed, in May 1965 he stood as a Labour Party Candidate, though he failed to win the Moortown Ward of Leeds City Council. Although he left the Labour Party at the end of the 1960s, he later worked for the Callaghan Government as Under-Secretary in the Energy Conservation Division for the Department of Energy in 1978–9. When Margaret Thatcher personally oversaw his appointment as her Chief Press Secretary in 1979, his curriculum vitae could hardly have reflected a history of staunch Conservative Party support.

When I pressed Ingham as to why, particularly during the first Conservative term of office, many political commentators believed some form of overt politicisation occurred in Whitehall, he replied:

> I think Mrs Thatcher would have got a worse reputation and indeed, in my view, an unjustified reputation, for political appointments, because of the way that some of the politicians around her gossiped about being 'one of us'. Civil servants in my experience, do not reveal their party political affiliation at all. (Ingham interviewed, 22 December 1994)

In light of the memoirs of Thatcher's ministers, Ingham's observation rings true. Her Cabinets never involved a harmonious coming together of like-minded individuals. The very fact that the term 'Wets' was coined for a particular faction within her Cabinet during the first term, indicated that division existed. The writings of

Francis Pym (1984), James Prior (1986), Peter Carrington (1988) and Ian Gilmour (1992), all testify to the sense of division in her Cabinets. They also reported a growing, if unspoken, sense of being outsiders, of not being 'one of us' – the phrase coined by the political columnist Hugo Young and applied to Margaret Thatcher's inner courtiers.[2] In such an environment, it was hardly surprising that these individuals, located at the periphery of the Thatcher Government, felt that those who 'held the ear of the Prime Minister', in particular, a number of top-serving Government ffficials, had become politicised. Indeed, this probably accounts for the popularity of the notion that overt politicisation did occur in Whitehall by many media and political commentators, during the first half of the 1980s.

On the evidence of both ministers and civil servants, it would appear plausible to reject the notion that this particular form of politicisation occurred. This then leads one to ask why, when the office of the Prime Minister was already burdened with an exceptionally heavy workload, should Margaret Thatcher wish to further increase her daily schedule, by paying unprecedented attention to the appointments procedure?

Why the Increased Interest: Undermining the Consensus?

When I questioned the mandarins on this area, there was general agreement that Mrs Thatcher was unhappy with the self-satisfied atmosphere which had evolved within Whitehall during the previous two decades. She was frustrated with the post-war consensus and the apparent belief in Whitehall that its role was to control the management of Britain's decline. Thus, she believed there was a need for change. As Peter Kemp put it:

> I think her approach to this was that she was a child of her time in the sense that she had come through from a consensus era of the fifties, sixties and into the seventies. She had perceived that Britain wasn't doing all that marvellously. She subscribed to the view that the Civil Service had something to do with this. She had been associated with senior civil servants in the 1960s who had been bright young sparks in the 1940s and who were very consensus minded. Cultured that way because they had to win the war. She had seen alongside this Britain going down, the public sector getting flabby and so on. She tended to blame people. She looked at the Civil Service and didn't

much like what she saw. These are pompous guys and they were men [emphasis on men] who thought they knew best. They thought they were running the ballast in society. (Kemp interviewed, 17 November 1994)

Rather than become involved in a long drawn out process of structural reform, Mrs Thatcher felt a quicker and more effective method of change, was to re-style the type of individual at the top of the Whitehall pyramid and allow the effect of this to permeate through the remaining tiers of the organisation.

Clive Priestley worked as Chief of Staff for Derek Rayner in the Prime Minister's Office between 1979 and 1983. When asked to explain Margaret Thatcher's increased role, he reinforced Kemp's observation:

I think she wanted signs of life, signs that the sap was still rising, signs of vitality and enjoyment. One of the things she reacted to was a statement attributed to Sir William Armstrong,[3] which was that the Civil Service was there to manage decline in an orderly fashion. She really did react to that very strongly indeed. She didn't like being patronised. She did like to feel people were genuine, that what they were saying to her was the genuine thing . . . I think she was impatient with individuals she felt belonged to an old-fashioned, wettish, supercilious breed. (Priestley interviewed, 14 November 1994)

John Cassels argued Mrs Thatcher was disillusioned by the type of official she believed had risen to the top of the Civil Service tree and the attitudes which such an individual spread throughout the rest of Whitehall. He felt:

She wanted change; she thought that Permanent Secretaries used to a consensus culture would be against it . . . She thought one of the problems of the country was that of the senior Civil Service. I don't think there was the slightest doubt about that. She had a whole range of things she wanted to change. I think she saw the senior Civil Service as being wedded to a kind of consensus and a kind of middle-of-the-road attitude which was against change. I think she thought that individual civil servants were prone to be satisfied with the way things were. Whereas there were others, elsewhere, who were more prepared to have a go at change. (Cassels interviewed, 20 December 1994)

When I questioned John Cassels on this disillusionment with the top tier of Whitehall mandarins, he elaborated, arguing that:

> She was in a hurry to make change in a way that most Prime Ministers are not. I think that she did feel more than most people that those who weren't with her, were against her. Not because they were against her or against Conservatives, but that they were for the status-quo, temperamentally. (Cassels interviewed, 20 December 1994)

Her response was to ensure that the officials who were appointed to the highest grades, would be capable of implementing her Government's agenda for change. Frank Cooper believed that: 'she was looking at people as individuals and saying "Is this chap likely to be able to effect change and is this chap really capable of making things happen"?' (Cooper interviewed, 20 December 1994). Bernard Ingham felt she wanted to take on those elements in Whitehall who lacked the commitment to the Administration's programme to rejuvenate Britain and replace them with people capable of implementing a new agenda:

> What she was interested in was whether people could get things done. Did they want to do things. This was a very important approach. In 1979–80, I experienced the interesting phenomenon in No. 10, that often when Mrs Thatcher wanted to do things the answer came back 'Oh no you can't'. There was enormous defeatism in the system. The Establishment was defeated. (Ingham interviewed, 22 December 1995)

What is important to note is Ingham's reference to the fact that from the outset Mrs Thatcher felt that Whitehall needed to be reformed. Kemp detected that she desired a new breed of official to be appointed, one which she felt she could rely on to work with her:

> I think she was sympathetic to people who she thought she could get on with and I don't suggest there is any sleaze about this sort of thing. It wasn't that they voted Conservative. The question is, did she feel she was comfortable with them. I remember talking to a senior member of here Private Office, and he made a paternalistic yet cynical comment: 'there are an awful lot of things in government she doesn't understand, but she takes it in through her finger-tips, like-all

good politicians, that this is a good idea, that that gives good vibes and she feels warm about it.' I think she is the same with people. It came in through her finger-tips . . . I don't think it is a wrong approach to be surrounded by people you feel comfortable with. These are advisers, and comfortableness is good, because it makes for better delivery, due to the chemistry between these people. (Kemp interviewed, 17 November 1994)

When I asked Peter Middleton, Permanent Secretary at the Treasury 1983–91, for his perception of Margaret Thatcher's approach, he argued:

It wasn't just a question of saying yes or no to people at random. She began to pick a particular sort of person. She wasn't so interested in people who sit there and analyse problems and say you can do this on the one hand, or you can do that on the other. Instead, she wanted people who would bring a more energetic approach to things and push the Government's policy forward. (Middleton interviewed, 16 November 1994)

John Sparrow, Head of the Central Policy Review Staff in 1982–83, echoed Peter Middleton's sentiments:

I don't believe it was politicisation. I think it was to get things done. The famous quote about Lord Young: 'He doesn't bring me problems, he brings me solutions', that sort of mind appealed to her and I don't think it was politicisation, it was action. (Sparrow interviewed, 15 November 1994)

Finally, Clive Priestley believed Mrs Thatcher targeted the most important positions in Whitehall and ensured the people installed were those she felt happy with: 'What she says very clearly in her own book is that, in effect, the effort to switch the system as a whole was not going to work. Therefore you found people and put them in key positions' (Priestley interviewed, 14 November 1994).

The mandarins made it clear that they believed Margaret Thatcher took a greater interest in the appointments procedure because she believed the Civil Service would have a residual effect on her attempts at reforming the nation. Therefore, the most pragmatic method of combatting this problem was to wait for a vacancy to arise at the highest level and then appoint an official she thought would display enthusiasm for the programme of change. Thus, instead of having an immediate clear out at Grades 1 and 2, with the likelihood of alienating a broad section of Whitehall, attracting widespread criticism from both opposition and media circles and, in all probability, triggering a constitutional crisis, she allowed time for the natural turnover of officials to take place. In so doing, she could oversee the appointment of individuals she felt she could work with effectively, whilst hoping not to attract any undue attention. William Ryrie concluded:

> She wanted to make real changes. She was a bit of a revolutionary in some senses. That is putting it a bit strongly, but I think there is truth in it and I think she felt that the Civil Service was going to be an obstacle. She wanted to make sure that there were people in charge who would do it in the way she wanted. (Ryrie interviewed, 19 June 1995)

Thatcher's New Breed of Mandarin

Having established that Margaret Thatcher had a desire to see a new breed of official appointed at the highest level in Whitehall, the next question I asked officials was, what type of individual did they feel she could work with? The Cabinet Secretary is the individual solely responsible for making the final appointment. He is therefore in a position to know more about the whims of Margaret Thatcher during the 1980s than any other person. I asked one ex-Cabinet Secretary what characteristics he felt she looked for, when they discussed a forthcoming appointment?

> When I was Head of the Home Civil Service, I was concerned to recommend, and Mrs Thatcher was concerned to approve, appointments of people who would be qualified, by experience and personality, to provide effective management as well as to provide good advice on policy formulation.

This official categorically accepted that there had been a shift in the type of individual Mrs Thatcher wished to see appointed during the 1980s, compared to those appointed in the previous decade. A switch in emphasis away from civil servants who were regarded as predominantly policy advisers, towards officials who were seen as effective managers and policy implementors. John Burgh, who served as a Deputy Secretary in a number of departments for over eight years, confirmed this analysis:

> I think it is right to reject outright politicisation. But I do think she went for the 'can-do' individuals and attached great importance to the managerial side. Basically people who would do things, rather than very good analysts. (Burgh interviewed, 18 November 1994)

Peter Kemp went as far as to define what he felt was meant by the Hugo Young quote 'one of us'. In so doing, he argued that what Mrs Thatcher was really interested in doing was putting together a team which could work effectively with one another:

> She divided people: the famous quote 'is he one of us' does not necessarily mean does that person agrees with what I am doing, because she was much too open minded for that sort of thing. Are we a team? Do we think the same way? Are we going to be able to exchange these views? That is why the Inghams and the Powells got on so well. I am sure both would have argued like mad with her over things, but it didn't harm them. (Kemp interviewed, 17 November 1994)

The majority of the officials I interviewed all referred to the switch from policy advisers to what was generally termed 'managerial/can-do' type officials. However, despite Kemp's attempt to explain Hugo Young's label 'one of us', most were uncomfortable with this label, believing it placed too much of a political slant on the Thatcher appointments. Instead, they used two basic terms to describe this switch: 'managerial/can-do' types; or 'positive/negative' individuals. Both labels effectively describe the same type of individual and refer to a new, high profile official whose main function was to concentrate on policy implementation.

Patrick Benner, Deputy Secretary in the DHSS, 1976–84, described the first of these two labels:

> 'Can-doers', that is right. If she saw a chap with first-class intellectual ability as well, you grabbed him. But if he had first-class intellectual ability, but would be totally incompetent at dealing with people, you scrubbed him. I think this sort of message was very much being taken on board. I was working on selection boards for administrators, up until 1990 and that was very much the atmosphere. (Benner interviewed, 6 November 1994)

Margaret Thatcher did not ignore those with highly developed intellectual capabilities, but if they were not enthusiastic administrators, their promotion prospects were hindered. As John Cassels noted:

> She preferred more cut and dried type individuals, than those who talk in terms of: 'Well, on the one hand and on the other'. Her famous remark about David Young applies there. Is this chap always going to be seeing both sides of the question, or is he actually going to come forward and say: 'Well, in my view, in the light of all this, is that we can do X, or we can do Y and I'll do X if you want it done'. She much preferred that. (Cassels interviewed, 20 December 1994)

Frank Cooper established rather an unusual reputation in Whitehall for being one of the few officials who advocated the need for civil servants to display much stronger personnel management skills. He also detected this shift, under Mrs Thatcher, away from old style policy advisers, arguing that:

> I think what was also happening was that people who were building reputations in the middle ranks, were producing schemes, policies and introducing plans in a way that worked. I think there was a distinct move away from chaps who were very, very brilliant, to doers and managers. People who performed and were capable of delivering things, progressively became a much more important element. (Cooper interviewed, 20 December 1994)

Charles Powell, her Private Secretary and adviser on Foreign Affairs 1984–90, agreed with Frank Cooper's conclusions that Margaret Thatcher wanted individuals who, in relation to policy implementation, 'could deliver results'. He argued that she resented the Establishment, which she felt had placed a stranglehold on existing latent, dynamic forces in Britain; her desire was to see a more meritocratic Service evolve:

> I would say the most important thing about her, stemming from her own background and experience, was that she was somebody who believed in people getting on through their own ability. Therefore, she wasn't interested in their social background and whether they had been to Oxbridge. She was interested in whether they could perform and she was very rigorous about that. She was very much the meritocrat. That was very important. She had a great preference

for doers, rather than elegant minute crafters. She wanted people who would get on and do things. (Powell interviewed, 16 November 1994)

Other interviewers emphasised her preference for positive officials. One therefore felt:

The words that were fashionable at the time were positive and negative. A distinction between those who actively promoted change and those who were more concerned with the difficulties. I suppose it is a fact that when governments are constantly changing, the civil servants who have to run quite big departments, probably tend to breed the kind of person who is ready to tell ministers of all the problems that stand in the way of change. Whereas, certainly after the Conservatives had been in power for sometime, Mrs Thatcher was looking more for people whose attitude was: 'Yes, we can of course do that. It might take a bit of time, but if that is what you want, we will find a way of doing it'. (Department of Trade official)

It would appear this official felt the important factor was the longevity of the Conservative administration throughout the 1980s. He suggested that the effect of this was to enable the Government to develop a clear identity, allowing officials to anticipate Government policy. This produced a generation of bureaucrats who saw their role in Whitehall as implementors, not critics, of policy. Bernard Ingham emphasised the same themes, but provided a slightly different explanation:

She felt, rightly in my view, that there was a lot that had gone wrong in the public sector and that it was negative. It certainly wasn't entrepreneurial, but of course it wasn't there to be entrepreneurial in many ways. But it was negative and defeatist. There is no doubt about that. There were parts of it that were obstructive. So I think she therefore placed a great prize upon those who were go-getters and would get things done. Of course they had to be able, or else there was no point in having them there. She found civil servants who were go-getters, wanted to get things done and would argue with her. She didn't want 'yes men', not at all. But also, she didn't want obstructive 'no men'. She wanted constructively critical 'yes, men', who would say 'we can't do it this way, but we can do it that way.' Once she found that, she was very defensive of them. She was very defensive of her own staff . . . She was enormously defensive of, interested in and determined to help those who were going to change Britain if you like. (Ingham interviewed, 22 December 1995)

I challenged Ingham further on what, exactly, he meant by his description of Mrs Thatcher's lack of tolerance of those who questioned or criticised policy. He replied:

Well on policy as well, they [officials] could simply say; 'If you do this, this will be the consequence'. Now I think that is perfectly reasonable and she would never have argued about people saying; 'Well, these are going to be the consequences of your policy.' She would then say; 'Well, how do we cope with that.?' They would then go away and see if they could cope with that. They would then come back, having drawn a blank and she would say; 'Well, you aren't trying hard enough'. Then they would presumably go away and come up with little of consequence and she might then say; 'Well, I am sorry but it isn't on is it.' It is a very wearing, negative process. This is why those involved have to be positive, not negative. People who try, try and try again. (Ingham interviewed, 22 December 1995)

The implication is clear: Margaret Thatcher was ruthless in her determination to have officials who were able to provide answers to the implementation problems of the policies of her Government.

I do not think you can distinguish between the two interpretations offered by the mandarins. They both emphasised the same point: Margaret Thatcher wished to see installed at the highest level of Whitehall those officials who were prepared to work enthusiastically with her Government and who were highly able implementors of policy and effective organisational managers. John Sparrow provided the best summation of these two labels and his conclusion was clear:

I don't think she wanted and I don't think that I observed that she went for people who could guarantee action twenty-four hours a day and never a moment to think. It is more the other way round; not wanting the people who think for twenty-four hours a day and never do any action. I think the people who came through certainly weren't devoid of the ability to think. They weren't devoid of the ability to differ, but they did have the ability to act. (Sparrow interviewed, 15 November 1994)

If one accepts the mandarins' comments that Mrs Thatcher adopted a greater interest in the appointments procedure in order to produce a generation of, as they put it, 'managerial/can-do', or 'positive, not negative' officials, then it seems sensible to label this new set of top-grade officials, 'managerially oriented, can-doers'.

An Uncritical Civil Service?

Of course, it is absolutely essential to point out that the emergence of a generation of higher civil servants whose primary function was to find ways of implementing government policy, led to two related problems. First, perhaps officials were becoming simply 'yes' men, unquestionably accepting Government policy. Second, if civil servants were employed for their skill as good managers, 'positive, can-doers', always searching for practical means to implement policy, then this downgrades their role as informed and sometimes sceptical questioners of government policy. In either case, one of the traditional, core roles of the Civil Service – the ability to criticise – would appear to have been eroded.

This vital role, constitutionally enshrined, was articulated by Brian Hayes, Permanent Secretary at the Department of Agriculture 1979–83, when interviewed for the 1981 BBC radio series *No Minister*, when he expressed the view that:

> I think the job of the Civil Servant is to make sure that the Minister is informed; that he has all the facts; that he is made aware of all the options. It is then for the Minister to take the decision. That is how the system ought to operate and that is how I think, in the vast majority of cases, it does operate.

In the same programme, Ian Bancroft felt it was the responsibility of a civil servant to 'confront politicians with reality'. Whilst Brian Cubbon (Permanent Secretary, Home Office, 1979–88) referred to 'a store of wisdom about what the facts are'. With 'yes' men or 'positive' type officials being introduced, the suggestion arises that officials were no longer making their minister's fully aware of all the facts.

When I questioned the mandarins on the first of these two concerns, no one believed that the 1980s was the decade of the 'Yes' official. Patrick Benner declared: 'Not in my time no. Wouldn't have dreamt of it happening, not at all' (Benner interviewed, 16

November 1994). While William Ryrie felt that: 'Is the question, to put it bluntly; "Would she like 'yes' men?", because that would not be fair to her. Rather, she did not want people who were just negative and simply pointed out all the obstacles'. (Ryrie interviewed, 19 June 1995)

However, the mandarins' positions were more ambiguous when asked if there was less willingness on the part of officials to say: 'But Minister'? Peter Middleton adopted a neutral position, arguing that:

> But that is a risk with any government. That is just one of the little problems of life in the Civil Service. It is particularly a risk with a new government, which always assumes that the people in the Civil Service are determined to follow the policies of the previous government. Therefore they do tend to be very sensitive, at the beginning, to anything that looks critical, especially if you suggest something that has already been done . . . (Middleton interviewed, 16 November 1994)

One only has to read the diaries of Barbara Castle or Richard Crossman to accept the validity of Peter Middleton's point. However, what Middleton does not acknowledge were the unique circumstances of the Thatcher Government. It has already been established that, compared to her predecessors, Mrs Thatcher had a more tangible effect upon the appointments procedure. Middleton's response to the question I posed was to use historical analysis to try to explain a unique set of circumstances. Thus, although his reply is probably true, in that, with all modern governments, new ministers regard the officials they inherit with a modicum of suspicion, he failed to address the question of whether Margaret Thatcher altered the traditional ethos of the Civil Service.

In general, the mandarins adopted two divergent positions on this question. The first group believed that even though 'positive, can-doers' were introduced at the highest level, officials still said 'but'.

Not surprisingly, one ex-Cabinet Secretary felt that:

> She looked for people who were 'doers' as well as 'thinkers'. I did not see this as a difference between 'positive' and 'negative' approaches towards policy implementation and I certainly do not believe that a vital characteristic of the Civil Service was being eroded.

Likewise, another official was not prepared to concede that a less critical service had evolved, justifying his position with a personal account of his experience during the Thatcher period:

I never saw any evidence of that at all. I think it would cut across the ethos of most of the civil servants I came across. In my own case, I think this is particularly true: in the Export Credits Guarantee Department, which is effectively running a business, I don't know whether I learnt it, or just felt it by instinct. I always thought my job was to help the minister to do what he wanted to do, but at the same time to explain the problems and to tell him if I thought something was a mistake, usually for a managerial reason. But I was perfectly happy to be over-ruled on a matter of policy. I thought that was part of a minister's job. I can't think of any situation where I held anything back. (ECGD official)

Frank Cooper acknowledged that Mrs Thatcher was very forthright in her views and determined to have her approach accepted. However, he denied that officials were no longer prepared to stand up and be counted:

I think you have to be seen to be critical, in a positive sense, rather than frustrating policy. She felt very strongly that her way of doing something was the best way of doing it. Frustration was where people got into trouble, or going on about what the policy ought to be . . . In my own experience, with various people in meetings, I think that they certainly expressed their views quite clearly and said what they thought. (Cooper interviewed, 20 December 1994)

Unfortunately, Cooper's comments focused solely on an official's willingness to criticise at the policy implementation stage and, even then, only in a positive manner. No reference was made to an official questioning the actual wisdom of a policy proposal. Peter Kemp also addressed this issue:

I think it is the role of the Civil Service to point out problems, but at the end of the day it is for ministers to decide what they are going to do. I think Mrs Thatcher's view was the civil servants have got out of balance with this thing. They weren't just saying this thing won't work, they were almost getting round to saying: ' . . . and this is a bad thing'. (Kemp interviewed, 17 November 1994)

Implicit in Kemp's statement was a belief that the role of civil servants is not to question the overall logic or wisdom of the policy with which they are presented, but to indicate to a minister where there may be problems in implementation and make positive suggestions about how these problems could be circumvented. It was Kemp's belief that, by the end of the 1970s, Mrs Thatcher felt that officials had risen above their station, too often criticising overall Government policy. This was an imbalance which needed rectifying. Bernard Ingham also dwelt on this issue. Not surprisingly, he was opposed to officials questioning broad Government policy. When I queried him on whether or not, if you have 'can-do' types, then the vital role of criticism is lost, he replied:

> Well, you are not if they say 'well you can't do it that way, but you can do it this way'. In other words, if they apply their critical facilities in a positive way. Frequently, I would say: 'if you do it that way you are going to have to be careful, because that might blow up in our faces'.

Ingham then went on to raise the interesting and highly pertinent point concerning who is actually responsible for making policy:

> I think this is where I have to raise serious doubts about civil servants. They aren't there to make the policy, they are there to implement policy. Now, they are there most certainly to draw attention to that which is not implementable, or which they have very serious doubts over. For example, I told Mrs Thatcher, at the Cabinet table, not at a Cabinet meeting, but with some people there, that there were two problems about the Poll Tax: one was that the duke in his castle would pay exactly the same as the pauper in his hovel. Now that is one thing we had to iron out. Then there is the argument that it is very difficult to collect. Well she was well aware of that one, but of course here you had a PM who didn't believe politics was the art of the possible – God no, Bismarck was a wet! To her, the point was, politics is the art of making possible that which she thought to be impossible. That is a much more challenging approach. Barbara Castle did exactly the same when she put forward *In Place of Strife*. That was an attempt to make possible what was thought to be impossible. (Ingham interviewed, 22 December 1994)

Those mandarins who believed that the introduction of 'can-doers' did not detract from the ability of top-level officials to criticise policy also felt that the role of the civil servant was not to question overall government strategy. They argued that officials could provide positive input at the policy implementation stage, but it was not in their remit to extend their advice further.

The second group of mandarins disapproved of the effect of introducing 'positive, can-doers' in the 1980s, as they felt it resulted in a less critical Civil Service and, with it, the loss of a traditional and important role for Whitehall. There were those who strongly believed the ability to criticise had been widely eroded. Thus, one official felt there were:

> less policy advisers, less independent thinkers and more operators of the machine, with the political goals very clearly laid down. They became operators of the machine, as opposed to, going back to the 1950s, policy advisers. (A Treasury official)

The point this official was making is clear: the Thatcher Government specified their policy programme and the official's role was to execute it in the most effective manner.

William Ryrie agreed with the point made earlier by Ingham, that Mrs Thatcher was deeply suspicious of the Civil Service she had inherited in 1979. However, when asked if he felt Whitehall had become less critical, his view differed from that of Ingham:

> I suppose the answer is probably yes, at least in the late 1980s, by the time it had become *Thatcherised*. I think there must have been some such effect, as against the old style Civil Service, that was very much detached, objective and always suggesting: 'Minister, if you do this, this will be the consequence; if you do that, that will be the consequence – you decide.' That wasn't quite the style that went down well with Mrs Thatcher. (Ryrie interviewed, 19 June 1995)

John Cassels also felt that top officials in the 1980s were less willing to criticise Government policy, but he rejected the notion that this was simply the result of the appointment of officials who were 'positive, can-doers'. He believed Margaret Thatcher's personality was a significant factor:

> I think she had an effect on everyone who worked with her and here I also include her Cabinet colleagues. They were frightened of her, weren't they? I think she silenced a lot of people, who in

other circumstances would have spoken up. You can accuse them of cowardice, and perhaps there were people who were cowardly from time to time, but you can only remonstrate up to a point. If you go beyond that point, you lose all influence. So it is a very difficult balance to strike. It is also a personality thing. Some people are very good at doing that and the more positive people are often worse at doing it, because their positive vision gets clouded. (Cassels interviewed, 20 December 1994)

Cassels's comments provided a number of interesting, yet contentious, points. Firstly, I question whether even Mrs Thatcher, with her renowned combative character, could effectively scare a number of top officials into silence. Any official who has scaled Whitehall's ladder is highly intelligent and should be more than capable of participating in heated argument. It is almost inconceivable that such individuals would be so intimidated as to be unwilling to express their own views. It is more credible that there was reluctance among officials to always be seen to be criticising Government policy. One must remember that the Thatcher Government was elected with a manifesto that clearly broke with the post-war consensus. There must have been a number of officials who were politically opposed to the proposed programme to be implemented. However, they still saw it as their professional duty, as neutral civil servants, to execute the wishes of the Government of the day. Not wishing to be regarded as individuals always opposing Government policy, it is only natural that in some circumstance they may have curtailed their criticisms, or even opted for silence, on a particular matter of policy. Cassels's comment, that positive-type individuals are often poor at spotting flaws in a policy as they are too intimately involved in the process, has a clear logic to it and deserves some credence. However, John Burgh felt that, under any administration, there was a tendency for a number of officials to tailor their criticism. He argued it was simply a matter of striking a happy medium, but that during the Thatcher Administration this medium had become unbalanced:

Another point concerns the tendering of unwelcome advice to ministers. In any government, for a senior civil servant, I think this is one of the most difficult judgements because certainly the way I operated and the way I was brought up, it was your task to point out to ministers the pitfalls of possible policies. One of the judgements you had to make is how often were you going to point out the pitfalls, before the minister lost confidence in you, because you clearly were not willing to perform, or were unenthusiastic about performing something that ministers wanted. That is a judgement you have to make, whatever government is in power. I think the change really was that critical advice or the pointing out of pitfalls was far less welcome and far less well received initially, by the Thatcher Administration, than was previously the case. (Burgh interviewed, 18 November 1994)

A Civil Service Commissioner adopted a more philosophical analysis:

I think there is a very real problem. She was attacking what she saw as the various bastions; these were part of the balance of the Constitution and if you view the Civil Service, as merely an organisation that gets on with the executive work within [Next Steps] Agencies, you are losing a very great deal, it seems to me.

It was clear this official's concern was for the unbalancing of the British Constitution, which he regarded as a delicate instrument, not to be upset. Mrs Thatcher's approach had done little too ensure the equilibrium was maintained.

In assessing the conflicting views of the mandarins in this area, one can conclude that a backlash occurred in the 1980s; Mrs Thatcher reacted to the Civil Service she inherited, believing they had overstepped the mark between providing helpful criticism of Government *policy* and continually criticising overall Government *strategy*. This was possibly a result of the drift in the policy-making process during the latter years of the Callaghan Government, caused by the lack of a working majority in the House of Commons. Thus, the Labour Government had lapsed into a state of 'gridlock', the term normally used to describe problems at the legislative stage of the policy process in the United States of America. Hence, in the 1980s, Margaret Thatcher wished to reinvent the role of top officials in the policy process. It was no longer their remit to criticise overall government strategy. She wanted her officials to concentrate on the policy implementation stage. To examine a policy proposal and provide practical suggestions for its implementation. Advice and criticism could still be tendered at this stage, but preferably in a positive light. The duty of top officials was to effectively and efficiently operate the machinery of government, instead of constantly identifying teething problems at the policy-making stage.

This had a cultural effect at the highest levels in Whitehall; officials were not as detached from Government as their predecessors, or as objective in the advice they proffered. Pointing out possible pitfalls in policy during the Thatcher era became less welcome. However, it would be wrong to overly exaggerate the impact of this on the whole of Whitehall, or on the policy process. Top officials did retain a degree of independence and objectivity, which ensured that rationality still played a central role. Under Mrs Thatcher the fundamental difference was a change in the stage at which officials became involved in the policy process, and a reduction in negative advice proffered.

A Thatcher Effect Ushers in a Cultural Change among the Higher Civil Service

What the series of interviews with the mandarins confirmed was that, during the 1980s, a 'Thatcher effect' did occur and this had a tangible impact on the highest grades of the Civil Service. One can reject the notion that any form of overt politicisation occurred. Mrs Thatcher had no interest in appointing top officials who could be identified as sympathetic to the Conservative Party. Her interest in the top appointments procedure was in order to introduce a set of officials, who I have labelled 'managerially oriented, can-doers'. The underlying reason for this was Margaret Thatcher's desire to see top officials concentrate on the implementation stage of the policy process and to appoint individuals who were efficient business managers. This, in itself, was a reaction to her perceived belief that the higher Civil Service, by the end of the 1970s, had become bloated with political advisers, intellectuals who continually criticised government strategy. She perceived a lack of able administrators, capable of taking government policy and devising effective means of implementation. However, as Cassels (interviewed, 20 December 1994) commented: 'The effect was not to produce a completely different breed of permanent secretary. Most officials had followed conventional career paths and I don't think it amounted to a revolution'. This did, however, affect the culture of Whitehall. It introduced a set of officials who were much more reticent to point out potential pitfalls in policy proposals. Thus, the 1980s witnessed a new generation of mandarins who could be characterised by a willingness to offer positive advice. This clearly contrasted with the previous generation of top administrators. Charles Powell concluded:

I think there was perhaps much more emphasis put on people who were positive and were capable of doing things, because I think she did very much want people who weren't particularly committed to her political philosophy, or anything of that kind, but who actually wanted to bring about change and showed themselves able to do things. I suppose the converse of that was that, extremely clever people who might have got two brownie points before simply for being clever, didn't under Mrs Thatcher. (Powell interviewed, 16 November 1994)

7

Personalisation of the Top Appointments Process: Cultural Change and its Contradictions

---

Don't tell me what; tell me how; I know what . . . I don't spend a lifetime watching which way the cat jumps. I know already which way I want the cat to go. (Margaret Thtcher, cited in Kavanagh 1990, pp. 247–9)

I N THE PREVIOUS CHAPTER, it was established that Margaret Thatcher had a tangible effect upon appointments to the highest grades in the Civil Service. She displayed an active interest in the appointments procedure, which culminated in her influence over the final appointment of a number of individuals to posts, she felt of strategic importance. Thus, during the 1980s, a new subset of officials was introduced to the senior grades in Whitehall. This group I label 'managerially oriented, can-doers'. Margaret Thatcher wished to see such individuals appointed, largely as a result of her view of Whitehall. This view was shaped by two separate, but linked, factors: first, her ideological outlook, based on New Right philosophy; second, her impression of the senior Civil Service, based on her formative experiences at the Department of Education and Science and her early encounters, as Prime Minister, with senior officials during her first term in office. The combination of these two factors prompted her to set about reshaping Whitehall into an organisation with which she believed she could work with. As a result, she developed her own unique approach to the senior appointments system.

In this chapter I will examine Mrs Thatcher's practical experiences in Whitehall which shaped her attitude to this institution. I will argue that these experiences prompted her to adopt a pro-active approach towards promotions, resulting in a paradigm shift in the way in which the top appointments procedure operated. I maintain that, from its origins in the late 1960s, up until 1979, the system was operated by the Civil Service, for the Civil Service. Senior officials determined both the means by which top appointments were made and the individuals to be appointed. Under Margaret Thatcher a switch occurred whereby the Civil Service was no longer in the vanguard. Visible problems in procedures arose, manifested by personnel unrest, as Margaret Thatcher instigated a Prime Minister-led system. The net effect was the transformation of the top appointments system, previously dominated by the mandarinate, to a new, more personalised system the Prime Minister could dominate. This allowed her greater control of the Civil Service, helping ensure that it did not envelop her.

This chapter then looks in more detail at the extent of, reasons for and effect of the personalisation of appointments. In particular, it examines whether there was an obvious change in the type of individual who was appointed to the most senior grades during the 1980s, compared to the type appointed in the 1960s and 70s. The final section considers a number of the contradictions created by personalisation.

Shaping a View of Whitehall: DES, Dinner and First-Term Meetings

In chapter 5, I examined Margaret Thatcher's views on the Civil Service, as seen by her ministers. Part of that chapter was devoted to an analysis of the ideological problems she had in comprehending Whitehall culture. This was based on her antipathy to the public sector; she could not understand why any individual who displayed the least signs of business acumen, or sound managerial techniques, would wish to work in the public sector. Further, she believed an institution like Whitehall perpetuated the post-war consensus, which she regarded as one of the causes of Britain's post-war malaise. This view was based on the neo-liberal, New Right agenda, orchestrated by, among others, Keith Joseph in the early 1970s. However, New Right theory, which so captivated Margaret Thatcher, was not the only factor that shaped her opinion of Whitehall and its officials. Personal experience, conditioned by her political ideology, also played a part. Three main episodes provided her with a practical insight, which affected how she believed the higher Civil Service operated and which reinforced her opinions of Whitehall: her experience in the Department of Education and Science 1970–4; the dinner party she held in May 1980 for all her Permanent Secretaries; and the series of departmental meetings she made during her first term in office.

The Department of Education and Science

The Department of Education and Science (DES), with a reputation for lower-quality staff than other, more glamorous, departments, did little to enhance Mrs Thatcher's opinion of the Civil Service, or the individuals who chose to work there. One Whitehall watcher observed of the DES: 'Officials from other ministries are the subject of commiseration when posted there. It is seen as an institution in which bureaucrats turn grey' (Hennessy 1989, p. 428). It is possible that if she had served in a department like the Treasury or the Home Office, the views she formulated on the Civil Service may have been discernibly different. Indeed, many individuals have commented on her astonishment at the abilities of the officials she inherited, on entering No. 10. However, the DES had a sobering effect on a politician with aspirations for higher office. As Hennessy (1989, p. 630) commented:

> Mrs Thatcher's spell at the Department of Education and Science in the wilderness years of 1970–74, when she said very little in Cabinet and was placed by Ted Heath in the 'blind spot' on the other side of the Cabinet Secretary, did nothing to lighten her dim view of permanent officials.

Her Permanent Secretary at the DES, William Pile, soon realised that his new Minister was quite unlike any master he had previously served and that Margaret Thatcher was not going to embrace her new officials with open arms:

> Within the first ten minutes of her arrival, she uncovered two things to us. One is an innate wariness of the Civil Service, quite possibly even a distrust; and secondly, a page from an exercise book with eighteen things she wanted done that day. Now these were two actions quite unlike anything we'd come across from predecessors and we later on, I think, saw that this was only the beginnings of the revelation of a character that we'd have to get used to

and that we hadn't run into before. (Young and Sloman 1986, p. 24)

Relations between the Education Minister and her Permanent Secretary were, at best, strained. At one stage, she approached Edward Heath to ask him to remove Pile. This, despite the fact that Pile had been appointed to Permanent Secretary at the relatively young age of fifty and was regarded as a Whitehall 'high-flyer'. Heath, having consulted William Armstrong, then Head of the Civil Service, refused her request. Pile felt that the problem lay in the fact that:

> We followed our old traditional course of speaking up for what the Department has always done or what we thought the Department should do, as opposed to what ministers were going to tell us to do. She thought that some of us were being obstructive. I regarded it as a necessary professional job to be done up to the point when the minister said to you that we're going to do the opposite. In which case I think we touched our forelocks and said 'Yes ma'am.' (Young 1989, p. 72)

Certainly, Mrs Thatcher's prejudices against the Civil Service and its culture were, in part, shaped by her experience in the DES during the 1970s. She was much scarred by her experience there and left the department with an unflattering view of those individuals who wished to work in the public sector. As Frank Cooper (interviewed, 20 December 1994) commented:

> I do not think that she ever changed her views. She was extremely friendly and social with most of the people she worked with. But I know she disliked bureaucracy. She did not believe it revealed the whole truth to her. She was very much in favour of ministers being more assertive, more directive and being seen to be leading from the front.

Margaret Thatcher included herself in this category and was determined not to allow the Civil Service to envelop her in the same way that, she believed, the Civil Service had enveloped a number of her predecessors. This led indirectly to the second episode which shaped her view of the Civil Service. During her first term as Prime Minister, she decided, on the advice of Willie

Whitelaw, to hold an informal dinner party for her Permanent Secretaries so as to get to know them better. What transpired was a disastrous night for all involved, which has become part of the mythology of Whitehall.

The Dinner

At the start of 1980, a number of colleagues had grown concerned about Mrs Thatcher's developing relationship with her Permanent Secretaries. James Prior and William Whitelaw had both spoken to her on separate occasions, to little effect, on this rather thorny topic. Finally, on 6 May 1980, Whitelaw, Margaret Thatcher's closest confidant, persuaded the Prime Minister to host a dinner party, at which those invited could get to know each other in more social surroundings, away from formal Government office hours. Clive Priestley, described the background to this dinner:

> She had thought very carefully on how to get them [the Permanent Secretaries] on board. She had had Whitelaw, Soames, Rayner, Bancroft and me in to talk about it, early in 1980. When she suggested, 'We could have a special meeting of Cabinet and the Permanent Secretaries could sit at the back', Whitelaw said, 'Oh no, they would not like that at all'. Mrs Thatcher then held a meeting in the Cabinet Room at No. 10 to discuss how to win the Permanent Secretaries over. It was attended by William Whitelaw [then Home Secretary, but present as Deputy Prime Minister]; Christopher Soames [then Lord Privy Seal and in charge of Civil Service matters]; Ian Bancroft, [then Permanent Secretary of the CSD and Head of the Civil Service]; Derek Rayner; and me. Michael Pattison, [Home Affairs Private Secretary], was in attendance. Prince Andrew, then visiting Whitehall for 'familiarisation', was a witness to the proceedings. Mrs Thatcher made the 'sitting at the back' proposal. Mr Whitelaw demurred, so instead she went for the generous idea of giving the Permanent Secretaries dinner at No. 10 [on 6 May 1980]; it was strikingly unsuccessful, both Ian Bancroft [Cabinet Secretary] and Lawrence Airey [Inland Revenue], sounding an important note of defiance or so it seemed to Mrs Thatcher. (Priestley interviewed, 14 November 1994)

Frank Cooper was a central, but silent actor in this episode. I asked him for his account of the evening:

That was an interesting experience really. She was determined to demonstrate, in public, that she meant business. She dressed herself very carefully, stunning black dress and nice jewellery and hair carefully done. First of all, there were far too many people there. You couldn't have a conversation around the dinner table. I am not sure whether or not Willie [Whitelaw] was there. Before dinner, she was perfectly normal and then she ate her dinner with a reasonable degree of normality. But the conversation after dinner, was when people started to have a discussion with her. She wasn't going to have a discussion. Her views were her views and that was that. I didn't say a word after dinner. I was sitting opposite her and I thought I am not going to get involved in this. I stayed silent. But some people took off and were asking her philosophical questions about policies, about this, that and the other. She got more and more domineering and sat there and it all went on a long time, until I got up and went to the loo. Someone then said quietly: 'I hope to God, Frank has gone to get the SAS, to get us out of here'. [Cooper interviewed, 20 December 1994]

It was the evening following the Iranian Embassy Affair, when the SAS had successfully stormed the building to release the hostages. I went on to ask Sir Frank whether it was the intention of Margaret Thatcher to send out a message to the rest of the Whitehall village by hosting the dinner party and why was she opposed to any open discussion.

It was supposed to get us all on the same wavelength. I think it was within her nature to oppose open discussion. She has got to sort of dominate any discussion and this became more and more marked. I think this was one of the elements that, years later, led to her undoing. I think some people were, for example, questioning her about basic Civil Service ethics. I can't remember exactly, but a couple of people went on a bit. I think that really stoked her up. She took off. It just went on and people were getting rather fed up with the thing. But I think the basic element, with both sides was, with twenty-five men and one woman round the table, you couldn't really have a discussion . . . I think there was an error on both sides. It would have been much better to have had a smaller dinner party. (Cooper interviewed, 20 December 1994)

One of the first individuals Margaret Thatcher met, the morning after the night before, was her Press Secretary Bernard Ingham. I asked him if the Prime Minister commented on the outcome of the dinner the following morning. Ingham recollected that the dinner was aimed at bringing one or two of the more erudite Permanent Secretaries into line with Margaret Thatcher's way of thinking:

> It was a very difficult occasion for some of them, for example Ian Bancroft, who was then Head of the Civil Service. If you go back to the file on *The Times*, he was being pretty jaundiced about it all. They were there to be alienated, bearing in mind what life was like at the time. She came to office, to actually govern by principle and to do things and to change Britain. That was very powerful medicine, because we hadn't changed for forty odd years. (Ingham interviewed, 22 December 1994)

Clive Priestley has his own interpretation of what Margaret Thatcher was attempting to achieve that evening. His comments provide a revealing insight into why it went wrong:

> She was profoundly turned off, at the famous dinner, when what she had tried to do was to get *the system*, the massed bands of the Permanent Secretaries, on her side. In effect, or as she understood it, they made clear to her they were not interested. It was an occasion influenced by two things – some of these chaps really saying, foolishly: 'We have been round this buoy before, you Ministers don't stay interested and you upset us terribly by going for these manpower cuts'. She was tired, it was the same day that the SAS had attacked the Iranian Embassy and she had that same afternoon come from a debriefing with the boys in black. So, once again, she had that contrast in her mind's eye – between these sweaty young men who had done this great thing and these rather grey-faced old loons who were really saying, she thought: 'we are not interested'.

Priestley argued that an important element is caught by this story, concerning the degree of self-importance senior officials attach to themselves:

> If you have become a Permanent Secretary, everyone tells you, you are terribly important. So, if you set that sense of self-worth and importance alongside the history, which they all experienced, of ministers not staying with reform, you can see why they were a bit

affronted by this over-energetic woman not using happy phrasing to them. Language is terribly important to them. They are specialists in language precision. (Priestley interviewed, 14 November 1994))

Finally, Donald Maitland was invited to the dinner as the soon to be Permanent Secretary at the Department of Energy. He was an official who spent the majority of his Whitehall career in the Foreign and Commonwealth Office and, maybe, understood more than some other of his colleagues, the occasions on which tact and diplomacy are the best course of action:

> As a head-of-department-designate I was invited to the dinner the Prime Minister gave for permanent secretaries at Number 10 on 6 May. I was seated well below the salt and was not required to contribute to the discussion. This was an uncomfortable occasion. My toes curled as my future colleagues raised one objection after another to the prime minister's propositions. Over the four years I had spent in Brussels I had learned from my European Community colleagues the virtues of the 'Yes, but . . . ' as opposed to the 'No, because . . . ' preface to a contrary opinion. If the Prime Minister had heard more of the former and less of the latter, she might have taken away a slightly less unfavourable impression of the top ranks of the Civil Service. (Maitland 1996, p. 241)

Whichever way one explains why the evening was such a disaster, it is clear that Margaret Thatcher's regard for senior officials was greatly diminished. The dinner was an unfortunate failure and it is ironic that an event, intended to improve relations between Margaret Thatcher and her Permanent Secretaries, instead alienated individuals on both sides.

First-Term Departmental Meetings

During the first term, Mrs Thatcher undertook a series of departmental meetings in order to get a feel of the work that various departments undertook and also for the officials who worked in them. Hennessy (1989, p. 633) describes these visits as: 'Occasions that were anticipated with about as much enthusiasm as an American Embassy waited for Roy Cohn and David Schine, Senator Joe McCarthy's aides, to drop by in their early 1950s'. Yet, for Mrs Thatcher, they were of a practical importance, for she hoped to show the rest of central government who was in charge. In fact, this was another attempt to ensure that the machinery of Government did not envelop her. As Young (1989, p. 158) commented:

> She was, at the beginning, incurably interventionist. This was partly by calculation, for only by poking her nose into every department's work did she think she could impress upon both the politicians and the officials that she was really in charge. But it was also a matter of instinct: the tendency of an indefatigable woman to suppose that nothing would be done right unless she personally saw to it.

Other prime ministers had undertaken a few, brief visits to the major departments in Whitehall, but none had done so in such a systematic manner. The reaction to the Thatcher sojourns depended on who you were in the Whitehall hierarchy. Young (1989, p. 161) concluded:

> These visits were not an unqualified success. They often had pleasing effects at the lower end of the departments. 'She went over very well with the cleaners and the filing clerks, a junior minister at Employment told me shortly after her appearance there. 'All that glad-handling reminded one what a good populist she is'. But the encounter with senior officials had been disastrous.

The senior officials I interviewed had their own views about the *benefits* of these departmental visits. Patrick Benner's impression of Margaret Thatcher's visit to the Department of Health and Social Security was that the whole occasion appeared to be a rather low-key affair:

> Those meetings were when she formed her opinions, but only very superficially. Each meeting tended to last only an hour and it was simply an open discussion. We just sat round, and the Secretary of State invited various individuals, mainly Deputy Secretaries, to say something or other about new areas of activity. Then there would be a general discussion and Mrs Thatcher would ask some questions. It was really quite superficial. (Benner interviewed, 16 November 1994)

Frank Cooper provides a more vivid account of the visit she paid the Ministry of Defence. He argued that she was against the upper part of the Whitehall hierarchy and instead wished to see 'young people and what they had done'. He did not believe Mrs Thatcher was the kind of person who 'sat back while everybody talked to her'. Instead he felt 'you were allowed to open the conversation and she sought to take it over'. Cooper asserted that was what she did at the MoD:

> People were trying to explain what their problems were and, then, after about three minutes, she sought to dominate the discussion. She scurried round and met a couple of groups who were working on some problem of one kind or another, but she didn't seem to be terribly interested in the problem itself. I think people were quite pleased with the outcome of her visit. The reason for the visit was to enable Mrs Thatcher to gain an impression of the smell of the department. Not so much of the individuals, because she knew the most senior people. She had met the military, already. I got to know her at the CSD, because of the Rothschild Report and I had met her at various social occasions, from time to time. I think some departments were strange to her. She wanted to look at the people there. I think that is true. I can't believe she knew anybody in MAFF. She did have her pecking order. Those she liked least, let us put it that way. I don't think that she left with any strong impressions of our department, but she was pro-defence.(Cooper interviewed, 20 December 1994)

Cooper accepts that certain departments were seen in a more favourable light by Mrs Thatcher than others. Charles Powell concurs with Cooper on her rating of individual departments:

> There are certain departments of government which she suspected of having a deep ideological bias, which was not one she was comfortable with. One was the FCO: an institution she never liked, because she thought it was there basically to give way to foreigners. There was this extraordinary contrast, in that she liked 99 per cent of the people she met in the FCO, but seemed to be incapable of associating them with the institution, which she disliked. Education she thought was a hot bed of socialism, lots of people committed to ideas she opposed . . . No doubt she was scarred by her time there and perhaps while there she should have done more to change it. I think parts of DTI were regarded as irredeemably interventionist and, therefore, fell under suspicion. The ODA she also thought of as a bunch of do-gooders. They give money away to unworthy causes. (Powell interviewed, 16 November 1994)

Yet, there were exceptions to the rule. One would have suspected that Margaret Thatcher ranked the Treasury near the top of her departmental 'pecking order'. However, William Ryrie was not convinced that her visit to this department was an overriding success:

> I remember her sitting in once and having a bit of an encounter with her about Cash Limits. I was trying to explain and, to some extent, defend the Cash Limits system that we had already. She thought it was no good at all and that we should go further . . . I think her view of the Treasury was that we were lot of fuddy duddies. (Ryrie interviewed, 19 June 1995)

Finally, in their memoirs, both Cecil Parkinson and Alan Clark noted that, on her visit to Whitehall departments, Margaret Thatcher went round marking-off peoples names on a check-list she carried with her. An official from the Department of Energy also witnessed these actions:

> She went around each department and, as she went around, she put a tick or a cross on her five-minute interview with officials she met. If you got a cross it would take a very long time to erase it. If you got a tick, you had survived.

His comments are very revealing, for they indicate how much attention Margaret Thatcher was paying to the individuals in the various departments. She stored this information and used it later, in an official capacity, when consulted on senior appointments. These actions also indicate that, from the start of her first term, Margaret Thatcher signalled her wish to take an active role in senior, personnel management within Whitehall.

The departmental visits, when coupled to the dinner party and her experiences in the DES, strengthened Mrs Thatcher's ideologically informed views on both Whitehall and its personnel. Yet, she had problems in reconciling these views, fully matured by the middle of 1980, with the staff she inherited and worked closely with in the Prime Minister's Office and Cabinet Office. Her antipathy towards, and suspicion of, many Whitehall officials, was countered by her surprise discovery of the abilities of the civil servants working closest to her. As Young (1989, p. 159) comments: 'What quickly impressed her was the willingness of the young men inside 10 Downing Street waiting to greet her to "work their backs off for her"', as one of them put it'. One senior, outside advisor to Mrs Thatcher commented, off-record, that she was astonished by the brilliant young men she found in No. 10 and wanted to promote them to other departments.[1] This presented a dichotomy for Mrs Thatcher: she was generally sceptical of the abilities of those working in departments. Yet, she discovered that the individuals located at the centre, in particular in the Treasury, the Prime Minister's Office and Cabinet Office, to be of outstanding ability. Mrs Thatcher carried this dichotomy with her into meetings on the senior appointments process.

Exerting an Influence: the Personalisation of the Top Appointments System

I have established that Margaret Thatcher was conditioned in her attitude to the Civil Service and its officials both by her ideological beliefs and by her personal experiences in Whitehall. The net effect was to instil in her a desire to control the Civil Service and make it an institution with which she felt she, and her Government, could work with. She learnt from the experience of previous administrations that, alone, structural reform was ineffective and so focused her attention on the composition of senior personnel within the ranks of the mandarinate. As Young (1989, p. 160) observed:

> She developed her personal intelligence system almost from the beginning. From her secure base, staffed by a corps of new-found friends, she could begin to neutralise and then slowly overcome the resistance of the bureaucracy. Perhaps she could even change the culture. But before that, for her personal position to be fully armour-plated, certain key appointments had to be put in place.

Thus, as I argued in the previous chapter, Mrs Thatcher used her official role in the appointments process to introduce a new type of official to the most senior grades. I labelled this type 'managerially oriented, can-doers'. To achieve this, she adopted a pro-active approach and this has led a number of commentators to suggest that the senior appointments process became personalised (RIPA 1987; Young 1989; Plowden 1994).

Using my interviews, I tried to unpack what was implied by the claims that the senior appointments process was personalised. The officials I spoke to suggested that what occurred was analogous to a chemical reaction. It was apparent that with certain individuals Margaret Thatcher met, there was an immediate connection between like-minds. The implication was she made almost 'knee-jerk' reactions to an individual; and the opinions she formed were difficult to change. She had a phenomenal memory. Thus, when asked for her views on a post to be filled in a certain department, she could produce the name of an individual she may have met for only a matter of moments. This individual would have so impressed her that she felt [almost always] he was the appropriate candidate for the vacancy. Of course, the converse of this was also true; an individual who Margaret Thatcher may have met only briefly, but who clashed with her, would find the chances of future promotion severely limited.[2] This whole notion of personalisation was further reinforced by the longevity of her time in office. No other individual politician, during the 1980s, perhaps in the entire post-war period, commanded the same overview of the senior officials working in government as Margaret Thatcher.

Addressing this issue, William Ryrie indicated the determination of Mrs Thatcher to surround herself with officials she felt she could work with; often individuals she had met briefly and to whom she had reacted immediately:

> I agree with the basic proposition that there was no overt politicisation. There was an involvement by the Prime Minister, in a way that was quite new. The disturbing thing was that that involvement included quite a lot of decisions which just reflected personal preferences. She was not very good at sitting down objectively and judging a person. It was a hunch – 'He's OK, or he's not OK'. Her judgements were taken far too much on that kind of basis and that is not a way to manage a big organisation. You need to be far more careful, rational and objective about it than that.

I pointed out to Ryrie that in any form of man-management, a personal agenda will play a role. The difference with the Civil Service is that it is a public service and it has to justify an individual appointment, in a manner, which may be unnecessary in the private sector. He agreed with this point, arguing that there was no such thing as 'total objectivity, but that every effort should be made to get somewhere near it'. Margaret Thatcher made no such attempt:

> I don't think she was trying to do that. She was trying to achieve a political agenda. She was the first woman Prime Minister. She

must have felt very much at risk and threatened in her early years. Nowadays, Thatcher is so established and such a strong figure that you forget how much she must have felt under threat in those early days. Was she going to succeed or not? She was driven by a desire to make sure she prevailed. I can understand that very well, but it didn't produce cool objectivity in these decisions. (Ryrie interviewed, 19 June 1994)

Ryrie's comments imply that Margaret Thatcher felt threatened by the Civil Service and this prompted her, when consulted, into an emotional, rather than a rational, response to an appointment to a vacant post. John Burgh detected a pro-active approach which set her apart from her predecessors:

Certainly, depending on who is the Prime Minister [and that is a very important factor in itself] the relationship and the Prime Minister's feelings about top civil servants would very naturally tend to enter into it up to a point. Some Prime Ministers would be more laid-back than others. Most were pretty laid back about top-level appointments. But she wasn't. She wanted to be involved. She wanted to interfere. She wanted to make sure that the right kind of people, from her point of view, were in the right post. She was able to watch them and, if necessary, to pick them. So, I certainly think, from that point of view, a quite significant sea-change occurred. (Burgh interviewed, 18 November 1994)

John Cassels felt that Margaret Thatcher simply used the existing appointments procedure to introduce the type of individual she wanted into the posts she wanted. This again, confirms her pro-active approach:

They are very personal decisions. I don't think she probably had a deep strategic purpose in the way she used approval. I think that each time it came up [and it looked like this too] she wanted people who were going to do a very good job. Her instincts, partly political no doubt, partly personal, led her to favour one person against another. Did she make any single change in the old procedure for appointing people? I don't think so. She just used what was there, to get what she thought was going to be the right person into the job. (Cassels interviewed, 20 December 1994)

However, Cassels saw no real harm arising from a more personalised system, comparing the Civil Service arrangements to those of the private sector. He argued that it was the Prime Minister who has got to approve the appointment and it is for a reason – that the 'Prime Minister needs this power and it should not be left in the hands of a civil servant'. He maintained that if a Prime Minister is going to exercise that power responsibly, it had to be done on the basis of what information was available:

> If you are wise, you will follow the advice of officials most of the time, but sometimes you will allow your own opinion to prevail. I think that is what she did. She certainly did that more than most Prime Ministers. It is hard to say that is wrong, tyrannical, or too personal. It is very difficult to see how to improve the arrangements. If you look at how big companies make up their minds about promotions, they are twice as personalised as that and yet they are deciding things far less important than the future of the country. (Cassels interviewed, 20 December 1994)

Frank Cooper agreed that, during the 1980s, the appointments procedure became more personalised, but felt this was a result of Margaret Thatcher's desire, discussed in chapter 6, to surround herself with positive, not negative type individuals:

> I think she had much stronger views than any of her predecessors, on what kind of person ought to become Permanent Secretary. I don't think it was political, I never thought it was political. I didn't think it was 'you have to be one of us'. She wanted people who were positive, rather than negative. Who were able to stand up for themselves. (Cooper interviewed, 20 December 1994)

Peter Kemp also felt the procedures had become personalised, but explained this transformation of the system by the need of the Prime Minister to feel 'comfortable' with those officials closest to the centre:

> I think it is personalised. We talk about a politicised Civil Service, in fact it was not that but a personalised Civil Service. For example, if I was asked the question – if Tony Blair gets to be Prime Minister, would he retain Robin Butler [something I don't wish to opine on], I would have answered on comfort grounds. I would say the question Tony Blair would have to ask himself is: 'Do I feel comfortable with

this man? Will he deliver that narrow balance between helping me
deliver what I want and at the same time advising me where I am
going wrong?' (Kemp interviewed, 17 November 1994)

Kemp was also keen to emphasise the degree to which chemistry
played a major role in Mrs Thatcher's attraction to a certain type
of individual. Particularly those not afraid to speak their mind:

> I think there was a natural chemistry thing, but also an element
> of speaking out or talking out, not just sitting there. She liked
> a conversation with people and she liked a view where people
> came along and were prepared to speak up. She wanted to feel
> there was someone she could trust. The old business that ministers
> would decide and servants advise is not a silly point, there should
> be truth in it. (Kemp interviewed, 17 November 1994)

Bernard Ingham agreed that chemistry played a vital role, but
he considered it just as important that a Prime Minister was not
surrounded by troublemakers, with negative attitudes:

> I think, inevitably, there is chemistry and I don't think this was
> because she was a female Prime Minister, that she was Margaret
> Thatcher, or that she wanted to get things done. I think this happened
> all the time. There are some people who can't get on with anybody or
> find it difficult to do so. You see it at all levels of society. It isn't that
> they are bad people, or that they are silly people, but it is that they
> do find it very difficult to get on with people. God knows, I find it
> difficult to get on with a lot of people, but you know very well that
> when you are there, it is your job to find a way through. Your job
> is to keep the system going, not to sink it. Your job is to make sure
> that what you propose will actually work. To that extent you are
> intensely practical, as well as having to think a great deal about it.
> But you aren't there to make life impossible. It is quite impossible to
> have people who are just causing trouble. For example, if you have
> a person in No.10 who is just plain bloody idle and negative, then
> quite frankly you have got to get rid of him, because it is such a
> small place, you cannot afford passengers, least of all disruptive
> passengers. (Ingham interviewed, 22 December 1994)

In the actual making of decisions, Ingham believed that Mrs
Thatcher's primary consideration was the personality of the individual. He was not, however, overly convinced of the success of her

approach. He argued Margaret Thatcher had a very mixed record for selecting people, but that she was:

> Better at choosing civil servants than she was at picking some other people, including ministers. I think she was undoubtedly swayed emotionally, by certain personalities, because some people have more appealing personalities, than others. (Ingham interviewed, 22 December 1994)

William Ryrie agreed with Ingham on the importance of personality, emphasising how quickly Margaret Thatcher made up her mind about individuals, on the basis of a first meeting. He stated that it became quite clear that she was influenced by personal considerations. He believed Mrs Thatcher formed a view or an attitude towards people and that: 'this occurred at the political level. She reacted well to certain people and badly to others. She tended to take that attitude from the first moment, and didn't change' (Ryrie interviewed, 19 June 1995).

John Burgh raised the issue of the longevity of her time in office, arguing that this enabled her to develop a deep insight into the officials in Whitehall. He felt this caused a number of problems, one of which was the accusation that the Civil Service was becoming politicised:

> The problem is the actual length of her term of office, which of course is crucial. She was the fountain head for twelve years. She kept on interfering with these appointments, which I don't necessarily disagree with, but the fact that she was able to do so for such a long period of course meant that more and more she picked people who were actually willing to get on and do what she wanted. (Burgh interviewed, 18 November 1994)

Charles Powell also used the longevity argument to explain the personalisation of the appointments procedure:

> She took an increased interest, for the very good reason: as time went by, she knew a lot more of the people being proposed for certain jobs, than she would have done early on. When you come in as a Prime Minister, after five years in Opposition, and before that a short spell in the Department of Education and Science, you are not going to know many senior Civil Servants. But after six, seven, eight never mind ten years as Prime Minister, you have seen most of

them. Therefore you develop a feeling about them, their performance and so on. So you are much more likely to have views. That was really what changed . . . it was knowing more of the candidates. She would have actually seen more of them in operating circumstance. They would have attended meetings with her or worked abroad with her. So she would have had a chance to assess, first hand, how they performed and therefore to develop views about them and their abilities. (Powell interviewed, 16 November 1994)

Another official felt it was the combination of both the longevity of her time in office and her ability to remember individuals, from only the briefest of meetings. He also argued that Mrs Thatcher did take a much greater interest, particularly in individuals. He commented on her phenomenal memory, which meant she had views on officials who had served her as far back as when she had been a junior minister. He argued that this culminated in her having:

very strong views on who should be chosen. Why was that? I think she was looking for people who would drive through the policies that she wanted and would not necessarily go back to the old days of the conventional wisdom of being in departments and working your way up. (An MoD official)

Similarly, another official echoed similar sentiments arguing that the concept of politicisation stemmed from Mrs Thatcher's perceived tendency to favour those officials with whom she came into close contact and felt 'comfortable with'. He believed this had been exacerbated by the fact that she was Prime Minister for such a long period. He personally felt there was nothing inherently wrong or unnatural in this, unless it could be demonstrated that it led to 'incompetent officials being placed unfairly in positions of power, or that in some sense it corrupted civil service standards'. However, he did not believe that that was the case.

The officials I interviewed provide a number of reasons why they believed the appointments system was personalised during the 1980s. One described this as the culmination of:

Margaret Thatcher's pro-active approach, whereby she used the existing system for her own ends, to introduce a positive-type of individual, who was not likely to *cause trouble*; the use of her outstanding memory; and the length of her tenure in office. The overriding factor which influenced her was chemistry: this was based, in part, on whether or not there was a connection between similar intellects on first meeting, and whether or not there was a degree of sexual tension.

If chemistry played such an important role, I asked the officials what was the catalyst. Their response was less clear. However, there was overall agreement that she preferred a younger type of official, the type often found in the Treasury, the Prime Minister's Office or the Cabinet Office. Thus, one official commented:

> When you turn the vague notion of the 'Civil Service' into particular individuals, she clearly became rather attached to those with whom she came into direct contact. I think it was an observable fact that a lot of youngish people were promoted, quite rapidly, up to Permanent Secretary after they had passed through the No. 10 / Cabinet Office circuit. (An Energy official)

This was part of the dichotomy referred to earlier and is examined in detail in the next chapter. However, this leaves two areas still to be addressed: first, the effect this had on the type of senior official who was appointed in the 1980s; second, the contradictions which arose from a system driven more by personal inclinations, than by rational decision making.

The Cultural Shift: A Changing Breed of Official

Margaret Thatcher's emphasis on introducing a number of officials to strategic posts and, in so doing, creating a new sub-set of senior civil servants, was intended to have a tangible effect on Whitehall culture. She argued that the old culture, which had embraced the post-war consensus, was a major factor in Britain's decline as a world power. She realised that previous attempts to change this institution, using structural reform, had failed. Whitehall had always been able to assimilate any such schemes. Instead, she argued for incremental personnel change as a means of addressing this perceived problem. Her use of the senior appointments process, and with it the personalisation of the system, was aimed at breaking down this culture, replacing it with a new one: the emphasis was to be on positive, policy implementors, who, rather than always seeing potential problems with policy initiatives, would be able to provide practical solutions. Her hope was that, by introducing a number of officials to the senior ranks who did not fit the traditional Whitehall mould of the mandarinate, their different personal skills and working methods would seep through the other tiers of the Civil Service hierarchy, both vertically and horizontally. The success of such an approach, would be seen in the transformation of the existing culture, so despised by Margaret Thatcher.

I asked the senior officials I interviewed whether or not they perceived any cultural change at the highest levels in Whitehall during the 1980s. In particular, did they witness a new generation of senior officials emerging, influenced by this injection of 'a new strain of blood' into their environment. To address this issue, I enquired if there were any discernible differences in the type of individual serving in the highest ranks of the Civil Service in the 1980s, compared with the preceding generation of the 1960s.

The majority of the officials I interviewed felt that there had been an overall change in the type of individual found at the highest grades, but that this change preceded Mrs Thatcher and was the result of wider, external factors. The situation had arisen that, because of all the economic, political, social and, most importantly, technological changes which had occurred in society in the post-war years, more was now required of a mandarin than the previous, rather antiquated, traditional role of a deep-thinking cerebral figure. New management techniques were appearing and, if the Civil Service was to take on board wider societal changes, the figures at the apex of their organisation had to adapt and update their operative techniques. The logical conclusion was that as society evolved, so the Civil Service had to evolve with it or it would be left behind.

Frank Cooper provided the historical overview of the changes occurring in this transitional period from the 1960s to the 1980s. He argued:

> I don't think that the cerebral element of the Civil Service was higher in the 1960s, than it was in the 1980s, but I think that it was significantly affected, because the world had changed and Whitehall also had changed greatly. The problems of actually coping with real-life issues had grown enormously. I think if you look back over the period since World War Two, there was continual change. The sixties, in many ways, were the watershed, because it was the end of the Empire and the European Community was coming up and all those kinds of things. That there was a much higher premium

put on 'can somebody run something, can he sort this or that out?' Problem-solvers, rather than policy-makers. I think the Civil Service, in a sense, became much more influenced by the need to have people who could solve issues and change things, rather than writing down classic bits of policy and translate them into legislation. (Cooper interviewed, 20 December 1994)

Cooper emphasised that for the Civil Service to evolve, it needed less officials whose main input was in the sphere of policy-making, and more individuals to focus on problem-solving, in particular at the policy implementation stage.

An ex-Cabinet Secretary, whose Whitehall career spanned both generations and who, in the 1980s was directly involved in senior appointments, agreed with Cooper:

> Though I have no direct knowledge about the process of choosing Permanent Secretaries in the 1960s, I think that it may have been true, as a broad generalisation, that the emphasis was primarily upon the contribution that the civil servant concerned would make to policy formulation and advice, as opposed to management.

Patrick Benner noted that these changes pre-dated the Thatcher era:

> This was a tendency that had been going on for a long time. It was not something new. The concern with management and doing had been increasing over a long period. It was some while since the Civil Service had just been a sort of policy-making body. Indeed, it never was. But this was a change that had been coming in for a long, long time. I think it may have intensified and probably did in the early eighties. (Benner interviewed, 16 November 1994)

One official dated this transition back to the mid-1950s and argued that the pace of change was increased in the 1970s. He felt this was due to the introduction of a number of government 'think-tanks', which caused the Civil Service to further reassess its role in the overall Government machine:

> In the period I was there, and I joined in 1955, I think towards the end they were not looking in Hugo Young's term 'Is he one of us, does he vote Conservative?' But they were looking for more the

'managerial-type school' to carry out what the policy was and to do so effectively. They were not looking, necessarily, for policy advisers and independent advice. Or less so than when I first joined the Civil Service. In relation to a change over a couple of generations, I don't think it was a cosy pattern. I think this is a function of the way the thing developed. Let us take my case: I went to Oxford in the early fifties and I think what was true of Oxbridge at the time, was that one of the best things it was thought you could ever do was to get into the Administrative Civil Service or the Diplomatic Service. You would be giving policy advice to ministers. You would be stretched intellectually. You would be with your intellectual peers and these were the attractions of going into it. I think for a very long time that was true.

This official then went on to argue that a fundamental change came about with the introduction of outside advisers and the establishment of a number of 'think-tanks' to advise governments:

Then I think over the years this started to change and it changed sharply under both Conservative and Labour Governments, when they were increasingly looking for advice from outside, rather than from inside. The development of 'Think-Tanks' and there are obvious ones like the Adam Smith Institute, I think the minister would be tending to increasingly want somebody to run the machine, and do it effectively, but not look to him for independent advice. That was a big change and that I think has had an effect to this day, on the calibre of the people coming into the Civil Service. I don't think they are as good as they were. Certainly not as prestigious and if you get governments, and I use this in the plural deliberately, that denigrate the Civil Service, then it becomes less attractive. It started under Benn, if you like, who politicised it and continued very sharply under Margaret Thatcher. Now those two things meant the quality of the person coming in, the type of person coming in, was totally different.

Similarly, another official also felt there was a shift, believing traditional policy advisors were not lost to Whitehall, but that they were counter-balanced by the introduction of a greater number of policy implementors. The net effect was to alter the culture of Whitehall:

My impression is that a different breed emerged, but I would not say it was a function of politicisation. It was more a function of the way the Service itself was changing. I think you can still find a distinction in the Service, between those advising ministers purely on policy, who can produce a polished draft and those who are involved very closely with external circumstances. They require different sort of skills. Through this period you are getting a leavening of the old, strictly first-class honours, academic type of administrative civil servant, with the post-Fulton types, who were entering through a different mechanism. They were coming up more from the grass-roots. Some people might argue this has involved a lowering of standards, post-Fulton. Suddenly, everyone became a Principal. Whereas in the old days there was a sharp division between the administrative class and the rest. There were certain changes on the part of the Civil Service, both as regards the type of job it was seeking to do and the sort of person with the caste of mind to do that sort of job, as distinct from the traditional regime.

Charles Powell also detected this change in the type of individual encouraged into the Civil Service, even when he joined in the 1960s:

The whole nature of the Civil Service has changed. I went into the Civil Service in 1963 and already, by then, I think there was a very distinct change in the sort of people coming in, the sort of people being sought by the Selection Board, on the grounds that the old model was now no longer enough. (Powell interviewed, 16 November 1994)

The impression the interviewers gave was that, in order for Whitehall to keep abreast of a rapidly evolving society, a shift had occurred in the make-up of the higher ranks of the Civil Service, and with it a cultural change in Whitehall – a change which pre-dated Thatcher. The first, tentative moves at encouraging the mandarinate to embrace new management techniques and to place more emphasis on policy implementation, date back to the 1960s. In an era which witnessed Plowden, Fulton and the reforms that succeeded it, these changes are not surprising.

However, for Mrs Thatcher, the pace of change was too slow and she was still sceptical about whether the mandarinate she had inherited had the appetite required to carry out her Government's programme. Her involvement in the appointments procedure, and with it the personalisation of the system, intensified the changing patterns in the make-up of the senior personnel in Whitehall – already partly instigated by the Service itself. She installed individuals into key posts to carry out specific tasks. This, then, still leaves the question open: did the introduction of a new type of individual in the 1980s make any impact at all?

An ex-Treasury official felt that the shift away, in the early 1960s, from great intellectual and innovative policy advisors, produced officials with less discernible characters. They were faceless characters, who were not prepared to stand up and be counted. The result was that the senior Civil Service Margaret Thatcher acquired was rather 'soft':

> I always felt, looking back, that the Permanent Secretaries of the 1940s and '50s were great men. Maybe that is an illusion of youth from when I first joined, but Permanent Secretaries appeared to be really powerful people who had views of their own. There are ways in which you can have views of your own and you can express your opinion forcefully and yet still be loyal. One permanent secretary, in a public lecture, used the phrase: 'I am just the Head of the Secretariat'. I thought that was a demeaning view of the role of a Permanent Secretary, but I think that is how a lot of them had come to think. Sir Edward Bridges in the 1950s wouldn't have said that. I think somewhere in those middle years we had gone a bit pale, a bit characterless, unwilling to express views strongly. You cannot just subordinate your own views when you are in a position like the Permanent Secretary of the Treasury, a central economic policy making role. Your own views have to count. No civil servant has ever resigned because he disagreed with policy profoundly. I think there should be cases where it does happen. The split between the political level, where all decisions are made, and the Civil Service level, which was a 'Secretariat' became too extreme in our system. (An ex-senior Treasury official)

Clive Priestley explained this lack of character as more a consequence of various Government attempts at reform which lost their initial impetus and so failed. The result was that officials were rather jaundiced. Every time a government took up the mantle of system reform, officials appeared only to carry out the job asked of them, without displaying any signs of passion or commitment. It was this which made them appear soft and rather characterless. Priestly felt that:

What you have to ask is; 'Is the management of Government a profession like other professions or is it something unique?' The answer to that is, it is still something rather unique and fluffy. In any other profession you find a governing council which governs that profession. This is not the case with the Civil Service. Whilst it is true, during the sixties and seventies, there was a movement towards new notions of government, like trading accounts, generally speaking, the number of people who thought about accountability, except in very general terms, were very few. Essentially, what the service is still doing, and the *Oughton Report* brings this out, is buying in its chunk of the nation's intelligence, which it still does, not train and educate, as it should. The pattern of career development is certainly very different now, from what it was twenty years ago, mainly because of the Executive Agencies. The pattern then was you were buying in what I call 'de-mountable intelligence'; you plug an individual into various departmental posts and positions and see how he performs. Whereas now the Government focuses on expertise in management. There were very few signs of this in the 1970s. Also, when Mrs Thatcher first came into office, senior people had been round that mulberry bush several times – with Fulton, Big Government under Heath and the early Wilson attempts at controlling the size of the Civil Service manpower. Each time it all fell flat on its face. So there were few merit points to be had from good management. (Priestley interviewed, 14 November 1994)

These comments implied that, compared to their immediate predecessors, Mrs Thatcher's new sub-set of officials introduced a tougher, more abrasive approach to the business of Government. *Characters* re-emerged in the corridors of Whitehall. I went on to ask the mandarins if they detected a more abrasive type of individual re-surfacing in the 1980s? Patrick Benner agreed and provided a personal example of this change:

Yes, I think that is true . . . I recently had an occasion to do an article for the new edition of the *Dictionary of National Biography* on Alan Marre, whom I knew because I worked for him. He finished up as Parliamentary and Health Service's Ombudsman. He was a very good example of that. He was a chap of very high intelligence, very much a policy man, a good negotiator and so forth, but at the end of his career he was in these posts which were quite high public profile and in them you had to be prepared to be abrasive and nasty to people. You couldn't be neutral, you had to come down on one side of the fence or the other. You had to deal with the press. You had to be shot at. He was one of the people who didn't like this, but he made the transition and he did the job. I think there were a lot of people like that who Mrs Thatcher promoted, but they weren't necessarily the people you would have chosen in the first place to do this sort of thing. (Benner interviewed, 16 November 1994)

When I put the same question to Peter Kemp, he agreed, though he provided a slightly different slant on what he felt had occurred:

Yes, I think what happened in the 1980s is that the Civil Service moved to recognising their job as delivering what ministers wanted. Can-do man was in and wait-a-minute man was out. The Government had been elected in 1979 and then re-elected twice, with large majorities. Ministers not only knew what they wanted, but often how to get there. The Civil Service role as ballast was sidelined. There was no room for it. The people had spoken. So officials buckled down and really got on with it. (Kemp interviewed, 17 November 1994)

Clive Priestley also felt a more abrasive individual appeared, but argued that their introduction was necessary, as it sent signals out to the rest of the Whitehall village that Margaret Thatcher really was serious about her programme of reform for Britain. He believed there was a need to distinguish between type and individual: the type was the same and remained the same as had been recruited for a long time. Within that type, there were all sorts of different individuals. Priestley felt:

That Mrs Thatcher very quickly detected a 'waiting game', because so many people had got 'stung' over the previous fifteen years. If anyone got excited about control, policy changed, or anyone got interested about management, ministers lost interest. But if ministers showed a sustained interest, then there was a slow change in attitude, a belief in the minds interested in those matters, that perhaps their day had come.

Priestley then provided an individual example, from the early 1980s, of a very senior mandarin coming to terms with what Mrs Thatcher required of the Civil Service:

It took Douglas Wass eighteen months, from June 1979, to realise that Mrs Thatcher really meant it [Government reform]. Derek

Rayner gently wooed him throughout 1980. At a dinner he had for Sir Douglas Wass, Sir Anthony Rawlinson and a few others in December 1980, Rayner told them: 'I neither want to, nor can deliver from outside the system, permanent change. It is only the system that can deliver that'. Having heard the discussion, Wass banged his hand on the table and said 'Yes – management's time has come'. From that flowed the FMI. So from that you see a sort of political sniffing of the wind by officials: 'Do they actually mean it? When we are convinced they mean it, we will get behind them and give it a lot of oomph'.

Priestley then contended that Margaret Thatcher had little time for the Establishment and the type of old-fashioned, paternalistic individuals associated with it:

> Mrs Thatcher did not like 'golden oldies'. One of the reasons why she did not go for Royal Commissions and so forth, was she did not share this general, British belief, that older chaps were necessarily wiser chaps. She inherited in Ken Stowe, an older Principal Private Secretary. She appointed in Clive Whitmore, a much younger PPS. I was quite young at that time and about to return to the DHSS on promotion. I think there was something about her feeling more comfortable with younger officials and she very much liked people who stood up to her. Tim Lankester was the Economic Affairs Private Secretary and she really liked to have a ding-dong argument with him, for example. (Priestley interviewed, 14 November 1994)

This evidence suggests that a cultural shift did occur and was facilitated by the introduction of a new set of officials. Senior civil servants were more abrasive in their approach, were prepared to be more outspoken in achieving their goals and were more committed to finding means of implementing policies. In the light of this evidence, I examined a number of contradictions in the personalisation of the appointments procedure.

Contradiction in the Personalisation of the Appointments Procedure

One area which remained unclear concerned Margaret Thatcher's reaction to officials who stood up to her and argued their case. In interviews, I was constantly presented with two conflicting views. One suggested that Margaret Thatcher liked individuals who stood up to her, stated their case and believed in what they were saying. She enjoyed informed argument, even if she did not necessarily agree with what was being said. She respected a person who was prepared to stand their ground. It was this type of individual who often 'caught her eye' and whom she singled out for future promotion. In contrast, others argued that individuals who stood up to Margaret Thatcher, and who stated their case in an informed and forceful manner, were effectively black-balled by her for future promotion. The most infamous case of this kind was that of Donald Derx (see chapter 5). I put this conundrum to the officials.

Again, most civil servants used chemistry to explain this apparent contradiction. John Burgh suggested that this single factor was responsible for producing a lack of consistency in Mrs Thatcher's approach towards appointments:

> You have to take into account chemistry and sex! You are absolutely right, this points to exactly the same thing, that there is conflicting evidence. For example, one case I know about, which points the other way [to Derx], is her relationship with Tony Parsons. Tony certainly stood up to her, but she liked him and that is chemistry and I think also there was inevitably, she is a woman after all, a certain kind of sexual element. To some people she responded well, she liked them and others she didn't. If somebody crossed swords with her and she didn't take to that person, that was the end. I don't think you will find any consistency on this matter. (Burgh interviewed, 18 November 1994)

Clive Priestley believed that chemistry was conditioned, not by what the individual was saying, but by the manner in which she or he said it:

> It is partly a matter of style. Firm-minded people like Donald Derx in the Department of Employment and Richard Jamieson in DES got up her nose because of what she thought was their manner. They seemed to her rather patronising, possibly they were unconscious of it themselves – 'We've been here a long time Minister, we have seen this before and let me tell you . . . ' Her time in DES left many scars on her psyche. (Priestley interviewed, 14 November 1994)

Peter Kemp agreed with Clive Priestley's explanation of this conundrum, though, rather than refer to 'manner', Kemp emphasised 'spirit' as the important factor:

Quite a lot of what she might have heard was not so much with her ears as her spirit. People with their mouths can say good thoughts, but if their attitude and their body language is arrogant or dismissive, then the person you are talking to, whether it is a man or a woman or politician will take this in. (Kemp interviewed, 17 November 1994)

Another official felt that Margaret Thatcher liked to argue over an issue, but that the individuals who really got on were those who displayed an enthusiasm for what she was trying to achieve:

If I were to take a view on that, I would say she enjoyed an argument, she was open to persuasion, but it took a long time and was very difficult, but in some cases it could well be held against you. If you wanted to say she didn't enjoy argument or you had to be totally subservient, that wasn't true. But that she would be more impressed if you were sympathetic, gave the impression that you were bursting with energy to carry out her plan, that she would like. Now, these are shades actually, but they are important shades.

Bernard Ingham argued that what was important was the actual clash itself, and that Mrs Thatcher was not shy of arguing. However, he felt she respected people who spoke their minds, so long as they did not appear to be negative. Only Charles Powell painted a significantly different gloss on why this problem arose:

There is an awful lot of tittle-tattle and gossip sometimes. That is always the trouble when you get a more presidential style of government. It is the people below who interpret the slightest sign from above, being a sign of disfavour and therefore inhibiting them from putting something or someone forward. I think there may have been an element of that: 'I don't want to row with the Prime Minister over this appointment, I'd rather have rows with her about this, that and the other, so I won't put forward a name which I think she might reject'. (Powell interviewed, 16 November 1994)

The personalisation of the appointments process led to what can be perceived as a degree of irrationality in a number of appointments and promotions made during the Thatcher era. Logically, when personal whims become the dominant factor, controversy naturally follows. The interviewees accepted that personalisation did lead to some degree of irrationality. As such, it was unsurprising that, during the 1980s, cases arose where individuals who stood up to the Prime Minister succeeded and there were others whose careers were effectively terminated. The overriding determinant in these circumstances appears to be, not what the officials had to say, but the manner in which they presented their case. If they appeared to Mrs Thatcher to adopt a negative manner, their chances of scaling the heights of the Whitehall hierarchy were severely reduced.

'If You Want to Get On, Catch Her Eye'

In this chapter I have established that Mrs Thatcher had, by introducing her own sub-set of officials to the highest grades in Whitehall, personalised the system by which senior appointments are made. I examined how her attitude towards the Civil Service, in her early days of office, was conditioned by her ideological outlook and the depth of experience she had working with Whitehall officials. These combined to persuade her that the senior personnel in Whitehall needed fresh blood, to assist her and her Government in their programme of reform. Her use of the appointments procedure, and with it, it's personalisation, produced a cultural shift at the highest levels in Whitehall. Senior officials were seen to be more abrasive and combative in their approach to their work. A generation of senior officials retired or left and the new personalities appointed, influenced the working methods of other colleagues. Thus, the rather 'soft' Civil Service that Margaret Thatcher had inherited became more robust. Personalisation also undoubtedly led to a less rational approach towards senior appointments. The net effect of this was that there were both winners and losers in the promotion stakes. 'Catching the eye' of the Prime Minister suddenly had a much more significant meaning.

The one area still to be addressed relates to the personalisation of the senior appointments system and it concerns Margaret Thatcher's potential use of the 'Centre' to influence the type of official who graduated to the most senior ranks in Whitehall. This issue warrants a chapter of its own and is examined next.

High-Flyers at the Centre: the Cat that Pinched the Cream or if the Glove Fits, Wear It

M RS THATCHER'S EXPERIENCE of Whitehall presented her with a contradiction she found hard to resolve. Her ideological perspective imbued her with a deep suspicion of the Civil Service. This was compounded by her formative experiences of working with Whitehall officials, which did little to endear the institution to her. However, on entering Downing Street, she was confounded by her experience of the officials available to serve her. As discussed in chapter 5, Margaret Thatcher found that the civil servants in her Private Office were some of the brightest individuals she had ever come across. They displayed a great deal of commitment and were of the calibre which she wished to see promoted to senior posts throughout Whitehall. In her memoirs she emphasised that, as a result, many of her former Private Secretaries went on to head departments (Thatcher 1993, p. 46).

Others have also commented on Margaret Thatcher's disposition towards officials who worked with her at the heart of the Westminster/Whitehall system of Government. One official suggested that Margaret Thatcher tended to favour those officials with whom she came into close contact and with whom she felt comfortable. He argued that quite a lot of youngish people were quite rapidly promoted up to Permanent Secretary, after they had passed through the No.10/Cabinet Office circuit. Again, as discussed earlier, Hugo Young observed that Margaret Thatcher's suspicion of Whitehall was offset by her surprise discovery of the abilities of her closest serving official and how willing they were to 'work their backs off for her' (Young 1989, p. 159).

It can be argued that Mrs Thatcher used the normal Whitehall practice of sending individuals to the centre for her own ends and, in so doing, personalised the appointments system, because she was attracted/deterred by certain types of individuals who caught her eye. This procedure, first evolved by the Civil Service Department after 1968, involved sending Grade 5, 6 and 7 officials to the centre (the Prime Minister's Office, the Cabinet Office or the Treasury) to provide them with a stage upon which to perform. These details are discussed in chapter 3.

There are two versions of this view that Margaret Thatcher used the process to single out individuals she felt ought to serve at the highest grades in Whitehall.

(a) *Thatcher hand-picks the 'creme de la creme'*: Here the view is that high-flyers within departments were sent to the centre to allow them the opportunity to perform at the cutting edge of politics. Such a process provided civil servants with the opportunity to excel in a more intense and demanding environment, whilst in the company of the political heavy-weights at the heart of British Government. At the same time, it also provided a pool of readily available talent from which Margaret Thatcher could target officials who caught her eye. Of course, this has happened under all modern-day Prime Ministers. Indeed, to an extent, the system is geared for this to occur. However, Margaret Thatcher differed in the degree to which she drew from this pool. This was probably a result of her almost instant attraction to a certain type of individual, coupled with the longevity of her period in office. The implication here is that, when consulted on an appointment to a newly vacated post, Mrs Thatcher would suggest the name of an individual who had passed through the centre and, in so doing, had caught her eye. Certainly, relative to the previous two administrations this would account for the larger percentage of officials with experience of working at the centre, who, under Mrs Thatcher, rose to the post of Permanent Secretary.

(b) *The socialisation/reconstruction effect*: This second version is a more subtle variation of the one presented above. On occasion, the Civil Service has been compared to a shoal of fish which, when receiving certain stimuli, navigates a new course. Alternatively, it has been compared to a very small, village-like community, whose antennae are sensitive to any change in its *modus operandi*. In fact, there are two interpretations of what happened. In the first view, individuals sent to the centre were astute and capable of discerning the 'en vogue' trends in their organisation. Being naturally ambitious, they would grasp which qualities were required for successful career progression and restructure themselves to meet those characteristics. This would make them prime candidates for further promotion. Thus, an individual capable of such reconstruction would rapidly graduate up the Whitehall hierarchy. In effect, the bright individuals sent to the centre were receptive to Margaret Thatcher's preference for enthusiastic, can-do, managerially-oriented types, and adopted this work mode in order to progress. In the second view, high-flyers, rather than being subconsciously socialised into this method of operating, reconstructed themselves into positive, can-doers. The implication here is that socialisation was an integral part of the programme of sending high-flyers to the centre. The net effect was similar – both the reconstructed official and the socialised official were attractive candidates for future promotion.

Determining a Centre Effect

I asked the officials I interviewed whether they were conscious that a higher than average number of officials, who had passed through the centre, graduated to the highest grades in Whitehall during Margaret Thatcher's time in office and whether they felt any form of socialisation had occurred? A retired Civil Service Commissioner agreed that, under Margaret Thatcher, a higher than previous percentage of individuals passed through the centre on their way to becoming a Permanent Secretary. However, not surprisingly for an official whose primary function was in the field of Civil Service personnel management, he saw this as resulting from the more effective and professional career planning of the 1980s:

> The procedure for making senior appointments involves bringing people into the centre, before they take on the most senior jobs. This is 'career planning'; you plan someone's career for 10–15 years ahead. It would be most unusual for someone to take on one of the top jobs in the Civil Service, unless he or she had some experience in the Treasury, the Cabinet Office or the Prime Minister's Office. So while you mention the 'socialisation effect', I think I would argue that this is an inevitable part of increased professionalism in career planning. It would be very difficult for a Permanent Secretary to operate unless he had a very broad knowledge of what that central machinery is like.

This was the only official I interviewed who argued that the influence of Margaret Thatcher was not responsible for the increased use of the centre. The remaining officials all felt that one or other of the two strands identified, fitted their view of Whitehall.

The Cat that Pinched the Cream

John Burgh believed that Margaret Thatcher was hand-picking those individuals she was attracted to, from the pool of talent available at the centre:

> I think that if you apply common sense, the chances are that this interpretation is absolutely correct. If you imagine people in their thirties, they are working in the Cabinet Office, they are working in No. 10, seeing the Prime Minister at work, year after year, knowing that she is responsible for promotion. However, more importantly, the Prime Minister sees these people and from this, spots the kind of personality she likes. She was very quick to make up her mind about people, very forthright in her judgement and she was able, through this, to pick the people who she thought would be the type of 'can-do' individuals she wanted. Not those who were always criticising or able to put up other options and try to introduce elements of doubt, where there was absolutely no element of doubt. (Burgh interviewed, 18 November 1994)

However, William Ryrie felt Margaret Thatcher had little bearing on the majority of officials' careers at the levels of grades 5–7. That is obviously the case with an institution the size of the Civil Service. Nevertheless, he did argue that certain individuals caught the Prime Minister's eye and that the prospect of this happening was greatly enhanced by their being geographically located at the centre of government. Ryrie argued that despite the fact that a meeting with the Prime Minister may only have been brief, she consciously assessed and remembered each individual and this could have a direct bearing on their future progress in Whitehall:

> I would find it implausible that the Prime Minister had much influence on the careers of many people at that level. There may have been odd cases, but it would have been very much a matter of chance; who at that level comes into contact with the Prime Minister. The great majority would only come into contact with the Prime Minister in a rather brief and passing way. I am sure

there were cases where the Prime Minister fingered someone who was good. But what happens is that departments can see who are their able people, send them for a bit of experience in the Treasury or the Cabinet Office. They were probably going to succeed anyway and this just gave them an extra boost. (Ryrie interviewed, 19 June 1995)

The Civil Service Commissioner, who earlier argued that the increase in the number of officials who passed through the centre on their way to the top was the product of more effective personnel planning by the Civil Service, accepted that lesser officials who came into contact with Mrs Thatcher left an impression:

> She couldn't and didn't pick the people at junior level; for example, secretaries in Cabinet Committees. Those people observed the way government was organised. But, at the end of the day, civil servants have to do what ministers want. Mrs Thatcher saw something of junior civil servants and she could identify people, who in her view were outstanding or not very good. So, when asked later if she wanted them at Grade 2, she would have views.

There is an obvious trend here. Those interviewed who felt Mrs Thatcher targeted officials from the pool of talent at the centre, emphasised the importance of officials catching her eye. Of course, by being positioned at the hub of British Government, the chance for an official to get noticed by the Prime Minister was greatly enhanced. This, coupled with the fact that these individuals had already been identified by personnel as high-flyers, helps explain the increase in those promoted from the centre during the 1980s.

There is an important subsidiary point which the above comment touches upon. If, for example, one uses the year 1990, in which there were 36 serving Permanent Secretaries and 140 Deputy Secretaries, it is clearly not feasible that, in a job which carries such a heavy work-load, a Prime Minister could devote a considerable proportion of his or her time to dealing, in detail, with all new appointments to these grades. As mentioned in chapter 7, Margaret Thatcher targeted a number of Whitehall posts, to which she believed it important to appoint a certain type of official. These would have included the majority of Permanent Secretaryships and a number of high-profile Deputy Secretary posts.[1] In the case of all other Grade 2s, when the Cabinet Secretary presented her with the short-list from SASC for her approval, she would simply ratify the Cabinet Secretary's primary recommendation. The rare occasions on which this did not happen would be when the name of an outstanding individual appeared on the list, who she had previously come across. In such cases, Mrs Thatcher would make clear to the Cabinet Secretary that the individual concerned was her preferred choice. Obviously, there was a higher chance of her having come across such an individual if he or she had at some stage served at the centre, rather than in one of the more *isolated* Whitehall departments. Charles Powell certainly felt this to be the case, arguing that it was all part of the general perception that the longer the Thatcher Administration continued, the more her style of government became presidential. The effect of this was for people to assume that 'she did virtually everything' and that everything was 'determined by Mrs Thatcher'. However, Powell used the example of the Scott Inquiry to indicate that:

> When they tried to determine in detail what she had and had not seen, you find that a lot of issues never came anywhere near No. 10, they couldn't possibly. The day is only 24 hours long and at certain levels things do not come up that high. My recollection is that the Cabinet Secretary of the day would say: 'We have got to fill the post of Permanent Secretary in the Home Office. With my colleagues I have considered three candidates: the first candidate is Mr A and his qualities are this, that and that, his experience is . . . Mr B has these qualities and this experience, rather younger, may stay longer in the job and Mr C comes from an entirely different department but nonetheless has . . . Having considered all these factors, we feel we are going to recommend the appointment of Mr A'. I think 90 per cent of the time she would have put a tick through it and we would send it back saying the Prime Minister has approved the proposed appointment and the Cabinet Secretary would then confirm it. There were a number of appointments in which she took a particularly close interest, e.g. the Permanent Secretary at the Treasury; but again, she would discuss them with the Cabinet Minister. (Powell interviewed, 16 November 1994)

There is a further element to this, raised by Frank Cooper – the longevity of Mrs Thatcher's period in office. Cooper believed that she obviously had no influence on who went to the centre. He argued that, in general, the arrangements were that people who went to the centre were expected to go further. But he confirmed the view that Margaret Thatcher got to know people at the centre, because 'she was there for eleven years':

She certainly met quite a large cross-section of people who had been in the centre. She probably must have had a better view than someone who was Prime Minister for only three or four years. Not only how the whole thing worked, but also of the people who were there. (Cooper interviewed, 20 December 1994)

Here, Cooper identified two important, but separate, issues. First, the length of time Margaret Thatcher was Prime Minister enabled her thoroughly to come to terms with the Whitehall system. Thus, not only was she able to play the Civil Service at its own game, using the system for her own end, but she was also able to gain an insight into the processes involved in Whitehall personnel management. This was an insight which Prime Ministers of lesser longevity could not have enjoyed. Second, due to the length of her administration, the natural process of Civil Service turnover allowed her to effect substantial change. Thus, before her time in office ended she was able to introduce the officials she wanted, whom she had discovered through contact at the centre and whose careers had matured. As one official argued:

The only person who would know the answer to that [Did Mrs Thatcher cream-off officials from the centre?] is the Cabinet Secretary of the day. I am not sure there would be anything terribly new if that had happened. It is only a function of human nature in a sense. One would identify high-flyers to start with, they would be identified by the system. Those high-flyers would then be given career paths that would take them close to the centres of power and to come into contact with top Cabinet Ministers. I think the difference between Margaret Thatcher and others is that she was there longer, so that a kind of natural process had time to develop. In fact, she was there so long, that in the end she knew much more about some of the departments and their policies than her ministers and quite a lot of the officials. This was also a result of her own capacity to work. She didn't need much sleep, she read voraciously and had a very retentive memory. A brief session with her was a memorable occasion.

Similarly, Peter Kemp provided an individual example of this process. In so doing, he opened up a further avenue for analysis. Kemp commented:

It would be interesting to pursue a similar line about appointments to the Rayner Scrutinies and the Next Step Agencies. These brought to prominence relatively junior civil servants whom she wouldn't normally have seen. With the Rayner Scrutinies, the scrutineers tended to be Assistant Secretaries, maybe Under Secretaries, maybe Principals, that sort of level. Relatively, low-level people. In the agencies, the Chief Executives also tended to be that sort of level and these are people brought to prominence and this created in her mind a sort of contrast between pin-stripped, male, white, genuine, civil servant, who she did not sympathise with, compared to these get-up-and-go-guys down the lane. People like Norman Warner in the Department of Social Security or Steven Curtis at Companies House. People she could actually enthuse to and she saw as can-doers. At a meeting with Steven Curtis at Companies House, she got on splendidly and the meeting ran well over time. At the end, she turned to Steven Curtis and said: 'I have had the most marvellous morning. I would not have thought I was in the Civil Service at all.' Steven Curtis replied: 'Ah, Prime Minister, that is the point, you have to understand you are.' That was a pretty brave thing for a junior official to say, but she took it extremely well. She said something like: 'You are absolutely right'. When she was exposed to real life and she got through this crust, she was happy. She once turned to me and said: 'There is no such thing as a bad Civil Servant, there is only a bad Civil Service.' I think at that stage Steven Curtis's cards were marked positively. She would have thought: 'That is one of the sorts of guys I want as a Permanent Secretary in due course.'[2] (Kemp interviewed, 17 November 1994)

There is an obvious conclusion to draw from Kemp's comments; the 'centre effect' did not necessarily have to be limited to the examination of those high-flyers relocated to the Treasury, the Cabinet Office or the Prime Minister's Office. It could be widened, to include those who had been appointed to carry out the Rayner scrutinies, or to be a Chief Executive of one of the newly established Next Steps Agencies. The suggestion here is that, like those high-flyers who had been transferred to one of the three departments at the centre and gone on to greater things, scrutineers and chief executives would also have enjoyed a much higher profile in their new posts and would have been located much closer to the heart of government. Thus, their potential to catch the Prime Minister's eye would have greatly increased. I asked Clive Priestley, an individual directly involved with the Rayner scrutinies, if he agreed with this version:

I think there is certainly an element of that. The two most famous scrutineers of the first wave were Clive Ponting and Norman Warner. Ponting was very interesting; he was sent on gardening duty by his department after his scrutiny. We got to know this, reported it to Mrs Thatcher. He was stunned that as a result, he was to be awarded an OBE in the Birthday Honours. Norman Warner was a different sort of story – this is where political reality overrides attachment to individuals. Both of those two gave her a presentation of their findings in her study in October 1979 and she amazed them both by saying they should present this to Cabinet two days later. Warner's scrutiny was about the payment of benefits and his recommendations were regarded by the National Federation of Sub-Postmasters as a living death.[3] Thatcher didn't have such a degree of loyalty to scrutineers as to lead her to neglect political realities, but she did look after them well. (Priestley interviewed, 14 November 1994)

Priestley confirmed that, though the link between the scrutineers and future promotion was probably not as strong as the one between the three central departments and promotion, a certain effect did occur. There is one additional element which contributes to the constitution of the centre; the now defunct Central Policy Review Staff (CPRS) which, it can be argued, also played a similar role. John Sparrow, the CPRS's last serving head, informed me that:

Yes, I came across it because the Civil Service secondments into the CPRS were not there because the departments were trying to get rid of them. It was a chance to expose somebody and give them the opportunity to grow. It was, in more ways than one, a fertiliser and water area. So we got good people and it doesn't surprise me that people working in these areas, the recruits into the scrutinies or the CPRS were successful. This, despite the fact that the CPRS fell under her displeasure, was dangerously apart from the centre, had people who were lured out to the flesh pots of the private sector, but those who stayed in the Civil Service, uniformly prospered. They were not in any way blighted by her attitude to the CPRS. They were marked for success, that is why we got them. The same is true of the Private Office and the Cabinet Office. They are all Civil Service nominations. (Sparrow interviewed, 15 November 1994)

It is clear from the views of the interviewees that there was a centre effect. The above account, in part, explains how and why this effect occurred. However, there is another version, which though more subtle, is potentially more powerful.

If the Gloves Fits, Wear It

There was no uniformity in the views of the interviewees as to whether or not a reconstruction or socialisation effect occurred. Indeed, in some cases they were happy to emphasise both processes. For example, this official initially felt that the 'socialisation version' was a convincing analysis. He argued:

> I am attracted to the notion of socialisation. Your high-flyer was always expected to spend time in the Cabinet Office, Treasury or the PMO, nothing new about that whatsoever. The very fact that he did spend time in the Cabinet Office, he was very close to a Prime Minister, who took a very keen interest in top appointments, gave it an added dimension.

However, when developing his argument, this official indicated that, although there was an element of luck involved, high-flyers had the natural talent to assess what was required of them in order to succeed and this was why they had already been identified by personnel as potential future Permanent Secretaries. This argument is further strengthened by the fact that, by the mid-1980s, it was widely accepted, throughout Whitehall, that the Conservatives were firmly entrenched in office. This fact was confirmed to me, in private information, by an ex-civil servant who took part in the 1985 Top Management Programme. He was candid in his comment that after six years of Conservative Government, civil servants were not able to discern a set of circumstances which would manufacture a Labour Government. Clive Priestley also confirmed this view, when he told me:

> If the Civil Service receives strong enough signals it will change direction. What progressively happened by the mid-1980s was that people did actually see, be it reluctantly, that this lot [the Conservative Government] were not actually going away. They did mean to reform the management of Central Government administration and those working in it. (Priestley interviewed, 14 November 1994)

The implication of Whitehall's acceptance that the Conservative Government was there to stay was obvious: those high-flyers who aspired to great heights needed to meet the requirements of a senior civil servant which were being solicited by Mrs Thatcher. Others develop this notion but emphasise reconstruction, rather than socialisation. As one official concluded:

> Immediately you join the Civil Service as a high-flyer, you know that you only have yourself to blame if you don't make it. Now there is a fair amount of luck involved. I think there was a certain amount of luck involved in being at the centre during the 1980s and catching-the-Prime-Minister's-eye. But I think you have made your own luck in the department, by being that kind of person in the first place. That is why they have sent you there. So there is a bit of luck, but there is also a lot of ability. I think there is a lot of natural talent and a natural way of presenting oneself.

Bernard Ingham felt a form of reconstruction occurred, although he was more direct in his analysis of the forces at work. When I asked him to comment on those individuals relocated to the centre, he replied:

> Given that it is an ant heap and that everyone is trying to climb to the top, I think you can imagine all kinds of things happening, because they are ambitious people wanting to get on. They knew that the way to get on with Mrs Thatcher was not so much to be able, although that mattered a great deal, but to be positive and active and give good advice. (Ingham interviewed, 22 December 1994))

Ingham makes an important observation here, arguing that those individuals identified as high-flyers would be the type who had ambitions to make a success of their career in the Civil Service. It is therefore logical to conclude that, to an extent, such types were prepared to meet almost any requirements, in order to succeed in their chosen career.

Senior civil servants during the 1980s needed to exhibit a positive, managerially-inclined, can-do approach. The ambitious type of official sent to the centre would attempt to meet such demands. Frank Cooper noticed this occurred in his own department, although there was a difference; in the Ministry of Defence high-flyers would be sent to Brussels:

> I don't think there was any doubt that there was a much higher cyclical round in the centre, but only in terms of a couple of years or

less. Again, I suspect this was one of those natural developments, in that, as the 1980s progressed, it became more obvious to people that they shouldn't sit in their own department. From your own point of view, it made sense to have a look outside. Being sent to the centre became much more of a prize and it became obvious that people who had had a tour in the Centre were much more likely to get on in their career. The same pattern emerged, as with those Defence men going to Brussels, because of NATO. It became standard practice to go there in the 1980s and those that went were mostly Assistant Secretaries, but I think with one exception they all became Under Secretaries, almost immediately on returning. So people could see it was a good thing. (Cooper interviewed, 20 December 1994)

Finally, Charles Powell also agreed with the reconstruction version, although he also believed that the most important factor was the longevity of the Thatcher Government. He felt that those being sent to the centre did sense the stimuli which was being transmitted and used those signals to convert themselves into the type of official who were attractive for future promotion. However, Powell contended that the vital element in all this was that Mrs Thatcher was in power long enough to make it clear what type of official she regarded as an effective public servant. Thus, the signs were clear:

> In any organisation people take their lead from the top. So, in the sense that they [officials sent to the centre] were probably more pro-active than the majority of civil servants, by nature they tend to be more ready to rush into the corridors of Whitehall to say: 'We want this, we want that' etc . . . I think that probably did occur, but I don't think it was a bad thing. What I see as the driving factor in all this is not any particular wickedness on the part of Mrs Thatcher or her ideology, it is simply the longevity of her time in office. It is the fact you so rarely get a Prime Minister who is in office for eleven continuous years, comes to dominate the whole process of government, from Cabinet colleagues downwards. There is an undeniable effect. Not all of it is willed or deliberate, it just becomes a case of different layers of government reacting to what they think the Prime Minister wants. (Powell interviewed, 16 November 1994)

On the basis of my interviews it is possible, I believe, to attach greater weight to the reconstruction interpretation than its socialisation counterpart. Undoubtedly, a high-flyer who was relocated to the intense atmosphere of the centre could not help but sub-consciously adopt the existing *modus operandi*. However, it seems more likely that the high-flyers consciously adopted fashionable behavioural patterns in order to further their career.

So Far so Good, but alas Cognitive Dissonance

The explanation of the 'centre effect' which emerges here, is clear. The two main factors were: the importance of catching the Prime Minister's eye and the need to be geographically located close to the centre. The centre effect was greater during the Thatcher period because of the length of time she had in office and because of her increased interest in the appointments process. Despite this, there is a version of this explanation which is more subtle and, potentially, more powerful. This revolves round the notion that aspirant high-flyers, sent to the centre, were either socialised and/or reconstructed themselves into a certain approach towards their job; they became hands-on, positive, can-do and managerially-oriented. As a result of such transformation, the potential for them to graduate up the Whitehall ranks were enhanced. This version sees similar forces at work, but suggests that the actual potential to catch the Prime Minister's eye was greater, as Mrs Thatcher discovered that there existed, near at hand, a pool of officials of the type she wanted. This particularly applied to those officials who, at some stage served as her Principal Private Secretary. As Bernard Ingham commented: 'I think you could identify anyone, in a sense, who had been Principal Private Secretary to the Prime Minister, as potential Permanent Secretary material sooner or later' (Ingham interviewed, 22 December 1995).

However, there is a potential problem with this explanation and it concerns the stage at which the high-flyers underwent the process of reconstruction.[4] There is a danger of cognitive dissonance. As we have seen, one might argue that the reason the individuals were originally selected as high-flyers was that they had already sensed the current trends in Civil Service operational patterns and, as such, had restructured themselves to meet those patterns. In so doing, they then stood out as potential high-flyers. Alternatively, it might be argued that these officials displayed a number of traits which persuaded departments that they were of potential Permanent Secretary calibre, but it was only on arriving at the centre that they were able to receive the requisite stimuli to reconstruct themselves in order to become attractive candidates for future promotion. To address this problem properly would have required a series of longitudinal studies, interviewing officials over a period of time, while Mrs Thatcher was still in office and after. My own interviews were conducted between 1994 and 1996 and, therefore, officials provided retrospective accounts Thus, the material from my interviews contains the clear potential for an element of historical re-evaluation, for which it is difficult to control. However, although this problem of cognitive dissonance must remain unresolved, we can conclude that a centre effect did occur. This was in large part a result of the personalisation of the appointments system during the 1980s.

Mandarins of the 1980s:
the Good, the Bad, the Unwanted and the Unaffected

Our doubts are traitors,
And make us lose the good we oft might win,
By fearing to attempt.

Margaret Thatcher (1993 p. 106) citing
William Shakespeare's *Measure for*
Measure in her memoirs

THE EVIDENCE USED TO assess a 'Thatcher effect' has been based on three main sources: a quantitative analysis of civil servant appointments and promotions throughout the 1980s; secondary information drawn from commentaries by academics and journalists; and qualitative data taken both from the numerous memoirs and biographies of ministers who served under Margaret Thatcher and, more significantly, from a series of interviews I conducted with senior, often retired, civil servants. I have argued that Mrs Thatcher took a more active interest than her predecessors in promotions and appointments to the most senior levels in Whitehall. She influenced the appointment of a number of officials to the highest grades in Whitehall and, in so doing, personalised the procedures. She intervened in an attempt to foster a new culture in the Civil Service: one in which officials spent more time dealing with the efficient management and implementation of Government business and less time on the more traditional and 'glamorous' side of senior Civil Service work – advising on policy-making. Mrs Thatcher was attracted to individuals who displayed enthusiasm and a pro-active approach to the implementation of her Government's policies. It was these types, often those who had spent a period of time working at the centre of Whitehall, who caught her eye. In so doing, they greatly enhanced their promotional prospects. This, I have argued, was the main thrust of the 'Thatcher effect' on the higher Civil Service.

In this chapter, I will present a series of *vignettes* depicting the various categories of individuals affected by this process. Of course, there are alternative means of presenting such case studies. The most obvious method would be to list all the officials I have identified by category and present the details of their Whitehall careers, alongside the evidence which justified their inclusion within that group. Such evidence would be drawn from all available biographical sources, making extensive use of evidence from my primary interviews, from the comments of ministers in their memoirs and the commentaries by academics and journalists. The advantage of this method would be its degree of comprehensiveness. However, I feel such an approach would, almost certainly, prove of little interest to the reader (unless they were a personal acquaintance of the said subject or revelled in detail). It could also be the case that detail would drive out analysis.

On this basis, I have decided to adopt a thematic approach. The individuals I have identified as having been affected by Margaret Thatcher are each different, but, nevertheless, they fit relatively comfortably into a number of broad, general categories. These categories are neither absolute, nor are they mutually exclusive. As such, I feel a more satisfactory means of presenting the individual case studies is by developing themes within the various categories. Thus, I used evidence drawn from my case studies to illustrate the themes. This, I hope, will not only be of interest to the reader, but, more importantly, prove an effective way of presenting a subtle and complex process.

The categories of civil servants generated from the numerous case studies discussed in this chapter are:

- those I regard as 'managerially-oriented, can-doers';
- those consistently accused of being 'overtly political';
- those disillusioned with the Civil Service, having been black-balled;
- those more *traditional* Deputy Secretaries who, during the Thatcher era, fitted uncomfortably with the newly-emerging generation of managerially-oriented, senior civil servants and,

as such, never reached the levels they may have done in another Whitehall era, i.e. the 'also-rans';

- the traditionalists who despite, rather than because of, the Thatcher era still scaled the heights of their profession, remaining there until retirement.

The final category is important because it indicates that the Thatcher effect was far from universal; it was often the case that civil servants took a traditional Whitehall path to the top.

Managerially-Oriented, Can-Doers

The officials in this category are those who displayed what Margaret Thatcher would describe as efficient management techniques and were also able policy implementors. I have referred to such officials in previous chapters as being positive types, who, when presented with a Government policy to be implemented, would look for the most effective means of executing that policy, rather than identifying any potential implementation problems. These were the type of individuals who would have spent time at the centre in Whitehall, for example serving Margaret Thatcher as her Principal Private Secretary. Whilst there, they attracted and impressed her and, later, through her intervention, their careers blossomed. This does not mean to suggest that the individuals in this category would not have made it to Permanent Secretary in another Whitehall era, but that their career flourished more rapidly during the 1980s.

One of the highest profile civil servants of the 1980s and an individual who all evidence suggests belongs in this category is Robin Butler, the present Secretary of the Cabinet and Head of the Home Civil Service. He enjoyed a dynamic rise through the senior open structure of the Civil Service, but the defining stage in Butler's career was the time he spent serving Margaret Thatcher as her Principal Private Secretary between 1982 and 1985. An *Observer* profile of Butler commented:

> Butler has not escaped criticism that he was a little too 'political' during the six years he spent as her Private Secretary . . . Others say he was more outspoken than some of his contemporaries . . . He tackled the Civil Service with the same zeal and sense of vocation that other people bring to the church. ('Sir Robin Butler: A Permanent Problem', *The Observer*, 13 February 1994)

As early as 1975, when Butler was only 37 years old, he had been singled out as a potential future Head of the Civil Service. Harold Wilson established a close working relationship with Butler, transferring him to the Treasury in 1976 to help bring public spending under tighter control. Hennessy (1989, p. 676) has labelled Butler a *Renaissance Prince*. Butler has also been credited with physical bravery – he was in the 'Grand Hotel', Brighton, on the night it was bombed during the 1984 Conservative Party Conference. The *Glasgow Herald* commented:

> His appetite for hard work is said to have saved her [Mrs Thatcher] life when at ten to three in the morning he asked her to read just one extra brief which meant she was still in her sitting room when the bomb went off. (*Glasgow Herald*, 14 July 1987)

Although it would be fanciful to suggest this had any direct effect on his subsequent promotion, it none the less indicates his capacity for work and dedication to the job.

SASC did not regard Butler as a great philosopher, in the mould of Burke Trend, one of Butler's predecessors as Cabinet Secretary. At the same time, it would also be wrong to see him as 'Thatcherite', as some elements of the British media did at the time of his appointment. However, Butler has been described as a doer; a man who, when given a task, ensures that it is properly completed on time. When asked to reflect on the abilities of Butler, one commentator replied: '[he got on with] the bread and butter of the job – ensuring that the flow of government business up through committees to the Cabinet itself goes forward as quickly and smoothly as it possibly can' (BBC Radio 3, 12 March 1986).

Butler was an official raised on the Northcote–Trevelyan model of a very able generalist. However, he was aware of the need for the modern Civil Service to be modified, in order to meet the demands of late Twentieth Century Britain. This attitude, incorporated in his approach to the post, won the approval of Margaret Thatcher. Thus, in 1988 when Robert Armstrong retired, it was Butler, not Clive Whitmore or Peter Middleton his most obvious rivals, who became the next *crowned Prince*. As Hennessy (1989, p. 641) concluded:

> If a Minister says 'I want this done', he is brilliant at calling a meeting, making it clear how he thinks business should proceed, consulting all the concerned departments represented round the table and parcelling out the work. He prides himself on it enormously.

Retrospectively, it can be said that Butler was always destined for the highest grade in his chosen profession and he was as likely to have made it under a Labour Government as a Conservative Government. However, like his predecessor Robert Armstrong, Butler has been accused of being too closely associated with both the Thatcher Government and, more latterly, the Major government. Also, like Armstrong, Butler has been called upon publicly to defend the Government over a series of incidents, notably: the Al-Fayed allegations; Norman Lamont's legal costs; Neil Hamilton's resignation; Jonathan Aitken's Paris hotel bill; and, most importantly, the Scott Inquiry into arm supplies to Iraq. At this last inquiry, Butler closely echoed the infamous Armstrong 'economical with the truth' gaffe, when he said: 'it was an accurate but an incomplete answer . . . The purpose of it was to give an answer which in itself was true. It did not give a full picture. It was a half answer. Half the picture can be true'. In the age of Select Committees and far greater media scrutiny of Whitehall, incidents are bound to arise which draw someone, in such a high profile post as Cabinet Secretary, further into the political arena. Few would ever accuse Butler of being an overt political pawn. However, the evidence suggests that, because of the Thatcher effect, his promotion to Cabinet Secretary was secured because he was the type of positive, pro-active type mandarin she wanted.[1]

A more unconventional Whitehall figure of the 1980s was Peter Kemp who, like Butler, can be placed in the managerially-oriented, can-do category. In 1988, after twenty years in the Civil Service, Kemp was appointed as Second Permanent Secretary in what was then known as the Office of the Minister for the Civil Service (the Cabinet Office). He was Mrs Thatcher's own choice to lead the Whitehall reform project – Next Steps. Kemp was appointed to this specialist job because, in Margaret Thatcher's eyes, he was the right person to establish and maintain the project. Kemp is a highly energetic individual and Margaret Thatcher was confident he would successfully channel the enthusiasm he had displayed for structural reform of Whitehall into the Next Steps programme.

Kemp never fitted the mould of a traditional senior civil servant. He was *not* an Establishment figure, even being regarded as an outsider by those who worked with him in the Treasury. His background was markedly different from that of his contemporaries. He did not hold an Oxbridge degree. In fact he had no degree at all, leaving his private school, Millfield, at sixteen and deciding against going to university. After a short career in the Royal Navy, he qualified as an accountant.[2] He entered the Civil Service late, joining the Ministry of Transport in 1967 at the age of 31 and then moving to the Treasury in 1973. He remained in that department until 1988, when he was hand-picked by Mrs Thatcher as the Next Steps project leader. Writing at the time of Kemp's appointment, David Hencke of *The Guardian*, commented:

> Kemp exudes enthusiasm for the job and a clear belief in what he is doing. In his role as creator of the quiet revolution, he was obviously delighted when John Reid, Labour MP for Motherwell North and a Member of the Public Accounts Committee, described him as the 'SAS of Whitehall'. (*The Guardian*, 30 January 1991)

It is implicit in Reid's observation that Kemp was regarded both in Westminster and Whitehall circles as a man of action. This was reflected in his rapid elevation, under Margaret Thatcher's patronage, to lead the Next Steps project. In an interview with Kemp, I questioned him on the circumstances surrounding his promotion:

> As far as I can see I drifted into it. The first time I really saw Margaret Thatcher was at a remarkable evening at Number 11 Downing Street in December 1981, when I was part of the team putting together the Autumn Statement. Lord Howe has a rather circumspect account of it in his memoirs [Howe: 1994, pp. 232–4]. It was not one for anyone to forget. After heading Geoffrey Howe's Central Unit I was promoted to deputy secretary and moved into Civil Service pay matters. This involved being a member of a joint ministerial/official committee which happened to be chaired by the Prime Minister, who took a great deal of interest in Civil Service pay. The ideas which we were developing to make the pay system more modern and relevant with more attention, for instance, to geography, skill, merit and local bargaining, were very attractive to her and it worked. So, I guessed that these personal encounters, coupled with the fact that dealing with the Civil Service pay was to do with Civil Service management in the round and the trade unions in particular, means that I was a very good candidate for the Next Steps job when it came up in the beginning of 1988. (Kemp interviewed, 17 November 1994)

Kemp's description of his involvement in the compilation of the 1981 Autumn Statement, his later involvement with Civil Service pay, and with a reputation as a proactive operator, is a classic example of a civil servant working in close proximity to Margaret Thatcher and catching her eye. So, when Margaret Thatcher was approached by the Cabinet Secretary about the appointment to the specialised post of Head of the Next Steps Project, she did not hesitate to recommend Kemp.

Another official confirmed Kemp's assessment of his appointment, arguing that the primary reason why Kemp received his rapid elevation was due to the enthusiasm he had displayed in his earlier Whitehall career, which singled him out in the eyes of Margaret Thatcher. He also made an interesting observation that, though Mrs Thatcher was unmoveable in her call for Kemp's appointment, it meant that an unconventional mandarin had reached the highest tier in Whitehall. A person who certainly did not fit the traditional pattern of senior appointments. As such, this official believed there was a down-side to the Kemp appointment:

> Peter Kemp was an accountant. He was also a man of great drive and ability. He certainly didn't fit in with the machine. He was hyperactive and full of ideas but there were doubts whether he was a good administrator. Surely it says something of the system that an accountant managed to get to the top, to do the job that he managed very well indeed. He was not a good Permanent Secretary, but he was a man who was very good at driving things forward. He drove the agencies forward, which I don't think many people in the Civil Service could have done.

As described earlier, the 1980s was an era in which, certainly as regards the Civil Service, an overriding theme underpinning Government reform was 'economy'. It is therefore ironic that an ex-senior official of that decade should argue that because Kemp carried the trappings of an accountant, he 'did not fit in with the machine'. However, the unconventional tag stuck and resulted, in 1992, in the sacking of Kemp, at the request of William Waldegrave, Kemp's final political master. The circumstances surrounding the sacking of Kemp are dealt with in chapter 10.

Another controversial intervention by Margaret Thatcher in the appointments procedure to ensure *her* man was appointed, concerned the elevation of Peter Middleton to the post of Permanent Secretary in the Treasury. The late Tony Rawlinson had been the Second Permanent Secretary in the Treasury since 1977. Although he was not regarded as the strongest candidate for the post vacated by the retiring Douglas Wass (see Hennessy 1989, p. 629), it was generally seen as an insult in Whitehall circles to promote Middleton over Rawlinson's head. However, in a partial defence of the Middleton appointment, Robert Armstrong and Frank Cooper argued in a letter to *The Times* (7 January 1993) that:

> Lady Thatcher certainly took an energetic interest in these appointments: she was keen to avoid any suspicion of 'Buggins's turn', and expected to be asked to approve appointments of people whom she could respect as having a combination of high intellectual ability and managerial effectiveness.

Certainly, Middleton possessed qualities of both high intellectual ability and managerial effectiveness and, as such, at Margaret Thatcher's behest, he received the top post in the Treasury. Anthony Howard (*The Times*, 22 December 1992) described Middleton's appointment as 'adventurous leap-frogging'. Hennessy (1989, p. 634) argued that, if SASC had got its own way, then either Brian Hayes or David Hancock would have received the top post at the Treasury. As it was, Middleton, an avowed monetarist who had been responsible for implementing the Conservative Government's medium-term financial strategy, was preferred. At the time of his appointment, Middleton was accused by many of being a Thatcherite; a man who: 'firmly embraced directives from the school of the New Right' (*The Guardian*, 18 January 1993). This was a distortion of the truth; although a confirmed monetarist,[3] his earlier Whitehall career was a testament to an obvious dedication to whichever party was in power. As Denis Healey (1989, p. 442) testified: 'I had an exceptionally able Head of Public Relations in Peter Middleton . . . He fully deserved his later promotion to Permanent Secretary over the heads of older men'. Similarly, Hennessy (1989, p. 630) commented: 'Middleton . . . has a sparky style and a can-do approach which appealed hugely to Labour Ministers in the Wilson and Callaghan years. It is possible . . . that he would have become No. 1 under a Labour Chancellor'. He was very much a: 'hands-on, can-do type of official, of the kind that appeals to Mrs Thatcher whatever their views . . . He does believe in getting from Ministers what the policy is and getting on with it' (Hennessy: 1989, p. 630).

Middleton's appointment was clearly not overtly political. It was his ability as an effective manager and administrator, and his well-documented monetarist views, which helped explain why he caught the eye of Margaret Thatcher. Unusually, Nigel Lawson's memoir provides a detailed account of Middleton's appointment:[4]

Within the Treasury, the consensus was that . . . the choice lay between two up-and-coming Deputy Secretaries, David Hancock and Peter Middleton. Hancock would almost certainly have won in a Treasury vote. I have no idea what his politics were. But the majority of Treasury officials, as indeed of Whitehall generally, saw themselves for want of a better description as social democrats. David Hancock certainly fitted that picture, however he actually voted. Discreet, civilised, knowledgeable in the ways of the Treasury and very Oxbridge, he was very much the mandarin's mandarin . . . He was not the official who said in a public lecture that the good civil servant should 'avoid the last ounce of commitment', but it was not hard to imagine his making the remark.

He was clearly not Margaret's type. In her eyes, the choice lay between Middleton and . . . Anthony Rawlinson, for whom she had a soft spot. He was not only the best looking – in a tall, wiry, matinée idol way – something that always cut a great deal of ice with her. He was also the one undoubted Tory of the three.

Geoffrey [Howe], however, strongly favoured Middleton, as did Leon Brittan, then Chief Secretary – and as I made clear I did, too, . . . [Rawlinson] . . . lacked the imagination and the intellectual firepower required. Margaret came to the same conclusion. [Middleton] had many of the other qualities she admired. He was not only an enthusiast for monetary policy. He strongly believed in supporting the government of the day – for instance in not thrusting an incomes policy down the throat of a Conservative Government which happened to be dead against the idea. Moreover his interpretation of the constitution was essentially Prime Ministerial, believing that all other Ministers and officials should toe the line. Margaret was also impressed by his support against the Foreign Office in the campaign to 'get our money back' from the European Community, and rightly regarded him as a doer and not just a talker.

A northern grammar school boy who had never been fully accepted as a member of the Establishment, Middleton had none the less succeeded in rising to the top of the establishment-conscious mandarinate, even though he was disappointed in his ultimate ambition to become Cabinet Secretary and Head of the Home Civil Service. (Lawson 1992, pp. 266–8)

In light of Lawson's comments, I asked Middleton for views on his appointment to Permanent Secretary in the Treasury and whether or not he saw himself as fitting into the 'can-do' bracket?

> I suppose so, but you never really know do you? It is very difficult to know what sort of person you are. Of course the one thing you don't know is the details of your own appointment. So I have no idea why I was appointed. I certainly didn't fall into a category of someone who deeply knew Margaret Thatcher. As to whether or not I was put in as 'Thatcher's man', I regard that as very strange. I would have only seen Margaret Thatcher on a few occasions, prior to my appointment; at meetings alongside the Chancellor, about four or five times. At the time, I was not well known by Margaret Thatcher. Of course, the individual responsible for my appointment, apart from her, was Geoffrey Howe, not Nigel Lawson, though Nigel was in the Treasury at the time.[5] (Middleton interviewed, 16 November 1994)

I pointed out to Middleton that Lawson, argues in his memoirs that Margaret Thatcher wanted Rawlinson, but that it was the combination of himself, Howe and Brittan that secured Middleton the promotion:

> Absolutely, well I don't know. I have never joined in this discussion, because I have absolutely no idea what the facts are. I have known about plenty of the appointments after me,[6] but very little about them before me. You have to remember there were a whole stack of appointments (the 1945 post-war intake), so a lot of people left. I always thought that, certainly towards the latter stages, it was between myself and David Hancock. I didn't actually think they would go for one of the existing Permanent Secretaries. What I don't know of course is what took place in SASC. When Robert Armstrong told me I'd got the job, he made it quite clear that it had all been done properly. I was recommended by SASC. Beforehand, there had been piles of stuff in the newspapers concerning the appointment. One of the things you discover, as you progress in life, is you know lots of things, but it is very difficult to find out what the influences are that affect your own career. It is quite difficult. I accept I was young for the post, but I think it is quite a good age for a job like the Treasury. I would ideally have liked to have stayed a little less long than I did. I think eight years is a long time, but I got into a rather confused period at the end: Nigel Lawson resigned; then John Major was appointed Prime Minister; then Norman Lamont came in. I had

to see both the Chancellors into their job. (Middleton interviewed, 16 November 1994)

Although he accepted he fitted the label of a 'positive, can-do' type official, Middleton was vague about the circumstances surrounding his rapid elevation in the Whitehall hierarchy. Other officials I interviewed had more pronounced views on this appointment. One official accepted that Middleton leap-frogged over four or five of his colleagues, but strongly refuted the notion that he was a straightforward 'Thatcher man'. An ex-Cabinet Secretary with knowledge of Middleton's promotion was also quick to refute any notion that, under Margaret Thatcher, Middleton became overtly politicised:

> There have been suggestions that Sir Peter Middleton was too closely identified with the policies of the Thatcher Government, but I do not think they are fair: he was hardly less closely involved with the policies followed by Dennis Healey as Chancellor of the Exchequer between 1976 and 1979.

If Middleton was not overtly political, he was certainly a positive-type official, as Charles Powell noted: 'One or two stood out as being energetic, possibly abrasive, action-oriented, Peter Middleton being one very clear case' (Powell interviewed, 16 November 1994). John Cassels agreed with Powell, arguing that, though Middleton leap-frogged over a number of his colleagues, his appointment came as no surprise:

> Peter Middleton was going to get to the top anyway and nobody was surprised when he became Permanent Secretary, even though he jumped a grade to get there. I think everybody thought he was going to make it. He was very bright and I think he was thought to be the best person for the job. I think his peers thought he was the best, apart possibly from the ones he jumped over. (Cassels interviewed, 20 December 1994)

William Ryrie agreed, arguing that it was these attributes which attracted Margaret Thatcher to him: 'She spotted him quite early. She liked him and he gave her the feeling that he was going to do what she wanted' (Ryrie interviewed, 19 June 1995). Another official concluded that:

> Peter was very, very bright, sharp and highly articulate. I would say
> he was an outstanding chap by any standards and deserved what he
> got. It would not be unfair to argue that he secured his promotion at
> a faster rate than was the norm.

Middleton enjoyed Margaret Thatcher's patronage in his accelerated rise to the top. There is little doubt he would have made it
to Permanent Secretary under a Labour Administration, but the
speed of his graduation through the Whitehall ranks owed much to
Margaret Thatcher's attraction to his aptitude for carrying out the
tasks asked of him, despite the obstacles, and his open embracing
of supply-side economics.

The three individuals I chose as representative of the 'managerially-oriented, can-do' type, all differ in the circumstances surrounding their promotions, yet they all benefited from the intervention of Margaret Thatcher in the appointments procedure to secure
their appointment. Their other common trait was that they were
all 'insiders', having spent the majority of their professional career
as public servants. There were few occasions on which Margaret
Thatcher intervened to ensure the appointment of an individual
from outside of the Civil Service. She reasoned that if one was to
intervene in the appointments procedure, it was politically sensible
for this to be done in a covert manner, through the more subtle
elevation of those already in Whitehall, rather than the more overt
and, potentially, more dangerous method of bringing in outsiders.
However, there were cases of outside appointments which fit into
the 'managerially-oriented, can-do' category'.

In 1982, John Sparrow was seconded to the Head of the Central
Policy Review Staff (CPRS) in the Cabinet Office. At the time
of his appointment, Sparrow was employed by Morgan Grenfell
and there were interesting circumstances surrounding his outside
appointment to the CPRS. In an interview, he informed me that at
the beginning of 1977, following Mrs Thatcher's elevation to Leader
of the Opposition, she wanted, among other things, to 'plug what
she regarded as a gap in her area of knowledge – what was going
on in the City'. She asked some of her friends in the City what she
should do about this and whether or not she should have a committee. This option was rejected and instead it was recommended
that she choose an individual as her 'expert' on the City. She asked
how to get hold of such an individual and the common consensus
was to approach Barclays Bank or Morgan Grenfell and have them
send someone along to be looked at. Sparrow pointed out that:

The first I knew about this [I was on the Board of Morgan Grenfell at the time] was at a Board meeting. We were told that this request was made and would we second somebody to be her adviser. That was all we discussed at the meeting and we agreed that we should provide the Leader of the Opposition with a fellow. I volunteered, because I thought it would be interesting and I was sent along to be interviewed by Margaret and had, what I thought, was a very jolly interview . . . I came away and waited for an answer and heard nothing. So I rang up the individual whom she had first approached for advice and asked if he knew when I was going to be told whether or not I was wanted on this assignment or not. He said: 'Oh good God, well I think she thinks you have got the job, I'll find out'. He came back to me five minutes later and said: 'it is perfectly all right, you have got the job, she didn't know she had the choice'. Quite interesting actually, in view of some of the things that have been said subsequently. The situation then evolved fairly rapidly. I stayed on at Morgan Grenfell, but I went to see her once a week and I wrote her a letter once a week. This went on throughout her period as Leader of the Opposition. The information I was providing was partly about what was going on, what the feeling about current economic issues were and a little bit of amateur economic analysis. Two very happy years.

Throughout the early stages of the new Conservative Government, Sparrow's contact with Margaret Thatcher was tailored down to a number of letters he sent her on economic issues which he regarded as important and on which he held views. However, this changed in 1982, when Robin Ibbs returned to ICI:

On this occasion, Robert Armstrong and Clive Whitmore saw me. They asked me if I would take over as Head of the CPRS. I didn't actually see the Prime Minister on that occasion, until after I had been appointed. However, I would be extremely naive to think she was unaware of what was going on. But she played no formal part in the appointment, this was strictly Robert Armstrong's area . . . [7] (Sparrow interviewed, 15 November 1994)

Sparrow went on to observe that his background had been in the City and he accepted that prior to his 1982 appointment, Margaret Thatcher 'knew me and to some extent trusted me'. He then commented that one of Margaret Thatcher's characteristics was her considerable personal loyalty. However, he emphasised that such loyalty did not necessarily imply that she 'promoted her friends, but that she is personally loyal to people through their ups and downs':

> I think the fact that I knew her and had worked well with her, helped.
> I assume that she had formed the impression that I was of at least
> average intelligence because if she formed the contrary impression,
> however much she liked me, I don't think she would have wanted
> me to be Head of the CPRS. I had something to contribute. (Sparrow
> interviewed, 15 November 1994)

I then went on to ask Sparrow if he had experienced any problems being appointed to such a high level and high profile post in Whitehall, having had no insider experience and whether or not existing servants resented his appointment?

> I was told beforehand that the big problem I would face would be
> huge opposition from the permanent Civil Service, that I would
> never be able to get anywhere. The problem actually was, that they
> offered me such a welcome that they almost enveloped me in their
> bear-hug. That is to say, they did not envelop me in the workload
> sense, but in the co-operation sense. They were very co-operative
> and remember that the CPRS was set-up to assist the Cabinet as a
> whole and hence the system as a whole. At all times it was helping
> one or other department, in its policy development. Retrospectively,
> I think that they wanted somebody to take over the job from Robin
> Ibbs and I did know both Clive Whitmore and Robert Armstrong
> before, but whoever they represented collectively, someone high up
> thought I could do the job of Head of the CPRS, which I will say
> immodestly, I think they were right about.

Sparrow then went on to argue that he never saw, nor felt that his appointment could, in anyway, be construed as political, at least not in the overt sense. He provided an interesting anecdote to supplement this view:

> I coined a phrase which one of these days I will get the *Oxford English
> Dictionary* to record, because it appeared in a headline on the middle
> page of *The Times*. Peter Stothard, now the editor, but then its political
> correspondent, rang me up, when my appointment was announced,
> to ask whether I saw myself as committed to Conservative Party
> policy. I said my job was to look at proposals within the remit of

government policy, but I don't see myself as personally committed to that. I would describe myself as 'semi-detached'. Stothard's headline was the 'Semi-detached Mr Sparrow etc' . . . Of course, about five years later, Bernard Ingham turned it into a term of abuse.[8] But it was a coinage and that was its first use. (Sparrow interviewed, 15 November 1994)

Finally, Sparrow addressed the issue as to whether it was the orientation of his economic outlook that had attracted the eye of Margaret Thatcher:

I have never described myself as a monetarist, largely because I have never understood what monetarism as one subject is. I don't belong to any particular school of thought. I actually think I have an ability to be dispassionate, which played a part in my appointment. What I couldn't do and I don't think I could ever do is possess the ability to be a member of the Treasury and oppose, for example, road programmes because they cost money and then get promoted to the Department of Transport and promote road programmes. I couldn't do that. I would have a view as to what would be the right thing to do and I would therefore be either appallingly bad in the Treasury, or appallingly bad at Transport. (Sparrow interviewed, 15 November 1994)

In relation to his CPRS appointment, Sparrow felt that what he possessed and what the CPRS required was the ability to rationally analyse issues and this was due to the adversarial environment in which Whitehall operated. He noted that it was Ted Heath, when in Opposition in the late sixties, that realised this could prove problematic, as no neutral view was being offered which said: 'Look, from the point of view of the Government as a whole, what about this?' As such, Sparrow believed this was the role Heath gave for the CPRS, or at least its original role:

It did change for a variety of reasons. At one stage, long before my time, it became a brainstorming operation. It was doing exercises long into the future. The core rule was always co-ordinating and cutting through the adversarial aspects in government. For that you do need to have some sort of ability, to stand aloof from the fray and say, right the essentials of this are . . . and cut out the partisan arguments and to try to look at the real issues. During the time I was at the CPRS, there was a complete spectrum of views. Half the members came from the private sector, half from the public sector. The CPRS always worked collectively, so one person's point of view only held so much sway. (Sparrow interviewed, 15 November 1994)

Sparrow's account of his chance association with Margaret Thatcher, his involvement with her as an outside economic consultant while in Opposition, and the formalisation of their relationship when she became Prime Minister, provides an interesting profile of how a top appointee's relationship with her developed. It is obvious that Sparrow was not appointed as an overt political sympathiser of Thatcherism. He earned the respect of Margaret Thatcher through his expertise of the workings of the City. As such, he was her number one choice when the time came to find a replacement for Ibbs at the CPRS.

Mrs Thatcher very much regarded Sparrow as a positive-type individual and his appointment was a conciliatory gesture to the CPRS, offering it a final chance to salvage itself.[9] The gesture failed and, within a year, she decided to abolish that particular branch of the Cabinet Office. At the time, the media were broadly scathing of Sparrow's appointment. For example, *The Economist* reported that:

Mr Sparrow has been advising Mrs Thatcher on City matters intermittently for some years [surprisingly, he sees Mrs Thatcher in the same mould of his political hero, Iain Mcleod]. But he enters the Whitehall jungle with little knowledge of the beasts who roam there. And it is these beasts, ministers and mandarins . . . who have been responsible for battering much of the Think Tank's recent work. (*The Economist*, 6 March 1982; material in square brackets in original)

Although with the passage of time the media became more conciliatory towards Sparrow,[10] he could not save the CPRS from abolition, despite the undoubted warmth of his relationship with Margaret Thatcher. Indeed, it is ironic that a man who was identified as 'one-of-us' during the Thatcher years, and who himself argued that Mrs Thatcher showed great loyalty to those she befriended and trusted, should be appointed to lead an organisation in its final death throes. However, the Sparrow case does provide an interesting study of one of the few outsiders appointed by Margaret Thatcher as a 'managerially-oriented, can-doer'.

Peter Levene represents a far more controversial outside appointment. Both the details and problems surrounding the Levene appointment have, in part, already been discussed in chapter 2. Levene was appointed from outside of Whitehall to be Chief of Defence Procurement. At the time of his appointment it was widely stated by the majority of the 'informed media' that this was an overt move towards the politicisation of Whitehall. Controversy followed: Levene had been appointed on a five-year contract, taking him beyond the next prospective general election, but breaking the tradition of what was meant to be a 'career Civil Service'. The situation was compounded by his salary – almost twice that of his contemporaries. Further, Levene had interests in a number of firms with Ministry of Defence contracts. Thus, special arrangements had to be made to ensure he was not privy to the files dealing with these contracts, despite the fact he was now the Chief Accounting Officer for the Ministry. This arrangement caused problems and widespread criticism.

Heseltine, with the blessing of Margaret Thatcher, had demanded Levene's appointment, as he regarded him as a very able individual, capable of introducing cost-cutting schemes, economies of scale and increased overall efficiency in the operating procedures within the department. However, his appointment prompted the question: how exactly was Levene to carry out an efficiency drive, when he had only limited access to the files in the department? The Public Accounts Committee were most concerned:

> The effect of the Government's decision is precisely to reduce the responsibility of the Accounting Officer to one of form without substance . . . we regard the arrangement as a serious breach of the principle of personal financial accountability to Parliament. (Ponting 1986, p. 223)

Media critics levelled the initial charge that Levene was an obvious case of overt politicisation. His background was that of a successful businessman; a graduate in economics from Manchester University, he progressed to become first, Managing Director and then Chairman of Joint United Scientific Holdings. He was also appointed Deputy Chairman of the merchant bank Wasserstein Perella & Company. However, the key to Levene's appointment was his relationship with Heseltine. As Minister of Defence, Heseltine had experienced close dealings with Levene; Joint United Scientific Holdings had a large contract with the MoD and Heseltine had witnessed at first hand, and come to respect, Levene's working practices whilst he was their chairman. He wished to see Levene's approach transferred to the ministry. The opportunity presented itself in 1985, when the post of Chief of Defence Procurement became vacant. The circumstances surrounding the appointment prompted Labour's Gordon Brown (*The Guardian*, 10 September 1992) to declare it: 'a further reinforcement of the incestuous relationship between the ministry and the arms world'. Although Brown's comment contained an element of truth, the main reason for Levene's appointment appeared to be his proven track record in running a company in the defence industry, along extremely efficient lines; in so doing, he attracted the attention of Michael Heseltine and, in turn, Margaret Thatcher.

The controversy surrounding the Levene case soon simmered down, as it was broadly recognised, both within and outside Whitehall circles, that he was performing a difficult job with notable success. However, the real significance of the Levene appointment was that it broke new ground. When the original appointment was announced, it fell outside the remit of the Civil Service Order in Council.[11] Heseltine had not secured permission from the Civil Service Commissioners for the Levene appointment. A Commissioner informed me of the official line that should be taken when a minister wishes to make an outside appointment. He stated that:

> No person can be appointed to a senior post without a certificate from the Civil Service Commission. We were suddenly told that irrespective of that, Peter Levene would be appointed to Defence Procurement, a Grade 1a post. We said: 'No, the law demands the following'. Mr Heseltine had struck this agreement with the Prime Minister and we said: 'No you don't. We are sorry, but we are not going to give our certificate. This post has got to have fair and open competition and that has not occurred'. Heseltine said: 'Do you mean to tell me that some potty little organisation like the Civil Service Commissioners can stop me'. We said: 'No, we can't, but the High Court will and we will go straight to the High Court'. So we then had a long period when all this was discussed; it was agreed this would not happen again and that certain safeguards should be introduced.

The official then pointed out that the situation in the mid-eighties was different compared to present-day arrangements in which complete control by the Civil Service Commission has disappeared:

> Ministers [today] can do very much what they like, subject to some safe guards. If, in fact, the Minister wanted to go to open competition,

we would have had no objection to that at all. The Minister could have specified the sort of person he wanted. Obviously we [the CSC] must abide by that. But during my time, we never had a single appointment where our recommendation was not accepted. We made it clear once or twice to ministers, that if they wanted their own man, then they could refuse our recommendation and they could go for their own chap, but we would publish the fact that the appointment was contrary to the advise of the Commission. That was always good enough. I think in the case of Levene, either Mr Heseltine was not aware of the procedures or, if he was, he thought they were so silly he was going to ignore them. If he did know the procedures, then he deliberately ignored them. He certainly took the line that he wasn't going to bother with them. It then had to be made clear that if he proceeded, then the Courts would become involved. The matter was finally settled by an agreement that this would not happen again. A statement was made in Parliament, that in future there would be no other appointments of this sort. This seemed to be the reasonable compromise. Can I say that Peter Levene himself acted impeccably throughout the whole of this. He offered to go through a selection procedure, if necessary. He was not the man behind all this.

I challenged the official that the whole saga of the Levene appointment appeared to outsiders to be a classic case of a Civil Service fudge, in order to ensure that there was no major political fall out from the event:

We had nothing against Levene, for all I know in an open competition he would have won, he had the exact qualifications sought after in that post. But what we wanted was a statement by the Government that they would never do this again and that the existing procedures would be operated. I felt it resulted in a sensible compromise, openly announced to Parliament. If one disagrees, it is, I suppose, wheeling and dealing. However, the arrangements following the Peter Levene case were announced to Parliament.

These revelations concerning the hidden aspects of the Levene affair highlight the many difficulties which can arise when a minister with a reputation for impulsiveness, backed by his Prime Minister, ignores normal Whitehall operating procedures. It also exposes the rigidity of the system. Few questioned the suitability of Levene for the post in question. Controversy surrounded

Heseltine's circumvention of the customary Whitehall procedures; he went ahead with a public announcement of Levene's appointment without insider approval.

The importance of the Levene case is that when a glitch occurs within the inner sanctum of British Government, the operation of Government machinery, at least to the outside observer, appears to continue to operate smoothly. However, behind the official façade, all is not as it should be and the Cabinet Secretary, as the senior Government mechanic, is called in to re-tune the engine. In the case of Levene, a fresh brand of oil was applied and the engine returned to its normal performance targets.

Levene was an outsider who was both pro-active and well-grounded in the methods of organisational management. Indeed, Levene himself agreed with this assessment, when giving evidence to the TCSC in 1994:

> Why was I brought in? It was to bring in some other ideas, to bring some outside ideas from the commercial world into what effectively was an organisation which had a very commercial purpose. (Treasury and Civil Service Committee 1994, Vol. II, p. 3)

His appointment was not directly the result of Mrs Thatcher's intervention, but rather, because of agitation from one of her more high profile Cabinet Minister's. However, she undoubtedly supported Heseltine in his choice. What is important about this case is the wider implications. The Civil Service Commission is not an organisation to be flouted. Following the fall-out from the Levene case, a series of changes were announced in the Commons. Hennessy (1989, pp. 372–3) paraphrases the Commission's 1985 annual report:

> Measures were being taken to provide that future appointments to the Home Civil Service which took the form of secondment from an outside organisation would be made in compliance with the Civil Service Order in Council and any regulations made thereunder. It was immediately clear that these developments represented a significant widening of what was considered to be the scope of our responsibilities, given the increasing use of inward secondments, often at senior levels in recent years.

Unfortunately, Levene refused to be interviewed, citing pressure of work. However, his subsequent appointment as the Prime

Minister's Adviser on Efficiency confirms that he continues to be regarded, at least in Whitehall circles, as an exceptionally able, senior civil servant.

The five individuals I have selected as representatives of the 'managerially-oriented, can-do' category, each displayed similar characteristics, which enabled me to group them together. More importantly, they enjoyed a degree of patronage from Margaret Thatcher, which was vital in securing their promotion to the highest grade in Whitehall. They received this support because they had proven records as pro-active, positive, managerially-oriented individuals and it was these traits which were attractive to Margaret Thatcher. However, in some cases, her intervention in the appointments procedure to guarantee either their promotion or appointment was problematic. For example, the appointment of both Levene and Kemp created difficulties. These two cases highlight problems encountered by the machinery of government when traditional Whitehall procedures are not observed. In these two cases, the problems resulted because the Prime Minister adopted an unfamiliar, pro-active approach towards the appointments procedure.

The Overtly Political

This category reflects the many accusations, in both political and media circles during the early years of the 1980s, of overt politicisation of the Civil Service. I uncovered no evidence of overt politicisation in the Civil Service during the Thatcher years; that is, there was no substantiated proof that, at any stage, Mrs Thatcher intervened in the appointments procedure to appoint or promote individuals on the basis of their being sympathetic to the Conservative Party. Of course, this does not mean that no Conservative Party sympathisers were appointed to the highest grades in Whitehall during the 1980s. However, Mrs Thatcher did not include in her criteria for assessing civil servants for a post an individual's personal political views. In the vast majority of the cases of senior appointments which came before Mrs Thatcher, she was probably unaware of the individual's personal, political outlook. However, a subset of 'overt politicisation' can be created; those individuals who, having already secured their appointment to the highest grades, became politicised through too close an association with the Thatcher Government. The three case studies I have selected as representative of this category, are individuals who, throughout the 1980s, experienced a high media profile. This is hardly surprising given that media coverage was, in part, responsible for their being associated with politicisation.

One of the most (in)famous senior civil servants of the 1980s was Margaret Thatcher's Chief Press Secretary, Bernard Ingham. Although he only rose to Deputy Secretary status, and even then belatedly, the Ingham case is enthralling and his promotion certainly came about as a result of Margaret Thatcher's active involvement in the appointments procedure. In chapter 6, I outlined Ingham's prior involvement in Labour Party politics. The circumstances surrounding his appointment to Chief Press Secretary, and the subsequent accusations of politicisation, are a central part of the controversy which surrounded his Whitehall career.

During the Callaghan Government, Ingham had been in charge of energy conservation, working (relatively) harmoniously with Tony Benn, the then Secretary of State for Energy. Young described how Margaret Thatcher first came across Ingham and the unusual circumstances behind his appointment:

> Under the new government, he [Ingham] was present among the thirty-five others when the Prime Minister [Thatcher] visited his department, on which occasion, he talked to her for all of two minutes. When, one day in late summer 1979, he was summoned from his desk in Downing Street, it was under the firm impression that he was going for an interview. He even thought he might not want the job of Prime Minister's Press Secretary, should it eventually be offered to him. On arrival in Mrs Thatcher's presence he soon realised that he was under a serious misapprehension. She immediately began to speak as though her and his acceptance were formalities already complete and began to instruct him in how he should approach his new task. If she had ever caught sight of him before, it could only have been through covert glances on her visit to his department. Yet in this fortuitous manner, devoid of the normal processes of rational choice, began one of the great enduring partnerships – as consistently close as she had with any other man – of Mrs Thatcher's years as Prime Minister. (Young 1989, pp. 165–6)[12]

This highlights Margaret Thatcher's method of making an almost instant assessment of an individual. As a result of the brief departmental meeting he was given a subconscious tick in her mental notebook of individuals. It was this tick which heralded his later appointment as her Chief Press Secretary. However, although they are revealing, the details of Ingham's appointment pale in relation to his subsequent career in Whitehall.

Ingham worked as press secretary for the entire duration of the Thatcher administration. Despite attempts by both Robert Armstrong and, later, Robin Butler, to ease Ingham away from the Press Office and back into the Whitehall mainstream, he steadfastly refused their overtures. Partly due to the longevity of the time he spent in this one post, his Whitehall career will almost inevitably be tarnished by accusations that he became politicised during the Thatcher years. Indeed, in an interview I had with Ingham, he accepted that he probably did become too closely associated with Mrs Thatcher. I asked Ingham if he felt anyone in Whitehall politicised themselves during the 1980s:

> I think in a sense you could say I did because I was there for eleven years. I must tell you I felt Mrs Thatcher was overall a very good thing for Britain. But my job was to support her. They tried to move me after five years. Robert Armstrong tried to move me to become Head of the Central Office of Information [COI] and I was profoundly unenthusiastic and said: 'I don't think that is for me, No. 10 is for me. In any case I have only five years to do'. I had done five years, I had been there long enough in Armstrong's view. I think three years is probably as much as you should do. I enjoyed enormously what I was doing, but I think it was a mistake to stay for eleven years. I got a lot of clobbering as a consequence. (Ingham interviewed, 22 December 1995)

Ingham went on to argue that he continued in the same post after five years because he found the job 'immensely satisfying'. He was reluctant to go to the COI because he suspected the job would bore him. However, retrospectively, he believed no one should be the Prime Minister's Press Officer for more than three years, as they would probably become a 'personality and a target'. I asked Ingham if his position became untenable after Margaret Thatcher's downfall in November 1990:

> I think in my case, I would have gone anyway, because I was eighteen months from retirement and I told them I was going. The first part was that, when she said she was going, I said I was going as well. I saw my way out, because it was becoming increasingly burdensome.

If she had stayed, I would have found it very difficult. I had reached the age of sixty. But when she went, I thought that was a natural break, I could then go. Departing from No. 10, with Mrs Thatcher still there, would have been very hard for me. You form a bond after eleven years. (Ingham interviewed, 22 December 1995)

I then asked Ingham whether or not he accepted that he had become too closely associated with Margaret Thatcher and therefore had no choice but to leave when she did:

Undoubtedly. I don't think there is any argument. I would defend myself on grounds of my professionalism and what I did while I was there. I am my own severest critic. So I think I gave her a good service to the end, but I think the fact of staying that long did mean I was politically identified and some would say far too closely identified. But none of my other ministers, whom I worked for, have ever really been critical of me. Also, for the last two years, when I became a Grade 2, because I did two jobs, [heading the Government Information Service, as well as being Press Secretary], people then said I had too much power and that sort of thing. Though it felt as though I did not have much power at all, bearing in mind that you could never do anything without consultation. It was never possible to do this, that and the other in this highly devolved system of Cabinet Government. I think I would be very happy to stand by what I did in those two years for the Government Information Service [GIS]. I think the truth is everyone felt I was identified with Margaret Thatcher. (Ingham interviewed, 22 December 1995)

Despite accepting that he probably was too closely associated with Margaret Thatcher, Ingham went on to point out that during his time as Press Officer, the media changed, becoming 'extremely suspicious of anybody there':

There are a means by which you can attack the Prime Minister. You only have to put a foot wrong and they will clobber you. You can't remain invisible anymore. Firstly, they want to quote you at every opportunity. Secondly, they want footage of you at every opportunity. You can't go in and out of the door without the cameras being there. So you became much more visible in the 1980s than anyone did before and that has its own problem too. (Ingham interviewed, 22 December 1995)

I then asked Ingham whether or not he had ever been guilty of interpreting what he thought were the musings of his Prime Minister, rather than only relaying to the media her actual views. As an example, I cited the case of the 1984 discussion of the floating of the free pound, in which Nigel Lawson claimed that Ingham's unsubstantiated comments produced a run on the pound:[13]

> What happened there was that I told the truth. What I was saying was that you are not going to throw good money after bad, because you can't buck the market. What I didn't say and what I couldn't say and what I ought to have said, was that we ought to put up interest rates. The *Observer* reached the conclusion that that is what would have to be done, because that day the Treasury had been too timid in putting them up by only one per cent. They should have put them up decisively and we wouldn't have had a problem. That was the real problem and, once again, this is what happens to press secretaries. They sometimes make mistakes, because they are coping with a problem that overwhelms them.

Ingham then went on to outline why, in his opinion, he gained the label of a 'reputation killer' in both Westminster and Whitehall circles:

> I got a reputation for slagging-off ministers because I called Francis Pym 'its being so cheerful as keeps him going' and John Biffen as 'that well-known, semi-detached member of the Cabinet'. I was actually trying to help them because Pym made a speech in the very same week that Geoffrey Howe said that the economy was coming out of recession, of insipid gloom. Well, he was like that. What the hell could I do when I had the Lobby saying how can you keep the Minister responsible for presentation in the Cabinet when he doesn't even know what his Chancellor thinks? How can he present policies? Bloody good question, I can tell you. So I said: 'Oh for god sake, you know very well'. Then, similarly, with John Biffen, he went on television in 1986 and said Mrs Thatcher was a liability to her Party and should be replaced by a collective leadership. A year later she had won her third General Election with a majority of one hundred. The Lobby were saying you can't have a Cabinet Minister who says that about the Prime Minister. Well, if she wasn't going to sack him what the hell could I do. I had to try to find a way of excusing his extraordinary behaviour. (Ingham interviewed, 22 December 1995)

Ingham was willing to accept that, in becoming too closely associated with Margaret Thatcher, he had politicised himself. His
defence of this position, though highly subjective, has some credence in terms of the longevity of his time in office. However,
it was his own choice, he enjoyed the job to such a degree that
he remained in the same post for eleven years, despite being
offered positions elsewhere in Whitehall. Thus, in part, Ingham
was responsible for the accusations made against him. He also had
difficulty distinguishing the thin line between being the *mouth-
piece* of the Government (through the lobby system) and being an
impartial, neutral, civil servant. Undoubtedly, there were incidents
where Ingham overstepped the line. A number of these have been
mentioned above. Yet, it was Ingham's involvement in the Westland
Affair which probably stood out as one of his most blatant *political*
acts.[14] Thus, it was Ingham's length of tenure in office, combined
with a series of high-profile political blunders, in which he lost
sight of his role as an impartial Government official, that justified
his being labelled a politicised bureaucrat.

It is difficult to examine the case of Ingham without also reviewing
the very similar career of Charles Powell. These two names from
the Thatcher era have become almost synonymous with each other.
Following his appointment as Private Secretary advising Margaret
Thatcher on foreign and defence affairs,[15] Powell did not enjoy
the same initial degree of access to the Prime Minister which
Ingham experienced. However, in the last years of the Thatcher
Government, Powell undoubtedly established himself as one of her
closest confidants. As Harris (1990, pp. 180–1) noted:

> Ingham's access to Thatcher was great, but it was as nothing
> compared to that enjoyed by her Private Secretary. Although Powell
> got off to a slow start when he joined the Prime Minister's staff in
> 1984, it was no exaggeration, six years later, to say that he saw more
> of her than any other person, including her husband . . . A telling
> demonstration of their relative status was provided in June 1988,
> when Ronald Reagan paid his farewell visit as President to see Mrs
> Thatcher. The Powells joined the Reagans, the Thatchers, the Howes
> and the Schultzes for the intimate candle-lit dinner; Ingham was left
> outside to hand out details of the menu to the press.

Harris's assessment of the Ingham–Powell relationship is a dem-
onstration of the power the two once held in Whitehall, despite the
fact that, nominally, they were only Deputy Secretaries:

What was once a most powerful axis – for a while, the nearest Britain had to a genuine Deputy Prime Minister – was eventually replaced by a well-attested, unmistakable, mutual *froideur*. Such are the squabbles of good and faithful servants. (Harris 1990, p. 181)

Another official also felt that the Powell relationship was a vitally important one, believing that their combined influence was one of the causal factors in the downfall of the Thatcher Government:

At a broader level, my personal opinion is that Margaret Thatcher had a very good instinct and some very clear policies at the start, but towards the end I think she started listening to department advice a bit too much and following her instinct a bit less. She may also have relied on Charles Powell and Bernard Ingham a bit too much. The interesting thing about Charles is how far the Foreign Office regarded him as a *renegade*.

Like Ingham, Powell often lost sight of his responsibilities as an impartial Government official. In an interview with *The Times*, as recently as June 1994, he outlined what he felt his public responsibility lay:

At Number 10 you have such a small staff, the Prime Minister has got to feel that you are on his or her side. You have got to cut departmental ties. Your loyalty has to be to the Prime Minister.

This explains the above comment as to why the Foreign Office regarded Powell a *renegade*. It is also a clear indicator of the primacy of Powell's commitment to the Prime Minister he served, over a broader responsibility to, as Robert Armstrong contends, the Crown as represented by the Government of the day. The implications here are clear: if conflict arose between the Prime Minister and the Government (as embodied in a collectively responsible Cabinet), Powell regarded his sole loyalty as to the Prime Minister and not the Cabinet or, more broadly, the public in general. Although, in the private sector, some might applaud such loyalty to one's immediate master, such loyalty goes against the grain of a number of the core values on which the Civil Service, as a public body, exists – impartiality, integrity and objectivity. In an interview, I questioned Powell on the principles of loyalty within Government. His priorities remained clear:

> I think it is quite simply a question of loyalty while someone is serving in a Private Office, particularly No. 10. It should never be seen that someone seconded from another department to No. 10 is there as that department's spy or agent. You cannot work the system like that. The Prime Minister has virtually no staff; every Cabinet Minister has thousands of Civil Servants at his beck and call, producing papers. Number 10 has got about ten people in the whole building, actually doing anything serious. While you are there, your loyalty is to Number 10, to the Prime Minister of the day, and I think that is extremely important. (Powell interviewed, 16 November 1995)

In addressing the issue of whether or not, on a number of occasions, Powell and Ingham breached the boundaries within which a public servant should operate, I asked Powell if he had politicised himself by becoming too closely identified with Margaret Thatcher:

> Traditionally, leaving aside Bernard for a minute, the Private Office job, in any Private Office, not just No. 10, is on a two-year rotation. People are rotated through and will only stay two and a half years. One way and another I was there seven and a half years. That is a very long time to serve in that sort of post. I personally am absolutely satisfied I wasn't political. I have never joined a political party. I have had no great urge to do so. I suppose you scratch me on the whole, you get conservative, with a small 'c', rather than socialist views. But equally if you stay that long as Private Secretary, you do become clearly identified with somebody, in the eyes of the system, the Civil Service, with Parliament and the press. That frankly was one of the reasons why I decided to leave the Government service. I actually thought it was not fair on the rest of the public service, which has very high standards in these matters, to confront them with the dilemma of my return as somebody who was tainted or identified with a political party and a person who had been in power. That is fair enough and I was very happy to leave. (Powell interviewed, 16 November 1995)

One can have some sympathy with Powell's argument that both he and Ingham were the product of a unique set of circumstances;

serving in specialised Whitehall posts, during an administration whose longevity in the twentieth century will not be surpassed. However, many would argue that the most substantial evidence that Ingham and Powell became overtly politicised was the fact both left Whitehall almost immediately after Mrs Thatcher's departure in November 1990. They both carried too much political baggage to try to start afresh under any new government, be it Conservative or Labour. The cases of both Powell and Ingham were inextricably linked. Their appointments were secured through the patronage of Margaret Thatcher and while in office both politicised themselves. It would also appear that both lost sight of the fact they were officially employed as public servants and not as key actors in an alternative Thatcher 'kitchen' Cabinet.

The third case of an individual who, having been appointed by Mrs Thatcher, politicised himself was Duncan Nichol, the former Chief Executive of the NHS Management Board. Nichol's appointment in 1989, to what is a Grade 1a post in Whitehall, subsequently proved to be highly contentious. His politicisation differed from that of Ingham and Powell because it was not the result of too close an association with Margaret Thatcher. Instead, there were a series of incidents in which comments Nichol made, linked him directly to the Conservative Party.

Although the controversy surrounding Nichol only came to the fore after the departure of Margaret Thatcher, it must be remembered that she was responsible for Nichol's appointment, at a time when the NHS was entering an intensive phase of reform. After the 1987 election, Mrs Thatcher had instigated a hurried Prime-Ministerial Review of the NHS, without consulting the BMA, which led to the 1988 White Paper *Working For Patients*. Nichol, previously the Regional General Manager of the Manchester Health District, was appointed to replace Leonard Peach.[16] A known convert to the principle of the dominance of market forces in the running of the Health Service, Nichol believed that the basis on which the Service was founded, free health-care for all at the point of delivery, was no longer sustainable. His appointment was made, so that, as an avowed free-marketeer, he could help promote the passage of the 1990 NHS and Community Care Act. At the heart of this Act was the division between purchasing agents and providers. Yet, it was not until the run-up to the 1992 General Election that public controversy surrounding Nichol first surfaced. This followed overtly political comments made by Nichol during the campaign. A 'leader' in *The Times* concluded:

But should any Thatcherite civil servant be retired? The answer is yes, where they have become too closely aligned with the politics of the Government. Duncan Nichol, the Chief Executive of the NHS, for example, should be required to step down because he has been ready to indulge in the politics of health administration – attacking Labour's policies, and presenting the Conservative changes in the most partisan manner. (*The Times*, 9 March 1992)

Nichol's comments so angered Robin Cook, then Labour's Health spokesman, that he was widely quoted as saying that in the event of the formation of a Labour Government, he would not be able to work with him. In January 1993, Nichol left to take a Chair at the University of Manchester, as Head of the Centre for International Health Care Management. At the time of his departure from Whitehall, *The Times* (4 January 1993) commented: 'Sir Duncan, aged 52, is regarded as having succeeded in holding together the NHS through the difficulties caused by the rushed introduction of the market system'. Although this may be true, Nichol was as responsible for creating those difficulties as he was for solving them. His post, though not at the traditional heart of Whitehall, is officially classified as a Grade 1a post and it would appear that Nichol, a Thatcher appointee, politicised himself while in office.

Ingham, Nichol and Powell all constitute cases of individual officials who, having been appointed at the behest of Margaret Thatcher, went on to politicise themselves. It is significant that only one of these individuals held a post above Grade 2. Certainly, and unsurprisingly, I came across no evidence of a Permanent Secretary in a major department, overtly politicising himself during the 1980s. The one potential, but incorrect, example of such a case, which arose at the end of the 1980s, was that of Terry Heiser, Permanent Secretary at the Department of the Environment. Heiser became embroiled in the Community Charge debacle and prompted Jack Cunningham, Labour's then Shadow Cabinet Minister for the Department of Environment, to declare publicly that he would not be able to work with Heiser as his Permanent Secretary. However, as Hennessy (1995, p. 130) correctly concluded:

Sir Terry Heiser, Permanent Secretary at the Department of the Environment, was even depicted in Labour Shadow Cabinet circles as being a keen Thatcherite, when anyone who knew him was aware that he was anything but.

Disillusionment by the Black-Balled

The clearest affirmation of Margaret Thatcher's active intervention in the appointments procedure does not appear in the 'managerially-oriented, can-doers' category. Instead, I would argue it occurs among the group of individuals who, for a variety of reasons, were informed that, while Margaret Thatcher remained Prime Minister, their chances of further promotion were negligible – the *black-balled*. It is not surprising that individuals in this category provided the strongest corroborative evidence of Mrs Thatcher's influence, given they were alienated from Whitehall by the Thatcher era and, as such, tended to harbour a degree of disappointment and resentment towards their former employees. Thus, they provided more information than those civil servants whose careers benefitted from Margaret Thatcher's tenure as Prime Minister.

The most notorious case, discussed earlier in chapter 3, is that of Donald Derx, an official whose career had been effectively black-balled by Margaret Thatcher. In their memoirs, both Prior (1986, p. 136) and Clark (1993, p. 22) emphasised Mrs Thatcher's disdain for Derx; this was the result of a clash during her first-term meeting at the Department of Employment.[17] When I conducted my interviews with senior civil servants, I asked them for details of this case and similar ones. From the information they provided, two further names regularly cropped-up – William Ryrie and John Steele. The common strand was that all three clashed with Margaret Thatcher during initial contact with her. In so doing, they all caught her eye, but in a negative, not a positive, sense. Thus, in Margaret Thatcher's mental register of Government officials, a large cross appeared beside the names of Derx, Steele and Ryrie. What is even more interesting, in these three cases, was that no attempt was made in Whitehall circles to conceal her disapproval. The Cabinet Secretary confirmed to each individual that, whilst Mrs Thatcher remained Prime Minister, their chances of further promotion were effectively non-existent. The advice given by the Cabinet Secretary was that if an opportunity arose for work away from the Whitehall village, it would be in the interest of all concerned, for them to move on elsewhere. If, of course, the Government could be of any assistance in easing their transition to civvy street, it would be

more than happy to oblige. Not surprisingly, all three opted to go
and each went on to a successful career elsewhere: Derx left in 1986
to take-up a Directorship at Glaxo Holdings plc; Steele moved on to
an auspicious career in Brussels, as Director General of Transport
for the EU and a consultant for Prisma Transport Consultants; and
Ryrie left to become Executive Vice-President and Chief Executive
of the International Finance Corporation at the World Bank. It would
appear that in all three cases the Government kept its promise and
did its utmost to soften the blow of having to leave SW1.

I have dealt with the case of Derx in detail in chapter.[18] When
I wrote to him requesting an interview, he declined my invitation
on the grounds that:

> The truth is that I do not normally contribute to excursions into my
> Civil Service past. So far as I am concerned it is closed. Obviously
> no historian can possibly accept the validity of this position and
> fortunately from your point of view few others seem to share it. So
> please forgive me if I decline your invitation, since I am sure that
> your study will not feel the loss. (Derx letter, 22 October 1994)

Fortunately, William Ryrie felt that his views were of some value
and therefore accepted the opportunity to comment on his Civil
Service career.

When Ryrie left Whitehall in 1984 he did so as Permanent Secretary at the Overseas Development Agency, one of the more
peripheral Whitehall departments. Hennessy (1989, p. 191) said of
Ryrie:

> He was an Assistant Secretary in the Treasury who rose to lead
> his own, Overseas Development department, and might well have
> headed the Treasury if Keynesianism had not acquired the status of
> heresy, at ministerial level at least, by the early 1980s.

Clearly, Ryrie displayed the type of credentials which in a previous Whitehall era might have led him to one of the great Permanent Secretaryships. However, the Thatcher Government was not
renowned for its receptiveness to demand-side apologists. I asked
Ryrie if he was disappointed at the treatment he had received:

> It may sound like sour grapes, but I am not disappointed that I didn't
> become a full Permanent Secretary, because only in those last two or
> three years before leaving, did I really understand something that I

think most of my colleagues had understood long before; the role of
a top official is purely an advisory role. You are not really expected
to be a leader, you are not expected to take charge, especially in the
Treasury where there is very little management function. The role of
the Treasury official is to advise ministers who take all the decisions.
(Ryrie interviewed, 19 June 1995)

In an earlier interview, John Burgh, an ex-Whitehall colleague,
provided an account of Ryrie's clash with Mrs Thatcher:

The one thing that was quite new was the Prime Minister went
round and met senior officials in the departments. It so happens I
didn't meet her when she went round, but other people did. Thus,
in relation to did anyone's career become impeded as a result of her
direct intervention, there are clearly two such cases. One you will
know, Donald Derx and the other was Bill Ryrie. Bill was widely
tipped, at one stage, as a possible future Head of the Civil Service
or Permanent Secretary in the Treasury. He crossed swords with Mrs
Thatcher when she was Leader of the Opposition, when she went to
Washington and also, when he was a Second Permanent Secretary in
the Treasury, responsible for the nationalised industries. I don't think
that pleased the Prime Minister. Bill did become Permanent Secretary
at the ODA and was told [it was while Douglas Wass was Head of
the Civil Service] that he couldn't expect any further preferment,
while she was at No. 10. (Burgh interviewed, 18 November 1994)

I asked William Ryrie to recollect his clash with Margaret
Thatcher. In particular, to outline the circumstances surrounding
his premature departure from Whitehall, with reference to the
Hennessy implication that the root cause was his association with
the *heresies* of Keynesianism:

I was not a Keynesian, it is in Geoffrey Howe's book.[19] I thought that
the budget of 1981 was too harsh. I still hold the view that damage
was done to the economy by the severity of the policy at that stage. I
think it raised the exchange rate to a level that did avoidable damage
to British manufacturing and industry. But, fundamentally I thought
the change was right; to give higher priority to getting inflation
down. To be tough fiscally. It was only a matter of degree. But I was
not, in the ordinary sense, a Keynesian, opposed to Mrs Thatcher's
policies. I thought the reduction of inflation was a crucially important
thing. I perceive the clashes we had in Washington and later, the

Treasury, as being quite a lot to do with personality and personal chemistry. She did not approve of the IMF or the World Bank as institutions at all. She had a view of the American economy which was not a view held by most economists. She had been briefed by Bill Simon, a man of the far right. She had accepted that view, so there was a basis for disagreement. I don't know whether it was just a disagreement or whether there was a personal factor as well. (Ryrie interviewed, 19 June 1995)

Ryrie then provided an account of his past association with Margaret Thatcher. He confirmed the Burgh story, that their first meeting was in Washington, not Whitehall. This occurred in 1977, when Margaret Thatcher was Leader of the Opposition, and Ryrie as the then Economic Adviserr in the Embassy. Ryrie was called upon to brief her twice:

One about the IMF and the World Bank, and the other would have been about the American economy. On both occasions, I think I got one, maybe two sentences out, then she took over and started briefing me. She didn't really want any briefing and I think some kind of relationship or attitude developed then. I had one or two other exchanges with her and Peter Jay during that time and I think a negative feeling developed then and didn't change. (Ryrie interviewed, 19 June 1995)

Ryrie then turned to discuss his return from Washington in January 1980 and his appointment as Second Permanent Secretary in the Treasury, a post he held for two and half years. He recalled that it was somewhere late in 1981 that he again encountered Mrs Thatcher:

I remember one about steel in which I think I said some things that she didn't approve of and the Head of the Civil Service called me in and just said, to my absolute amazement: 'Bill, the Prime Minister would like you to take the position of Comptroller and Auditor General'. I nearly fell off my chair. Of course the meaning of saying 'would you be Comptroller and Auditor General' was clear. I was being kicked upstairs and something didn't fit with my personality – I probably appeared absolutely disinterested. So I asked what happened if I refused and he said: 'I am afraid you probably will not get any other advance in the Civil Service, so long as Mrs Thatcher is Prime Minister'. The Head of the Civil Service was very reserved about it, and I went straight over and saw [X] who was much more open about it and said: 'Yes, this has been coming for some time. She doesn't want to give you further promotion'. I was at the stage where, in the normal routine of Whitehall, I might have been sent out to be head of one of the major Departments. [X] said: 'You are not going to get that so long as she is there'. I was still thinking of my career in Civil Service terms. People had spoken of me as a Permanent Secretary, but now I was being told I would have to go and try and find something outside. I was told I could have the ODA and I said: 'No, thank you'. Then, after a while, I thought maybe that would not be a bad jumping-off point. I was being side-lined in the Treasury. Not completely, I was able to do quite a few things, but I was not in the inner circle of Treasury Ministers, so I agreed to take the ODA. (Ryrie interviewed, 19 June 1995)

These comments indicate that Hennessy's linking of Ryrie to a Keynesian disposition as the causal factor in the rift with Margaret Thatcher, was not entirely accurate. It was also a personality clash which grew from a series of less than amicable encounters:

It is possible she thought I was a kind of Keynesian, but I don't think that was really what it was all about. I think it was about personality. I was not really regarded as being a supporter: 'He is not going to really go out of his way to find out what I want done and get it done'. I was told that she had said that she was not prepared to see me made a full Permanent Secretary and therefore I took it for granted that SASC could not put my name forward. There is no doubt at all, in these questions of Mrs Thatcher's relationships with the senior Civil Service and with her own political colleagues, that personal preferences played a considerable part. (Ryrie interviewed, 19 June 1995)

The Ryrie interview confirmed that Margaret Thatcher was prepared to make clear to her Cabinet Secretary (as the Chairman of SASC) which individuals she was not willing to consider for promotion. This is primary evidence that she actively interfered in the appointments procedure. In addition, it suggests that it was personal chemistry and first impressions which were vital in determining an official's future progress in Whitehall. The John Steele example is further evidence of this, as one official highlighted while we were discussing the Derx case:

I don't know the details of the case but I would have said that pre-Thatcher, Donald Derx would have become a Permanent Secretary. There is also the case of John Steele, who was a Deputy Secretary in the Department of Trade and Industry. He was very well thought of and was again expected to be a Permanent Secretary. He went to a meeting with Keith Joseph, on something to do with steel. Margaret Thatcher asked a question which he didn't answer, as he wasn't sure on the detail and she basically said: 'never let me see that man again'. So, it was suggested to John that he went to Brussels. (An Energy official)

This evidence has serious longer-term implications for Whitehall. These three cases indicate that Mrs Thatcher intervened to ensure that certain individuals did not reached the apex of Whitehall. In addition, through her Cabinet Secretaries, she actively encouraged these officials to leave the Civil Service and seek a career elsewhere. The ramifications of such actions are grave: Mrs Thatcher unwittingly(?) reduced the range of individuals from whom her successor could draw, whilst also restricting the broad range of intellectual types in Whitehall. Her actions were self-seeking; they were a means to an end, which in a long-term, broader context smacked of myopia.

The Also Rans

Another, broader category to emerge from this study was a set of officials who, though competent Deputy Secretaries, were not able to adjust to the changes in the Civil Service augmented by Margaret Thatcher. As such, they were rejected as serious contenders for a Permanent Secretaryship. There are three representative cases I have selected from this category, whose anonymity, for obvious reasons I have maintained: one was a Deputy Secretary in the DHSS, the second official served in the Department of Energy and the third in the DTI. All were university graduates, two from Oxbridge and one from the LSE. They each entered the Civil Service at the outset of their professional careers and remained there for thirty years. I do not wish to suggest they were individuals who, in a different era in Whitehall, would inevitably have become Permanent Secretaries. However, they represent a more traditional type, career civil servant who led thoroughly respectable Whitehall careers. Yet, when nearing the pinnacle of their careers, they discovered that their more traditional approach to a civil servant's job was out of step with the newly fashioned Whitehall trends of the 1980s. The DHSS official reconciled himself to a Civil Service which was vastly different to the one he had joined in the late forties. In contrast, the other two officials developed strong antipathies to the developments.

The DHSS official became a public servant in the late 1940s, when he entered the Ministry of Health. After a sound, if unspectacular, rise through the ranks of Whitehall, which included the all important spell at the centre serving in the Cabinet Office, he rounded-off his career as Deputy Secretary in the Department of Health and Social Security. In total, this official spent well over ten years at Grade 2, without achieving the last step-up the Whitehall ladder to Permanent Secretary. The length of his tenure as a Deputy Secretary was far longer than the Whitehall norm. In an interview I asked him whether or not he felt increasingly out of step with the new trends of the 1980s:

> I think looking back, the right assessment is a 'good number two but not such a good number one'. I think it is a question of personal qualities. Have you got the energy, self-confidence or force to stand up to the demands of the top job, which are pretty considerable. Looking back, I actually think that those doing the appointments job got it about right. I think I was a good number two, but, though I could have done the number one job, I would have been less good. My own view is that it was a fair outcome.

The official's assessment of the final stage of his career was interesting: he accepted that though a good Grade 2 official, he did not quite have what was needed to make the final step up to Grade 1. His assessment of the qualities a Permanent Secretary required to function effectively were also revealing: 'energy, self-confidence or force'. These traits can all be associated with the type of pro-active Permanent Secretary who surfaced in the 1980s – the hands-on, energetic, can-doer. In accepting that these qualities were not part of his own personal make-up, the official was being brutally honest in assessing his character. It was obvious from my interview, that he had reconciled himself to this fact a long time ago and displayed no obvious signs of disappointment in falling one step short of the Whitehall *Gods*.

Similar to the DHSS official, the Energy official spent nearly all his professional life in the Civil Service. After spells in the Treasury (the centre) and a number of other Whitehall departments, this official was appointed to a senior grade in the Department of Energy. He remained a servant in that department for seven years, before, prematurely, turning his back on Whitehall. When interviewing this official, I asked him whether he had become disillusioned with the newly emerging Whitehall of the 1980s and had, therefore, decided to leave, or if he was simply seeking new horizons elsewhere?:

> It was a mixture of both. I was in my early fifties when I left. Now for one reason or another and much to one's own surprise, you find yourself at some stage, near the top of the pile and people say: 'you know the next job coming is Permanent Secretary'. Now all my career, for one reason or another, I have been involved in interface with industry, which I enjoyed. If you had asked me earlier what my chosen career pattern would have been, I would have liked to have been Permanent Secretary for two years and then gone out to industry. It happened that Lawson offered me a job and I snapped at it. At the time, that managed to fulfil a number of things. But undoubtedly the Civil Service changed, and changed greatly. Of the years I was there, the first fifteen were splendid. Progressively though, I thought the role of the senior civil servant was getting less interesting. His impact on policy was getting less and it was getting a much more frustrating job. So, it is both of those reasons you mentioned. But again; Lawson and I hardly ever agreed about anything. Yet, we had the highest regard for one another and so he selected me for this outside post and Thatcher said 'yes'. It is characteristic of Lawson that, provided you were prepared to argue, and he didn't think you were a fool, he respected your arguments and had a good regard for you. I am bound to tell you that, though as you may have gathered already, I am far from being a natural Tory supporter, Lawson was the best Secretary of State I have ever worked for, but nevertheless we argued everyday.

I questioned this official as to whether or not he became frustrated by the majority of his advice being ignored at ministerial level and if this created a sense of alienation:

> Well the sense of alienation and the sense, after a time, of saying you've done all the briefing, you have got it ready and the Minister messes up the Press Conference. Frankly he doesn't do it as well as you think you could do it.

This official is a classic example of the traditional type of civil servant who scaled the Whitehall ladder, thoroughly enjoyed the role of policy adviser to his minister, but who did not wish to immerse himself in the more laborious task of administrative management. This became apparent when I asked him to compare the Civil Service he joined in the 1950s, to the one that evolved during the 1980s:

> That it has changed I have no doubt. That it has changed dramatically, I think it has. In my own personal view, it has changed for the worse and this will be regretted, but that could be an old man growing older. I can't prove it. I do have to go back to my old University [Oxbridge] quite a lot. Now, in the early 1950s and 60s, they would talk about bright young people going into the Civil Service. They never talk about that nowadays. The managerial line is the one now taken. In a way it is a reflection of how society has changed. If you look at recruitment at one time, the Civil Service did prefer intellectuals. Now some of those were outstanding and they would be brilliantly analytical, but they could not run an agency. Now, I think ministers are in danger of losing some of the great independent thought and advice they used to receive.

Although not a known Conservative sympathiser, as a professional civil servant this official maintained he would have been prepared to work willingly with the Conservative Government during the 1980s. However, it was obvious throughout our interview that he had become alienated by the changing role of the senior civil servant under Mrs Thatcher; the shift away from policy-making, towards the 'efficient' management of the service. Alienation bred resentment and this, coupled with the fact that he found he was becoming increasingly marginalised in his own department, meant that the returns, in terms of job satisfaction, were diminishing. In such an environment it became increasingly apparent that further opportunities for promotion were limited and so, when the chance presented itself, he opted out.

The third case runs along parallel lines to that of the Energy official. This official was an individual who, in another era, had the potential to become a Permanent Secretary. However, in the 1980s, he found himself, as a high-ranking DTI official, in an environment which had vastly changed from the one he had joined thirty years earlier. He therefore opted to leave, accepting that, as things stood, he would not become a Permanent Secretary. This official joined the Board of Trade in the early 1950s. He followed the path of a typical 'Whitehall high-flyer' of his generation, spending the next three decades working in a variety of departments. However, despite almost reaching the hierarchical peak of Whitehall, he left early believing that, under Margaret Thatcher's Government, he could no longer work as an impartial, neutral, civil servant. I questioned this official on the final stages of his Whitehall career and his increasing sense of alienation from the institution he had joined in the 1950s:

> I certainly would not have been comfortable working with the Thatcher Government. I was offered a job at . . . which I accepted, as I was increasingly disenchanted with being a civil servant. I would have felt miserable serving in the eighties.

I then asked the official whether it soon became obvious to him that, under the new Thatcher Administration, he was not going to be appointed a Permanent Secretaryship:

> I don't think I would have made it to Permanent Secretary. I think the reason for it is the top civil servants, the Bancrofts of this world, didn't think I was 'sound'. The reason why I think this, is because my minister informed me this was the case. Likewise, I didn't have a lot of respect for the minister I was working for . . .

This official differed from the Energy official in that he predicted that the newly elected Government, led by Mrs Thatcher, would put an immense strain on his own approach to being a professional senior civil servant and so he decided to leave early. He also appreciated his capacity to climb a grade higher to Permanent Secretary was severely constrained by the changing attitudes in the Civil Service. Thus, the official opted to go, rather than become side-lined in the new regime.

This category, like the black-balled category, suggests worrying, longer-term implications for the Civil Service. Both the Energy and DTI officials had become unhappy with an institution visibly different to the one they joined three decades earlier. Realising their limited chance of progressing in such an environment, they voted with their feet and opted to leave. As discussed in chapter 8, by the mid-1980s it had become apparent to the majority of those in the senior Civil Service that the Conservative Government was, in the medium-term, there to stay. As such, the remodelling of Whitehall was set to continue. In the light of this, what we don't know is the extent to which Deputy Secretaries, Under Secretaries and Assistant Secretaries who disliked what was happening to the organisation they had joined, opted out during the 1980s. Again, the net effect was to reduce the range of individual talents, available to fill Whitehall posts in future generations.

Traditionalists who made the Grade

This final category contrasts directly with the previous one: here, I present two cases of individuals who followed a traditional White-hall career path, did not display the more fashionable traits asso-ciated with the mandarinate of the 1980s, and yet still achieved Permanent Secretary status. This is an important category in two respects. First, it highlights the fact that an outstanding, yet tradi-tional, civil servant, could still scale the organisation's hierarchical ladder during the 1980s. Second, it demonstrates that the Thatcher effect, while crucial, was not universal.

The first of the two cases in this category is that of Michael Quinlan, who in 1983 was appointed Permanent Secretary in the Department of Employment and, five years later, became the Per-manent Secretary in the Ministry of Defence. Ironically, his appoint-ment to Employment was viewed, at the time, as having been at the expense of Donald Derx.

The bulk of Quinlan's career was in the Ministry of Defence and it was while serving as a Deputy Secretary in that department that it is believed he caught the attentions of Mrs Thatcher:

> Thatcher was particularly impressed with his work on strategic nuclear weapons and was said to have been especially taken by his [anonymous] disquisition on deterrence theory and the British strategic nuclear force in the 1981 Defence White Paper. (Hennessy 1989, p. 636)

However, it is hard to see Quinlan as an official who displayed pro-active, managerially-oriented tendencies. He is a cerebral-type figure, devoted to analysing and criticising Government policy, rather than rushing head-long into various implementation options. As such, one would assume his character was not the sort which nor-mally attracted the attention of Margaret Thatcher. Yet, as Charles Powell commented:

> There were some very reflective senior civil servants appointed by Margaret Thatcher. The excellent Permanent Secretary at Defence, Michael Quinlan, was an archetypal intellectual, being a great writer

on nuclear weapons and so on. He was entirely the opposite of a can-doer and not an action man at all. (Powell interviewed, 16 November 1994)

Clive Priestley also suggested that Quinlan was not the usual type of official Margaret Thatcher was attracted by:

When she first met him, she took against him because they had a profound disagreement on policy matters and he had a high-pitched voice. But in the end she was convinced that he was the right man for the job and he finished up as Permanent Secretary in the MoD. (Priestley interviewed, 14 November 1994)

It was Frank Cooper, Quinlan's predecessor at the Ministry of Defence, who explained why, despite Quinlan's character, Mrs Thatcher believed him to be the best individual for that particular post:

She certainly, initially, was very dubious about Michael Quinlan, but she did, particularly after his arguments on Cruise and Pershing missiles, come to greatly respect his intellect and his quiet way of arguing and, of course, his total commitment to the nuclear deterrent. She thought that he was a very clever chap and you need clever people thinking about these kinds of issues. I think she did respect him, because he is not naturally the kind of person she would take to. (Cooper interviewed, 20 December 1994)

Quinlan's appointment is an example of rationality triumphing over emotion: Mrs Thatcher would possibly have preferred a more pro-active type of official to be appointed to the post of Permanent Secretary at the Ministry of Defence, if a suitable one had been available. Thus, although initially she frowned on Quinlan's more reserved, dispassionate approach to his work, he was still the one outstanding candidate for the job.

Like Quinlan, Angus Fraser was not the type of individual who, in most circumstances, would have attracted the admiration of Margaret Thatcher. Despite this, in 1983 Fraser was promoted to Permanent Secretary in HM Customs and Excise from Deputy Secretary in the Management and Personnel Office. Having entered Customs and Excise in 1953, as an Assistant Principal, Fraser's career followed what can only be described as a traditional path through the various ranks of Whitehall.

Fraser was never regarded as one of the new breed of 1980s Permanent Secretary which the Thatcher effect nurtured. John Cassels said of Fraser:

> Certainly the Civil Service Department used to attract people like Angus Fraser, who were brought in from other departments. He is an interesting case because he was not beloved, I guess, of Mrs Thatcher and still made it to the top. Obviously, there were some people in the Civil Service who she did not think well of and yet still made it to the top. I think that perhaps might have been, and in my view deservedly so, the case of Angus Fraser. (Cassels interviewed, 20 December 1994)

Despite Fraser's renowned *cerebral* approach to his work and a reputation for allocating an unusually large proportion of time to the consideration of the viability of Government policy, he still managed to reach the grade of Permanent Secretary. Indeed, his reputation in that post grew to such an extent that, in 1988, following Robin Ibbs's return to the private sector, Fraser was appointed his successor as Adviser to the Prime Minister on Efficiency and Effectiveness in Government. He had developed into one of Mrs Thatcher's closest advisers, without shedding a critical approach to Government policy and also, despite some obvious personal differences between the two. Clive Priestley commented on Fraser's second promotion:

> When it came to the succession of Robin Ibbs as adviser, she appointed Angus Fraser, who was serving as a Chairman of the Customs and Excise Board. This showed how open her mind could be on some appointments. She could sometimes be influenced less by thinking about categories, than her experience of individuals. (Priestley interviewed, 14 November 1994)

What the cases of both Quinlan and Fraser highlight is that, in appointments to Grades 1 and 2, all of which required the approval of Mrs Thatcher, the final decision would, in the majority of cases, have been based on SASC's assessment of the most suitable individual available. The Prime Minister simply gave her approval to the preferred candidate on the SASC short-list presented to her by the Cabinet Secretary. However, this was not the case if the appointment involved was to a post which Margaret Thatcher felt of strategic importance, or where an individual appeared (or in some cases did not appear) on the SASC short-list about whom she held strong views. Those views may have been either positive or negative and were often the result of the briefest of encounters with a particular individual. Either way, in such cases, Mrs Thatcher's impression had a direct bearing on the outcome of the final appointment. However, Quinlan and Fraser provide examples of individuals who were the outstanding choice for senior ranking posts in Whitehall and who had not crossed swords with the Prime Minister. This, despite the fact that neither possessed some of the more fashionable traits associated with the mandarinate of the 1980s.

10

The Blue and the Grey: Whitehall and Major

(John Garrett) *Is it not the case that we are in the process of moving from a unified Civil Service of some 30 main departments to a Civil Service which consists of 30 Ministerial Head Offices, about 150 Executive Agencies and Units, hundreds of quangos, like TECs, trusts and corporate bodies, and thousands of contracts with private contractors, all of whom are trying to make a profit? Would you agree with that description?*

(Sir Robin Butler) *Yes, I do not think that that is an inaccurate description; nor do I think there is anything that is contrary to the traditions of the Civil Service which is in it. I think that is the way in which one could see a lot of companies and a lot of other organisations outside have gone.*

(Robin Butler submitting evidence to the Treasury and Civil Service Committee: 1994, Vol. II, p. 52)

IT IS NOW OVER SIX YEARS since John Major replaced Margaret Thatcher as both Leader of the Conservative Party and Prime Minister. Major has surprised a number of Whitehall watchers by not only picking up the mantle of Civil Service reforms bequeathed him by the Thatcher Government, but also dramatically increasing the pace of reform. As Willman (1994, p. 64) noted in *The Major Effect*:

Majorism has intensified the pace of change in the Civil Service. Far from stifling the revolution, Mr Major has spurred it on and backed more radical measures. Indeed, one of his most significant bequests to his successor is likely to be a Civil Service vastly different from that created by the Northcote–Trevelyan reforms 140 years ago and largely unchanged until recent years.

By the election year of 1997, one has witnessed the rapid expansion of the anti-statist, NPM programme through the proliferation of Next Steps agencies, the increasing contracting-out (privatisation) of Government business and finally the Citizen's Charter. This last initiative has been regarded by many (including Major), as his Government's 'big idea'. Indeed, as the above quote from Robin Butler indicates, the pace of change has been so great that the Civil Service he will leave behind can no longer be regarded as a unified entity.

In this chapter, I will examine John Major's less interventionist approach to the top promotions system. I will argue that the quantitative evidence from the Major appointments indicates that a more traditional, but increasingly meritocratic, generation of officials were appointed. Yet, a fundamental change in top appointments has occurred in the post-Thatcher era. There has been a sharp rise in the number of outsiders introduced to the highest ranks in Whitehall. Of course, this is a corollary of the partial opening up, in the 1990s, of senior Whitehall posts to outside competition. However, a second, and perhaps more disquieting, trend has seen both the resignation and the sacking of senior ranking officials. In my view, this reflects the failure of a number of the Thatcher generation of mandarinate appointees to endear themselves to the Major generation of ministers. As Barberis (1996a, p. 217) observed: 'The hue of Thatcherism seems to have gotten into the timber of Whitehall. It has coloured the roles of permanent secretaries and their relationships with ministers under the Major Government.'

Major Consensus towards the Appointments Procedure

Although academics have continued to scavenge over the remnants of the Thatcher era and offered varying interpretations of the scope and limits of 'Thatcherism', there remains a notable scarcity of academic literature concerning the Major administration. Nevertheless, much has been written in media circles about John Major's more conciliatory and consensual approach towards the office of Prime Minister. Indeed, in John Major's effort to be seen as 'his own man' and to carve out a distinct identity for *his* Government, he has portrayed himself, at least publicly, as willing to listen and heed the advice of others. It was clear from the earliest days of the Major administration that the new Prime Minister wished to be seen as the leader who rekindled the flame of consensual Cabinet Government. Thus, while one could attach the motto *praesto et persto* to Mrs Thatcher's style of leadership, in the Major period, one witnessed the restoration of the more traditional notion of governing – *primus inter pares*.

Whether the private face of Major is consistent with the public mask, only time and the predictable surfeit of new ministers' memoirs can tell. However, it certainly appears the case that, at least in relation to the appointments procedure, John Major has been willing to adopt a consensual approach. When the Cabinet Secretary presents the new Prime Minister with a short-list of two or three names, in order of preference, for a vacancy to one of the highest two grades in Whitehall, he seldom, if ever, rejects the prime candidate. On the rare occasion when this did occur, Major certainly had no need to go beyond the remaining names on the list. Thus, following an earlier epoch in which pro-activity and personalisation had become the key words to describe the prime ministerial approach towards the appointment of the mandarinate, under Major there was a marked reversion back to a more traditional, passive and constitutional style.

My evidence concerning Major's involvement in top appointments was gathered from interviews I conducted with individuals who served at the highest level in Whitehall during the 1990s.[1] They all provided first-hand accounts of the workings of the top appointments procedure and of John Major's personal involvement. However, as three remain Whitehall employees and the others have only recently retired, they must remain anonymous.

These interviews emphasise that, following the SASC negotiations stage, Major never once rejected, outright, the short-list of officials presented him by the Cabinet Secretary. He certainly took an interest in the top promotions system, but rarely queried the suitability of the candidates being offered him for appointment. As one official put it:

> Although I was not privy to the private conversations between John Major and Robin Butler [the Cabinet Secretary and Chairman of SASC], it was quite clear to the remaining members of SASC that our recommendations were, in general, being adhered to.

Another official noted that, unlike in the 1980s, the Major generation of senior appointments provoked very few murmurs of disquiet amongst the senior Whitehall ranks and, in parenthesis, quipped that this was always a clear indicator of a Prime Minister willing to listen to the advice tendered him:

> I think, looking back at the Thatcher era, there were a number of appointments that caused more than the odd eyebrow to be raised. Under Major and despite the increase in chaps being brought in from outside, I'm thinking here of your Bichards,[2] there was a general feeling that the right chaps were being chosen for the top jobs.

The qualitative evidence from both the media and the officials I interviewed would suggest that John Major readily accepted the recommendations that his Cabinet Secretary offered him. In order to verify this evidence, I conducted a quantitative survey of the Major generation of appointments, identical to the surveys presented earlier in chapters 4 and 5 of the previous Thatcher and Labour Administrations.[3]

The Major Generation of Permanent Secretaries

If one accepts that the criteria for the Major generation of mandarin appointees is the same as that for the Thatcher generation, then one's interest remains in analysing only first-time appointments to the most senior grade (1/1a) in Whitehall.[4]

Table 10.1   Number of first-time promotions to Grades 1/1a (1980–95)

1980	1981	1982	1983	1984	1985	1986	1987	1988	1989	1990	1991	1992	1993	1994	1995
9	4	8	13	11	8	6	8	4	7	6	4	7	6	4	6

Table 10.1 indicates that in relation to the Thatcher administration, there was no irregular rise in the number of first-time appointees to Grade 1/1a between 1991 and 1995. More importantly, of the twenty-seven first-time appointments to Grades 1/1a in the Major period, none enjoyed any form of accelerated promotion. The normal pace of Whitehall promotion, as established in chapter 4, has been maintained throughout the nineties. Where there has been a

significant change has been in the number of outside appointments. Of the 27 first-time appointees, eight (29.7%) were from outside the service compared to 9 (10.7%) out of 84 first-time appointees between 1980 and 1990. There were eight cases of outside appointments during the Major administration (see Appendix E). As this list of individuals indicate, almost all outside appointments under Major, like those between 1980 and 1990, have been to specialist, technical, posts. The only outside appointment which can be construed as controversial was that of Michael Bichard, which I discuss in greater detail later in this chapter.

Table 10.2   Demographic profile of first-time appointments to Grade 1/1a

	1980–90 Nos:[%]	1991–95 Nos:[%]
Average Age of Newly Appointed Official	53.8	51.8
The Number State Educated	6 [7%]	5 [18.5%]
The Number from Private School	78 [93%]	22 [81.5%]
The Number from University [excluding Oxbridge]	25 [29%]	13 [48.5%]
The Number from Oxbridge	51 [61%]	12 [44.5%]
The Number without University Education	8 [10%]	2 [7%]
The Number of Women	1 [1.1%]	2 [7%]

Note: The total number of first-time appointees to this grade between 1980 and 1990 was 84; for the period 1990–95 it was 27.

Table 10.2 presents the comparative, demographic breakdown of the Thatcher and Major generation of first-time appointees. The figures indicate that during the 1990s a slightly younger breed of *male* officials were appointed to the highest grade. They were privately educated, but as likely to have attended a plate glass or redbrick university, as to have come down from Oxbridge. One can partially account for the decline in Oxbridge domination of the mandarinate by the increase in the number of outside, especially overseas, appointments made during the 1990s.

Table 10.3 First-time appointments to Grade 1/1a, with experience of the centre (1991–5)

	1991–95
Cabinet Office	3
Treasury	2
Cabinet Office/Treasury	6
PPS to the Prime Minister	1
No Centre Experience	15
Total	27

Between 1980 and 1990, 59 per cent of first-time appointees had experience of the centre, prior to their promotion to Permanent Secretary. As table 10.3 indicates, only 12 (44%) of the 27 appointees of the Major Government passed through the centre on their way to the highest grade in Whitehall. This is a notable fall of 15 per cent and marks a return to the pre-1979 level of 45 per cent. These figures are important, as they substantiate the argument that, unlike in the 1980s, when Mrs Thatcher personalised the appointments procedure by using the centre more intensively, under Major this has not been the case. This evidence substantiates the idea that during the 1990s John Major reverted to the traditional role of the Prime Minister as a passive conferrer of senior appointments.

Outsiders Find a New Home in Whitehall

Although the evidence I have compiled would suggest that John Major did not set about personalising the mandarinate in the manner in which his predecessor had, one distinct change in the make-up of top personnel in the 1990s has been the increase in outside appointments. As Robin Butler noted when giving evidence to the TCSC in November 1993: '8 out of the present 35 Permanent Secretaries were appointed from outside' (Treasury and Civil Service Committee: 1994, Vol. II p. 51). The main factor accounting for this change has been the tentative moves towards the open advertisement of Civil Service vacancies.

Throughout the 1990s, Next Steps, market testing and contracting-out have eroded the Northcote–Trevelyan notion that the Civil Service should be a career-oriented, unified and centralised organisation. The Conservative Administration, particularly under John Major, has been responsible for undermining these core principles on which Whitehall has operated for over 100 years. The introduction of market forces to the structural and operational framework of the Civil Service created a cogent logic for the extension of these principles to the management of personnel at the core of Whitehall. Thus, as noted in chapter 3, a series of personnel reforms were introduced in the 1990s: the Efficiency Unit's *Career Management and Succession Planning* (1993); the White Paper *Continuity and Change* (1994); the *Treasury and Civil Service's Fifth Report: The Role of the Civil Service* (1993–94); and the second White Paper *The Civil Service: Taking Forward Continuity and Change* (1995). Gradually, but in the view of many people far too slowly, the system was making the crucial change from appointing a person to the career to appointing him or her to the job.

Accepting that the rationale driving Conservative reform was a commitment to market forces, then if this principle was to be applied to Civil Service personnel, one might have expected an open competition for all new vacancies in Whitehall. However, as with the majority of previous Whitehall reforms (particularly those which deal with personnel), the mandarinate was partially successful in assuaging some of the more radical proposals. Thus, as Theakston (1995, p. 156) observed:

> The [1994] White Paper was a clear compromise between the hard-line reformers [the Government] and the consolidators [the mandarins] . . . The government envisaged that most of these top posts would continue to be filled by insiders . . . The White Paper . . . would allow only that departments and agencies will always *consider* advertising openly posts at these levels when a vacancy occurs, and then will use open competition whenever it is necessary and *justifiable*.

These 'watered-down reforms' have produced a rise in numbers, but, as my earlier list of outside appointments indicates, the majority of these have been appointments to technical, specialist, posts. However, there is one appointment, that of Michael Bichard, which requires more detailed scrutiny, as it has posed a series of questions concerning Whitehall's future. Theakston (1990b, p. 33) noted this when he pondered the post-Next Steps generation of mandarins:

> The really interesting question is how different in backgrounds
> and career experiences will be the most senior bureaucrats in the
> post-Next Steps Civil Service? If there are more outsiders, transfers
> between executive agencies and policy-making departments and
> more emphasis on management experience, then the future 'Sir
> Humphreys' may be a very different breed.

As of December 1996, Michael Bichard is the only agency Chief
Executive who has been appointed to a Permanent Secretaryship.
However, his case may provide some interesting pointers for
the future. Bichard's earlier career was spent working as Chief
Executive, first with Brent Borough Council and subsequently with
Gloucestershire County Council. In 1990, he was appointed Chief
Executive of the Social Security Benefits Agency under the new,
open, arrangements for selection. In March 1995, following another
open competition, he was appointed Permanent Secretary in the
Department of Employment, becoming the first chief executive
from a Next Steps Agency to cross the divide into the traditional
mandarinate. Appointed at the age of 48, he remains one of the
youngest Permanent Secretaries in the Civil Service.

The Whitehall correspondent for *The Times*, Nigel Henderson,
wrote of Bichard's initial appointment:

> The appointment is being seen as something of a breakthrough. Some
> have even described Mr Bichard as 'an outsider', Whitehall-speak
> for anyone who has been a civil servant for less than a decade and
> who has work experience outside the governmental machinery. (*The
> Times*, 6 March 1995)

More surprisingly, in Autumn 1995, following a major upset in
the Whitehall promotion stakes, Bichard beat Tim Lankester, a
career civil servant, to the top job following the amalgamation
of the two departments of Employment and Education. Even in
the 1980s, when a departmental merger occurred, the permanent
secretaries affected would always be accommodated within the
Whitehall community. However, prior to the departmental merger,
Lankester was informed by the Cabinet Secretary that he would
have to openly compete alongside Bichard, for the one available
permanent secretaryship. He declined to do so.[5]

With the Bichard case, it is unclear whether the appointment of a Chief Executive to the ranks of the mandarinate is a one-off, or whether his case ushers in a new, less predictable, pattern for appointments to the highest grades in Whitehall. Moreover, the Bichard case is important, because the Rubicon between Permanent Secretary and Chief Executive has now been crossed. This raises three further questions: first, how well equipped is a trained administrator to work successfully in what may prove an alien and highly-charged, political, environment?; second, is it possible for an outsider, not educated in the principles which shape and guide a senior mandarin and encapsulated in the notion of a 'public sector ethos', to distinguish between the public and private good?; third, there is the potential that outside appointees, often on short-term contracts, may be chosen on the basis of a similar ideological outlook to the incumbent government.

Fall-Out from the Thatcher Appointees

The final area of controversy surrounding the Major era and senior appointments concerns a number of highly public 'fall-outs' that have occurred between the senior mandarins appointed by Margaret Thatcher and the Cabinet Ministers appointed by Major in the 1990s.

The most notorious incident was the sacking of Peter Kemp in 1992 by William Waldegrave, then Minister at the Office of Public Service and Science. The event had a whole section devoted to it in the 'Summary and Recommendations' section of the TCSC 1993–94 Report:

> In July 1993, Sir Peter Kemp was required to leave his post as Second Permanent Secretary at the Office of Public Service and Science following a request by Mr Waldegrave for a Permanent Secretary with different skills. Sir Robin Butler was unable to find an alternative post for Sir Peter Kemp within the Civil Service, and Sir Peter was therefore required to take early retirement. Mr Waldegrave explained that he came to the conclusion that the establishment of the Office of Public Service and Science required a Permanent Secretary with different skills from Sir Peter Kemp, with greater emphasis on the traditional administrative skills of a departmental Permanent Secretary as opposed to the project management skills which had been Sir Peter Kemp's great strength. Mr Waldegrave took the view that this was his 'right as a Departmental Minister'. Sir Robin Butler

said he 'would very much have liked to have found another post for Sir Peter at Permanent Secretary level elsewhere in the Civil Service' and that he 'sincerely tried', but that he was unable to find a post which matched Sir Peter Kemp's blend of skills [sic]. He therefore found it necessary to ask Sir Peter Kemp to retire early on 'the terms that go with early retirement'. Sir Robin Butler thought that 'the terms were fair and in my heart and conscience I did not feel I was doing him an injury'. Sir Robin admitted to concern that an impression might have been given that Sir Peter Kemp's departure from the Service might undermine the independence and impartiality of the senior Civil Service, but was confidant that such concerns were misplaced. The departure resulted from the job having changed, not from the advice which Sir Peter Kemp had given: 'if he had given even the most craven advice, it would have made no difference to the situation'. Sir Peter Kemp indicated that he had sought to persuade Mr Waldegrave to continue with their working relationship on the basis that 'we should both try again'. He was concerned that the different skills which the Minister had sought had not been clearly indicated to him. Following Mr Waldegrave's final decision, he was left with the impression that those concerned did not fall over backwards to find him another post. He disagreed with Sir Robin Butler's contention that the terms of his departure were fair and criticised aspects of the handling of his departure which he felt had been inadequate or insensitive. (Treasury and Civil Service Committee: 1994, Vol. 1, pp. cvi–cvii)

As the above quote indicates, the official gloss given to the sacking emphasised that Kemp had been an individual with the necessary qualities to launch Next Steps, but that, once the programme was up and running, a different individual, with a contrasting range of qualities, was required to consolidate the progress already made. Of course, official versions rarely reflect the reality of an event.

Kemp's departure was unprecedented in Whitehall circles. He was summoned by Robin Butler on 8 July 1992 to be told his services were no longer required and that he was to be made compulsorily redundant. Butler was acting at the behest of William Waldegrave who had approached John Major to seek permission to remove Kemp from his £80,600 a year job. Richard Norton-Taylor, wrote of the sacking in *The Guardian*:

Mr Waldegrave is understood to have told Mr Major that he wanted Sir Peter removed so he could appoint his own man as Permanent

Secretary to his new ministry. The minister is understood to have told colleagues that he had difficulties working with Sir Peter and also wanted to move on to a more radical agenda. (*The Guardian*, 22 July 1992)

Two years after the sacking, I asked Kemp about the details surrounding his own departure, but he did not wish to be drawn, believing the subject was now closed. However, in a more recent interview, and with the passage of time, Kemp was prepared to shed more light on the event. While saying he was still puzzled, he thought there might have been two sets of reasons:

> The first reason was basically that I fell out personally with William Waldegrave. He had come from big departments – the Department of Health was his most recent – and he wanted big department style. And, up to a point, he was right; the OPSS, as it became, was a slightly bigger department than the old OMCS. It was not unreasonable to suggest that different skills might be needed, though we were scarcely given the chance to test this. But I believe that there was more to it than just that. Perhaps Waldegrave did not enjoy having something of a star on his staff. And the second reason may have been because I had my own views about how we should go forward with reforms, such as the market testing exercise – something which in itself I thoroughly approved of – which were not apparently attractive to people like Peter Levene who was in charge of the thing or to Waldegrave himself. Neither of them ever really understood the Civil Service. Whichever way up it was, Waldegrave did not want me, and was not prepared to let us both try harder to get on; and when that happens it is right and proper that it is the official and not the minister who has to depart. The difficult bit that followed on from this was that contrary to what has happened to other people on previous occasions of this nature, no attempt at all seemed to be made to find me another job, so I had to leave. (Kemp interviewed, 16 April 1996)

Historically, in the few isolated cases when a Permanent Secretary could no longer get along with his minister, he was normally transferred to another department. There was the occasion, in November 1981, when Ian Bancroft was effectively sacked from the Civil Service, following the abolition of the Civil Service Department. It was true that Bancroft and Margaret Thatcher did not regularly see eye-to-eye. However, a compromise was sought and he was able to end his career in Whitehall with dignity intact. The Kemp affair differed because there was no obvious attempt at conciliation. The Government formerly accepted that they were sacking Kemp. As Theakston (1995, p. 136) points out, what was even more surprisingly to outsiders was that: 'Whitehall's elite did not close ranks to protect him'. However, as the Kemp interview highlights, this was no ordinary clash of personality between a minister and his official, as it also involved Levene, another very senior mandarin. Hence, the elite failed to step-in and resolve what eventually became a very public falling out. Something had to give; in this case it was Kemp, the 'unconventional' figure, who had always been considered, even by his own staff, an outsider.[6]

The importance of the Kemp sacking was that, for first time, the Government signalled to its higher civil servants that they no longer enjoyed security of tenure. Elizabeth Symons, the FDA general secretary, said of the sacking:

> It is an unprecedented and wholly undesirable development that a neutral, impartial and, above all, efficient and effective civil servant, who has rightly earned public recognition for his achievement, has found there is no longer a job for him to do. (*The Guardian*, 23 July 1992)

Not surprisingly, Kemp also felt his undignified departure from Whitehall sent out worrying signals concerning the future security of tenure of an increasingly demoralised mandarinate:

> It was quite a precedent. Previously, people had bent over backwards to keep Permanent Secretaries in jobs. The echoes go on; it has been written that my precedent would enable a future Labour Government to sack top advisers. (Kemp interviewed, 16 April 1996)

This is a key point that Kemp touches on: his dismissal does have wider implications for the Civil Service. It could be the precursor for future sackings of the Conservative generation of senior civil servants by a government of a different political hue dissatisfied with their inheritance. If this were the case, then two of the fundamental Northcote–Trevelyan principles on which the Civil Service was founded, permanence and impartiality, would have been dismantled.

In fact, since the Kemp sacking, there have been no further public sackings of senior civil servants of the Thatcher generation.

However, in November 1993, Geoffrey Holland the Permanent Secretary in the Department for Education, resigned from the service. Afterwards, claims were made (which were denied by his department) that John Patten, his Education Secretary, had stopped talking to him. This was followed, in May 1994, by Clive Whitmore announcing that he was prematurely leaving his post as Permanent-Under-Secretary in the Home Office for a job in the private sector. *The Observer* reported that:

> Sir Clive Whitmore has made it clear in private that he is dismayed by the low standard of political competence displayed both by Mr Howard [his Minister] and the Government as a whole. He has contrasted ministers' performances with the defter touch of senior ministers during the Thatcher heyday. (*The Observer*, 6 May 1994)

Since these two resignations, and the Lankester affair, there has been no additional political fall-out and at present it appears that, under Major, there will be no further sackings or resignations from the Thatcher generation of civil servants. However, what these cases indicate is that the 'Thatcher effect' resulted in a shifting of the goal-posts that has had profound ramifications for the Major administration. A precedent was set, whereby, if a Prime Minister actively intervened in the appointments procedure, then the mandarinate bequeathed to future governments could potentially prove ill-suited. If this proves to be the case, then one of the core, constitutional principles on which British Cabinet Government has always prided itself, the smooth transition from one administration to the next, without the exposure of a seam, may no longer hold.

11

Conclusion: Whitehall's Political Poodles?

'What is the advice I have to offer you? You have to clear your slate. It is six years since you were in office . . . The primary duty of the Liberal Party is to wipe the slate clean'. The Earl of Rosebery, speaking to a Liberal audience at Chesterfield, 16 December 1901. Sir H. Campbell-Bannerman replied at Leicester: 'I am no believer in the doctrine of the clean slate'. (Cited in Butler and Butler 1994, p. 266)

The Conservatives and Whitehall

IN THIS BOOK, I have argued that during the Thatcher administration there was no evidence of an increase in the number of cases of accelerated promotion or officials being appointed from outside the Civil Service to Grades 1, 1a or 2. I rejected the notion that Margaret Thatcher had appointed civil servants who were sympathetic to the Conservative Party. However, she did promote a number of officials I have labelled 'managerially-oriented, can-doers'. To do so, she was much more closely involved in the appointments procedure than her predecessors. This resulted in the system becoming personalised. One element of personalisation was a centre effect. Officials who were socialised or, perhaps more accurately, reconstructed into can-doers, while at the centre, went on to gain high office in the 1980s.

Despite personalisation, in the majority of cases Margaret Thatcher approved the preferred candidate on the SASC short-list. However, when she regarded an appointment as strategically important, or she held strong views about the individuals on the SASC short-list, she was more likely to intervene directly. In such cases, her partiality affected the outcome and the result was often the unexpected appointment of an individual who was not generally regarded as the front runner. It was these appointments which triggered much of the debate about the politicisation of the Civil Service.

In contrast, John Major has been willing to accept a more traditional, passive role in the appointment of officials to the highest grades. Although Major has displayed an interest in the top promotions procedure, he has tacitly accepted the list of recommendations presented him by the Cabinet Secretary. Paradoxically, on the broader matter of the reform of the Civil Service, the Major administration has, if anything, been even more radical and dynamic than the Thatcher administration. A corollary of this has been a rise, despite insider resistance, in the number of outside appointments to the highest grades in Whitehall during the 1990s.

Today's Civil Service is a vastly different institution to the one the Conservatives inherited in May 1979. It has been systematically reduced in numbers, has undergone dynamic, structural, diversification, including increased open competition at all levels, and has had its pay structure overhauled to mirror private sector practices. At the senior levels in Whitehall, the greatest change has occurred in the shift from policy-making and management to focus on efficiency and costs of service delivery. As Smith (1996, p. 164) concludes:

> The other power shift is from professional power to managerial power. In the past, the key officials in the government were the professional policy advisers, and it was these professionals who managed the departments from the top to the delivery of services. Increasingly, Permanent Secretaries are becoming policy managers rather than policy advisers. Simultaneously, in the delivery of services it is now a distinct set of managers, the chief executives [of Next Steps agencies], who are in control. It is an interesting indication of this shift that several chief executives now earn more than Permanent Secretaries.

The consequence of this shift in the role of officials from policy formulators and advisers to efficient managers involved in cost delivery is profound. Throughout the twentieth century, Britain has operated within the framework of the Haldane model, derived from Lord Haldane's (1918) *Report of the Machinery of Government Committee: Ministry of Reconstruction*. This report, as Hennessy notes (1989, pp. 296–7), was presented in two parts: first, it dealt with the relationship and functions of Cabinet and Parliament; subsequently, it examined the formulation of policy. Hennessy describes the key phrase in the second part:

> Haldane came up with the one-liner with which his name will always be associated. It was embedded in a paragraph of contrived understatement: ' . . . we have come to the conclusion . . . that in the sphere of civil government *the duty of investigation and thought, as preliminary to action,* [Hennessy's emphasis] might with great advantage be more definitely recognised'. This phrase has been something of a *beau idéal* in the British Civil Service ever since. (Hennessy 1989, p. 297)

What this phrase encapsulates is the notion that at the heart of the core executive, civil servants, *as advisers*, have an indivisible relationship with their masters. As Foster and Plowden (1996, pp. 76–7) argue, the Haldane model, unlike its European and US counterparts, portrays the relationship between politicians and administrators as being 'intrinsically linked' – a relationship which derived from the Northcote–Trevelyan report:

> The Government of the country [cannot] be carried out without the aid of an efficient body of permanent officers, occupying a position duly subordinate to that of the Ministers who are directly responsible to the Crown and to Parliament, yet possessing sufficient independence, character, ability and experience to be able to advise, assist, and to some extent, influence those who are from time to time set over them. (The Northcote–Trevelyan report was reprinted in Cmnd 3638: 1968, pp. 108–19)

On this basis, Foster and Plowden (1996, p. 77) argue that: 'the British system embodied a system not of rules but of advice. As cabinet ministers constitutionally still acted as advisers to the sovereign, so they in turn were advised by the Civil Service'. They contend that, traditionally, officials were in a position in which they could advise a minister on any subject and, as such, there was no requirement for the separation of power between the two. This contrasted directly with the Wilson model, established in the United States, which argued for the explicit separation of the roles of these two sets of actors, with the administrators focusing solely on implementation. The Haldane or British model, underpinned by Northcote–Trevelyan, does not recognise a separation between politician and public servant. Instead, a minister can expect, and it is constitutionally demanded, that his or her officials will advise on the necessary and relevant facts concerning an issue or a policy and make the minister aware of existing precedents and law. This provides both a practical and constitutional constraint, in order to protect against the arbitrary (ab)use of power by a minister. Foster and Plowden (1996, p. 77) conclude that:

> In theory and largely in practice, civil servants are privy to almost all decisions ministers make, able and encouraged to advise them on every aspect of that discretion, not only in terms of their meeting of their own political objectives but also as a safeguard against illegality and impropriety. Since the Northcote–Trevelyan reforms, this has been the corner-stone of the British administrative tradition, and it could not be more different from the Wilsonian principle. It has also proved more workable. Any separation, by creating agencies or other arm's length bodies, creates uncertainties for the maintenance of the Haldane principle.

If one accepts that, for much of the twentieth century, the Haldane model has operated, largely unimpeded, then I would argue that this model has been seriously undermined during the last eighteen years of Conservative administration. Foster and Plowden (1996, p. 77) believe that the introduction of agencies has created *uncertainties* between the politicians, at the heart of the British executive, and the administrators located away from the centre. They argue that this has eroded the core principle of the Haldane model, which supports integration, not separation. However, I would contend that there is a further more subtle, but potentially more powerful effect, which may prove even more damaging to the Haldane model. This effect concerns *mind-sets* and the reluctance of present-day officials to offer independent advice to their minister. Today, officials are either unwilling, or alternatively are unable, to curb the exercise of arbitrary power by ministers.

The Erosion of the Haldane Principle: 'Mind-Sets' and a Less Critical Civil Service

The Northcote–Trevelyan Report of 1853 was responsible for establishing the principles and guidelines to which, for the majority of the twentieth century, the Civil Service rigidly adhered. Indeed, this Report eventually led to the Order in Council of 1870, which established the fundamental principles associated with the British Civil

Service – anonymity, impartiality and permanence. As Hennessy (1995, p. 122) noted:

> The 1870 Order in Council . . . created a permanent career public service, recruited free from political or personal patronage on the sole basis of ability as revealed through that great Indian Civil Service – competitive examination.

Hennessy argued that the 1870 Order in Council had, as its introduction intended, acted as a barrier against any 'political abuse of patronage'. The circle was completed in the 1990s when:

> Both the Government's Civil Service White Paper, *Continuity and Change*, released in July 1994, and the House of Commons Treasury and Civil Service Committee's report on *The Role of the Civil Service*, published the following November, begin with unequivocal reaffirmations of it [the Order in Council]. (Hennessy 1995, p. 122)

As this book has shown, one of the effects of the Conservative administration has been to call into question the principle of impartiality. Yet in the majority of cases, where this occurred, the accusations were directed at *individual* civil servants rather than at Whitehall *per se*. Although a few of the less well-informed commentators argued that there was broad politicisation, the majority of the better commentaries were more circumspect. Since 1990, a further dimension has been added to the debate on politicisation. It has been suggested that the longevity of the Conservatives in power has undermined the neutrality of the Civil Service.

It is now eighteen years since the Conservative Party were elected to office. One of the implications has been that no one under the age of 37 working in Whitehall has served a non-Conservative government. This has prompted increased concern about the 'mind-set' of a growing proportion of officials. On 24 May 1992, the BBC News and Current Affairs programme *Analysis*, hosted by Peter Hennessy, discussed these wider implications in a programme entitled *Bluehall SW1?*[1] A disparate collection of views were expressed during the programme. Not surprisingly, Robin Butler and William Waldegrave defended the status quo, arguing that the spirit of Northcote–Trevelyan lived on in the Civil Service of the 1990s. Others, including the late John Smith, were more ambivalent. Smith believed that the Labour Party would have to review the situation when taking over the reins of power. More radically, some observers felt that eighteen years of Conservative rule had turned Whitehall 'bluish', but in a subtle manner. Thus, Oonagh McDonald suggested:

> I don't think it's the problem that people often suggest: that you will have . . . a group of Tory civil servants around you. But you will be so used to looking at the world in a particular way and they will be so used to having collected their particular range of options for consideration, it's going to be quite a shock to take a wider view, to look for other solutions and to think freshly about the issues. So I think this is a serious problems. (P. Hennessy and S. Coates 1992, p. 9)

Hennessy concluded that:

> If the government does change in the 1990s, it will be essential that the seam does not show. Any suspicion that a 'Bluehall' has become established will not simply imperil the Civil Service. It will inflict lasting damage on our system of government as a whole. (Ibid., p. 19)

The whole debate was brought further into the public domain in December 1992 by the appearance of Lord Callaghan, the last serving Labour Prime Minister, on the BBC2 programme *Behind the Headlines*. While being interviewed about the actions of the then Permanent Secretary at the Treasury, Peter Middleton, in relation to the Treasury's involvement in the Norman Lamont/Miss Whiplash affair, Callaghan argued:

> The Civil Service has now reached the stage where it is simply a *fiefdom* of the Conservative Party, the Conservatives having been in power for so long. Traditionally, the Civil Service has acted as a buffer between politicians and the public. A conscientious civil servant was capable of saying 'no minister'. This is no longer the case. The Civil Service has been 'socialised' into becoming simply a further branch of the Conservative Party.

Callaghan reiterated these same comments when giving evidence to the TCSC in Session ,1993–4. It was implicit in Callaghan's observation that civil servants were no longer prepared to provide their ministers with negative, but nevertheless essential, advice; a service their predecessors had always been prepared, and unafraid, to offer.

Of course, this can be seen as a legacy of the Thatcher era, given her desire to see pro-active, positive types officials who were not going to produce a lengthy critique of Government policy. Nicholas Monk, the retired Permanent Secretary at the Department of Employment, on the Radio 4 *Analysis* programme 'Running Britain' (21 November 1996), disagreed with this viewpoint. Monk argued that:

> The changes [in personnel] have not been very large . . . Most people you still see around ministers are lifetime people . . . Just before I was leaving [1995], when the Senior Management Reviews were impending, I didn't see people suddenly ceasing to say what they thought.

As this book has shown, there has not been a high turnover in personnel in Whitehall. 'Life-time people' have remained the norm. What Monk's point fails to address is the cultural change in Whitehall during the 1980s, the longevity of the Conservatives in office and the effect this has on mind-sets, or what Peter Hennessy, in the same radio programme, refers to as 'thought colonisation'.

Obviously, one consequence of any Civil Service failure to criticise Government policy might be less effective policy. Indeed, Butler, Adonis and Travers (1994) contend that the whole saga of the botched attempt to reform local Government finance in the mid-1980s might have been avoided if Terence Heiser and other senior officials at the Department of Environment had been prepared to stand up to Baker, Patten, Ridley and Thatcher and highlight the shortcomings in the Community Charge.[2] More broadly, it could be argued that, in the 1990s, such incidents as Jonathan Aitken's Paris hotel bill, Neil Hamilton's resignation and, most notably, the Arms to Iraq affair, which all reflected poorly on both the Government and the Civil Service, might have been avoided, or at least better handled, by advice from a more critical Civil Service.

There was no uniform view among the civil servants I interviewed on whether or not eighteen years of Conservative Government had affected the conceptual framework in which officials operated. It came as no surprise to be told by a previous Cabinet Secretary that:

> If there were to be a change of government at the next General Election, I do not believe that there would be any problems on this score for three reasons: (1) the commitment of civil servants to the ideal of an impartial, non-political, professional civil service ready

and able to serve the duly constituted government of the day remains very strong; (2) the present generation of top civil servants are all old enough to have served the 1974–9 Labour Government, often in positions of responsibility if not at top level; (3) if the electorate decided that 'it is time for a change', civil servants would readily, as a matter of professional duty and ethics, unreservedly accept the consequences of that decision, and would very much want to make the relationship with new Ministers work as well as that with the old had worked, more particularly because the new Ministers would for the most part have had no direct prior experience of ministerial office.

This official was not prepared to accept that the mind-sets of officials had changed during eighteen years of Conservative Government. In his view, the various incidents I cited earlier were simply a set of unfortunate, but isolated, cases and not the result of a less critical Civil Service. Frank Cooper's response was more phlegmatic:

> I think it is obviously going to create problems in both directions. But it depends very much on the style of a Labour Government, whether they change things a hell of a lot and no doubt we shall get complaints of the Civil Service being biased, or whatever. But I think the answer is that, in 1979, the Civil Service welcomed a change in government and I can't believe that the present Civil Service would be anything but delighted at a change in government. It is excruciatingly boring when you get the same government in power for so long. You can heave a sigh of relief when there is a change of government. The Civil Service is much more apolitical than people give it credit for. (Cooper interviewed, 20 December 1994)

Cooper obviously felt that, despite the longevity of government by one party, civil servants have been able to maintain a degree of detachment in their work. Indeed, this comment reflected the majority view of the officials. However, in contrast, William Ryrie believed that the length of tenure of the Conservatives presented a serious problem:

> I think one party in power for a very long time does tend to leave a mark on the Civil Service. The John Major mark is not a particularly strong one. The Thatcher mark is a strong one. I don't think it is altogether beneficial. (Ryrie interviewed, 19 June 1995)

Ryrie felt that the shift in the agenda towards efficient management, sound administration and policy implementation had had a residual effect on the workings of Whitehall. Similarly, Peter Kemp argued that the fact that no official under the age of 37 had served another government was worrying:

> I am very glad you made that point. The powers of the Civil Service, the place where power and knowledge meet is very narrow in any large organisation and in the case of the Civil Service is around the top Assistant Secretary and the bottom Under Secretary. This is, as you say, approximately 35–40 years of age. Chaps who joined from university, in about 1979, will be about there now. They will never have any other experience . . . I think, in that sense, the Civil Service has been politicised. This was not in a crude way, but they have all worked for a government for a long time, which knew what it wanted. (Kemp interviewed, 17 November 1994)

It is probably the case that civil servants, more than most other groups of professionals, have a tendency to be protective of the institution they serve. It is therefore not surprising that the officials generally felt that, despite the length of time the Conservatives have been in office, the Civil Service would still be able to display the characteristics of a political chameleon, if, and when, another party comes to power. However, clearly there are significant potential problems.

The notion that a paradigm shift in the conceptual framework of the British Civil Service has occurred is a cause for great alarm amongst those who wish to defend the Haldane model. I would argue that further testament to the erosion of this model can be found in the manner in which Conservative ministers have viewed the role of their officials. Indeed, in the months preceding the 1997 election, two alleged examples of the Major Government misusing, or wishing to misuse, their officials occurred.

Heseltine's 'Cheerleaders'

On 24 August 1996, Michael Heseltine sent a signed memorandum to the Prime Minister proposing that the names of officials who were 'supportive, service-providers' should be made known to the media. Heseltine hoped that such an initiative would help to counter what the Government regarded as a growing imbalance in media coverage of the Conservative Party in the lead up to the 1997 General Election. Robin Butler, the Cabinet Secretary, rebuked Heseltine, informing him that it would be constitutionally improper for civil servants to be involved in the promotion of Conservative Party activities. Butler pointed out to Heseltine that the proposal directly contravened the *Code of Practice for the Civil Service*, which had been updated and republished as recently as January 1996. The issue was then laid to rest until 10 November 1996, when the original memorandum was leaked to the press. Heseltine was accused of calling on public officials to act as 'cheerleaders' for the Government:

> Michael Heseltine will be challenged in the House of Commons today to explain the circumstances in which he ordered senior civil servants to promote Conservative policies. Sir Robin Butler, the Cabinet Secretary, intervened to prevent the Deputy Prime Minister using Whitehall officials to draw up teams of 'cheerleaders' to praise the Government's achievements. The Prime Minister had endorsed the plan. (*The Times*, 11 November 1996)

John Prescott, Labour's Deputy Leader, argued that this was: 'a further blatant example of an abuse of government power . . . a blatant interference in the impartiality of civil servants'. While the Liberal Democratic Leader, Paddy Ashdown, told GMTV's *Sunday Programme* (10 November 1996): 'I take heart from Sir Robin's actions. I don't take heart from the fact that one of the very few checks and balances we have now left in our democracy is the integrity of the Civil Service'. Finally, the General Secretary of the First Division Association, Liz Symons, said that: 'it was inappropriate for civil servants to be asked to identify people to be proponents of Government policies and that Sir Robin had been right to reassert the political neutrality of the Civil Service' (PA News, 10 November 1996). Heseltine defended himself on BBC Radio 4's *World This Weekend* (10 November 1996) arguing that, in response to the initial suggestion, he had immediately accepted the advice of the Cabinet Secretary: 'The moment he did that, I agreed that was the position'. However, the key issue here is that Michael Heseltine even considered making such a proposal. This point was made in a letter to *The Times*:

> It is remarkable that Michael Heseltine should have even contemplated ordering civil servants to promote Conservative policies.

Throughout the past 17 years of Conservative administration, he has been the one minister who has consistently displayed an interest in, and understanding of, the machinery of government. As such, more than any other of his ministerial colleagues, he should have been aware of the constitutional and broader political implications of 'using Whitehall officials to draw up teams of "cheerleaders" to praise the Government'. Heseltine's actions would appear to be further indication of a covert form of politicisation of the Civil Service. Personalisation of Whitehall has created an environment . . . in which there is little incentive for officials to offer their ministers critical advice. (Richards and Hay 1996)

Treasury Pawns?

A second, alleged, misuse of civil servants by the Major Administration occurred on 21 November 1996. This followed a publication by Conservative Central Office identifying 89 policy pledges by the Labour Party which, it claimed, would cost the taxpayer over £30 billion. Labour reacted by accusing the Government of using public servants to help in the compilation of the document which, they argued, should have been a purely party exercise. Once again, Sir Robin Butler was called on to defend the neutrality of Whitehall. Whilst the Chief Secretary to the Treasury, William Waldegrave, accepted that civil servants had assisted in the preparation of the document, he argued that the exercise was conducted in accordance with existing guidelines concerning the costing of opposition policy. Ironically, it had been Robin Butler who had outlined what the procedures should be in an internal Cabinet Office memorandum – *Guidance on Guidance* (1990). However, as *The Times* reported:

> In a strongly worded statement the First Division Association, which represents senior Civil Servants, expressed deep concern at 'the extensive use of civil servants to cost alleged Labour Party policies . . . Baroness Symons, General Secretary of the First Division Association, telephoned Sir Robin to protest about the use of civil servants in preparing the document. (*The Times*, 21 November 1996).

The First Division Association President, Martin Brimmer, later argued that the document, published by Conservative Central Office, about Labour's spending policies, did not assist ministers in carrying out their duties as ministers of the Crown. He argued that the existing Civil Service Code was clear in that ministers have a duty not to use public resources for party political purposes. Brimmer concluded: 'Its purpose appears to be as party-political propaganda and the use of public money in its preparation is highly questionable' (PA News, 20 November 1996).

It is part of the character of the British polity that, as a General Election approaches, the incumbent party's energy focuses upon short-term political interests, rather than on the broader, long-term, demands of government. However, when a party in office uses public officials for party political activities, then it is no longer acting within the existing, constitutionally established, constraints.

Centripetal Pressures and the Implosion of Haldane

What these two separate but similar cases illustrate is a government which after eighteen years of office can no longer discern the traditional limits placed on its executive power. Further, it leads one to conclude that the Haldane model has been severely undermined. This model is constructed on the notion that, constitutionally, the role of Cabinet is to act as an adviser to the Crown, while, in turn, the Civil Service advises the ministers who make-up Cabinet. Therefore, ministers and civil servants co-exist in a finely-balanced, symbiotic, relationship. Yet, the equilibrium has been upset by two conflicting pressures which have led to the implosion of the Haldane model. First, the present Civil Service, for the reasons stated, is no longer willing to offer its masters the critical advice which is the basis of its constitutional role. Second, the longevity of the Conservatives in office has left the Party unable or unwilling to identify the parameters with which a Government exercises power. These two centripetal forces have distorted the relationship between ministers and officials: the Cabinet has neglected the confines of the Haldane model; Whitehall, by not offering the necessary critical advice, is no longer fulfilling its side of the relationship. A MORI survey in April 1996 for *The Observer*, confirmed this. The survey, based on the responses from 1,911 civil servants revealed:

> widespread concern that the need to tell long-term Ministers what they wanted to hear has politicised the service beyond recognition. Of those responding to the Survey, 73 per cent say Conservative ideology has 'now become part of the Civil Service culture', while

one in 10 say they have been asked by a Minister or superior to act in
a political manner which breaches civil services rules of impartiality.
(*The Observer*, 14 April 1996)

Whitehall's Political Poodles?

The Liberal Party's landslide victory at the 1906 General Election
left Arthur Balfour the leader of a small, and seemingly ineffectual,
Opposition. However, speaking at a pre-election rally in Notting-
ham, Balfour declared that: 'the great Unionist Party should still
control, whether in power or in opposition, the destinies of this great
Empire' (Zebel 1973, p. 151). In Balfour's view, the Unionists could
use the same tactics against the Campbell-Bannerman Government
which he and Salisbury had employed in the previous two decades;
once again, the House of Lords was to become a theatre of compromise. Indeed, Balfour did use the dominance of the Unionists in the
upper Chamber to block the Liberal's legislative programme. This
obstructive action prompted David Lloyd George to declare:

> The House of Lords has long ceased to be the watchdog of the
> Constitution. It has become Mr Balfour's poodle. It barks for him.
> It fetches and carries for him. It bites anybody that he sets it on.
> (Zebel 1973, p. 152)

The analogy with the present is far from total and it would be
misleading to conclude that, similar to the House of Lords in 1907,
Whitehall in 1997 has been overrun with *Conservative* poodles.
However, there is cause for concern that the current Civil Service
has become too willing to follow an unfettered master.

Appendixes

APPENDIX A   ABBREVIATIONS OF DEPARTMENTS

BIR	The Board of Inland Revenue
BL	British Library
BM	British Museum
CEC	Crown Establishment Commissioners
CO	Cabinet Office
CPS	Crown Prosecution Service (Department of the Director of Public Prosecutions)
CSD	Civil Service Department
DEMP	Department of Employment
DEN	Department of Energy
DENV	Department of the Environment
DES	Department of Education and Science
DETCS [DENVTCS]	Department of the Environment and Transport Common Services
DH	Department of Health
DHSS	Department of Health and Social Security
DHSSCS	Department of Health and Social Security Common Services
DI	Department of Industry
DITCS	Department of Industry, Trade and Common Services
DNS	Department for National Savings
DPCP	Department of Prices and Consumer Protection
DSS	Department of Social Security
DTI	Department of Trade and Industry
DTR	Department of Trade
DTRAN	Department of Transport
EAD	Exchequer and Audit Department
ECGD	Exports Credits Guarantee Department
FCO	Foreign and Commonwealth Office
FORC	Forestry Commission
HMCE	Her Majesty's Customs and Excise
HMLR	Her Majesty's Land Registry

HMSO	Her Majesty's Stationery Office
HMT	Her Majesty's Treasury
HO	Home Office
HoC	House of Commons (Department of the Clerk of the House)
HoL	House of Lords (Department of the Clerk of the Parliaments)
HSC	Health and Safety Commission
LCD	Lord Chancellor's Department
LOD	Law Officers Department
MAFF	Ministry of Agriculture Fisheries and Food
MoD	Ministry of Defence
MPO	Metropolitan Police Office
MSC	Manpower Services Commission (Employment Department/Training Agency)
NAO	National Audit Office
NIO	Northern Ireland Office
OAL	Office of Arts and Libraries
ODA	Overseas Development Administration
ODPR	Office of the Data Protection Registrar
OFT	Office of Fair Trading
OPCAHSC	Office of the Parliamentary Commissioner for Administration and Health Services Commissioners
OPCS	Office of Population Census and Surveys
OWS	Office of Water Services
PMO	Prime Minister's Office
RFS	Registry of Friendly Societies
SFS	Serious Fraud Squad
SO	Scottish Office
TSD	Treasury Solicitor's Department
WO	Welsh Office

(PS) = Permanent Secretary/Deputy Permanent Secretary
(DS) = Deputy Secretary

APPENDIX B   CONTACT ADDRESSES FOR ACCESSING DATA SETS

For readers interested in examining the complete data sets of officials appointed between 1974 and 1996, these can be obtained by contacting the author at:

Department of Political Science and International Studies
University of Birmingham, Muirhead Tower
Birmingham, B15 2TT.

APPENDIX C NAMES OF OFFICIALS INTERVIEWED

Below is a list of the officials I have interviewed who were willing to have their comments directly attributed.

Benner, Patrick – Deputy Secretary at the DHSS, 1976–84.
Burgh, John – Deputy Secretary at the Department of Trade, 1979–80.
Cassels, John – Second Permanent Secretary at the Management and Personnel Office, Cabinet Office, 1981–3.
Cooper, Frank – Permanent Secretary at the Ministry of Defence, 1976–82.
Ingham, Bernard – Head of the Government Information Service, Prime Minister's Office, 1979–90.
Jenkins, Kate – The Efficiency Unit, Prime Minister's Office, 1986–8.
Kemp, Peter – Second Permanent Secretary at the Cabinet Office, 1988–92.
Middleton, Peter – Permanent Secretary at the Treasury, 1983–91.
Powell, Charles – Private Secretary to the Prime Minister, 1984–91.
Priestley, Clive – Chief Secretary to Derek Rayner in the Prime Minister's Office, 1979–83.
Ryrie, William – Permanent Secretary at the Overseas Development Agency, 1982–84.
Sparrow, John – Head of the Central Policy Review Staff, Cabinet Office, 1982–3.

APPENDIX D OUTSIDE APPOINTMENTS FOR GRADE 1/1A UNDER MRS THATCHER

The nine cases of outside appointments under Margaret Thatcher:

1980
Terence Burns was appointed to Chief Economic Adviser and Head of the Government Economic Service from the post of Professor of Economics at the London Business School.
Robin Ibbs was seconded to the Central Policy Review Staff from a post at ICI.

1982
Montague Alfred was appointed to Chief Executive of the Property Services Agency, Department of the Environment from a post at Caxton Publishing Holdings Ltd.
John Sparrow replaced Ibbs as Head of the Central Policy Review Staff from a post at Morgan Grenfell Group.

1984
Anthony Wilson was appointed to Head of the Government Accountancy Service, the Treasury, from a post at Price Waterhouse.

1986
Peter Levene was appointed to Chief of Defence Procurement, Ministry of Defence from a post at Joint United Scientific Holdings.

Victor Paige was appointed to Second Permanent Secretary at the DHSS from a post at the National Freight Corporation

1989
Alan Hardcastle was appointed Chief Accountancy Adviser to HM Treasury from a post at Peat, Marwick, Mitchell and Company.
Duncan Nichol was appointed to Chief Executive of the National Health Service from Regional General Manager of Manchester Health Authority.

APPENDIX E OUTSIDE APPOINTMENTS TO GRADE 1/1A UNDER JOHN MAJOR

The eight cases of outside appointments under Major:

1991
Alan Budd, appointed Chief Economic Adviser to the Treasury and Head of the Government Economic Service from the post of Professor of Economics at the London Business School.
Malcolm McIntosh, appointed Chief of Defence Procurement in the MoD from the Australian Department of Defence.

1992
William Mclennan, appointed Director of the Central Statistical Office and Head of the Government Statistical Service from the post of Deputy Australian Statistician.

1993
David Davies, appointed Chief Scientific Adviser, MoD, from the post of Vice-Chancellor, Loughborough University of Technology.

1994
Alan Langlands, appointed Chief Executive, NHS Executive [Gr.1a] from the post of General Manager of NW Thames Regional Health Authority.

1995
Michael Bichard, appointed Permanent Secretary, Department of Employment from the post of Chief Executive of the Social Security Benefits Agency.
David Holt, appointed Director of the Central Statistical Office and Head of the Government Statistical Service from the post of Professor of Social Statistics, Southampton University.
Robert May, appointed Chief Scientific Adviser to the Government and Head of the Office of Science and Technology from the post of Professor of Zoology at Imperial College, London.

Notes

Preface

1 Private information conveyed to the author by Peter Kemp, January 1996.

Chapter 1

1 See chapter 2 for details on Mrs Thatcher's approach to reforming the Civil Service and the greater importance she placed on changing personnel, rather than attacking the institution.

2 The details of the senior appointments procedure are discussed in chapter 3.

3 For details of the position of civil servants in relation to public political activities, see *Civil Service Management Code – Personnel Management* (1993). In section 4.4.9 'Political Activities' it is stated that: 'Civil Servants at Grade 7 level and above . . . must not take part in national political activities. They must seek permission to take part in local political activities and must comply with any conditions laid down by their department or agency.' While section 4.4.11 stated: 'Civil Servants must not take part in any political activity when on duty, or in uniform, or on official premises.' Finally, section 4.4.15 stated: 'Civil servants who are not in the politically free category and who have not been given permission to engage in political activities must retain at all times a proper reticence in matters of political controversy so that their impartiality is beyond question.' Certainly, from a Whitehall perspective, it would appear they were attempting to take a comprehensive approach to ensuring that the notions of impartiality and neutrality were not eroded.

4 A result of the post-war intake reaching the age of retirement.

5 For example, Hoskyns wrote an article for *Parliamentary Affairs*, 1983, vol. 36, 'Whitehall and Westminster: An Outsider's View', in which he was highly critical of the residual attitude of Whitehall to reforming itself and prescribed a series of radical steps to transform the Civil Service into more of a business organisation.

6 Two years later, Hennessy (1995, pp. 129–30) further reassessed his position on the vexed question of politicisation when he argued: 'There was not, I believe any serious politicisation even in the high days of

Mrs T. and her 'ism'. There were problems, however, associated with having an ideological government [by British standards] in office for so long . . . I have some sympathy with those whom it would be wrong to see as 'grovellers' but who, nevertheless, have been criticised by name for being too accommodating of ministerial wishes.'

7 On 24 May 1992, The BBC News and Current Affairs programme *Analysis*, hosted by Peter Hennessy, discussed the wider implications of the longevity of the Conservative Government in Bluehall SW1? A transcript of this programme has been published: *Strathclyde Analysis Papers* 1992, No. 11. A similar version of the *Analysis* programme, this time chaired by Peter Kellner and entitled 'Running Britain', was repeated on 4 November 1996, during the run-up to the 1997 election.

Chapter 2

1 See G. K. Fry (1984) 'The Development of the Thatcher Government's 'Grand Strategy' for the Civil Service: A Public Policy Perspective', *Public Administration*, vol. 62.

2 For example see Drewry and Butcher (1991) or Middlemas (1979).

3 Cmnd 4506 (1970), *The Reorganisation of Central Government*, London: HMSO.

4 L. Chapman (1979), *Your Disobedient Servant* Penguin, London: Penguin.

5 Figures taken from Cmnd 8293 (1981, para. 9).

6 Figures from Hennessy (1989, p. 598).

7 Cmnd 8616 (1982) *Efficiency and Effectiveness in the Civil Service: Government Observations on the Third Report from the Treasury and Civil Service Committee, 1981–82*, London: HMSO.

8 See J. S. Cassels (1983) *Review of Personnel Work in the Civil Service: Report to the Prime Minister*, by J. S. Cassels, London: HMSO.

9 See *The Seventh Report from the Treasury and Civil Service Committee*, HC 92 1985–86, paras 5.13, 5.18.

10 For example, employees from Price Waterhouse, ICI and the Halifax Building Society were interviewed.

Chapter 3

1 RIPA 1987, *Top Jobs In Whitehall: Appointments and Promotions in the Senior Civil Service*, London: RIPA.

2 The bulk of the information in this first section is based on information I gathered, while interviewing a high-ranking official in the Office of Public Service.

3 Private information from an interview with the OPS Official (14 November 1994).

4 Prior to this White Paper, the Senior Open Structure was confined to Grades 1–3. In future, the new Senior Civil Service will incorporate Grades 1–5.

5   Statistics taken from the Efficiency Unit (1993, p. 32).

Chapter 4

1   RIPA (1987), Plowden (1994) and Barberis (1996a), all testify the need
    for this requirement.
2   In defence of Theakston and Fry, they address this limitation, explain-
    ing that the intention of their survey was to update the Harris and
    Garcia survey, which itself only examined Grade 1 officials.
3   By December 1996, Ann Bowtell and Rachel Lomax had both been
    appointed to Grade 1. Also, Dame Anne Mueller had been appointed
    Deputy Permanent Secretary at the Cabinet Office in 1984 and, later,
    went on to be Deputy Permanent Secretary at the Treasury, 1987–90.
    Although these appointments indicate that some progress has been
    made, a structural imbalance still persists in British Government. As
    Barberis (1996a, p. 119) concludes: 'There is evidence . . . that in recent
    years certain groups, most notably women, have failed to advance such
    claims upon top posts, as might have been expected'.
4   For details of 'Clarendon Schools', see Theakston and Fry (1989, p. 132
    ff.1).
5   This can partly be accounted for by the standard age of retirement for
    Permanent Secretaries being lowered to 60 during this period.
6   If, for example, a researcher is sifting through information from the
    Civil Service Statistics (CSS), he or she will discover that the statistics
    vary year by year. These statistics have traditionally been presented in a
    format involving a three-year comparison. However, statistics provided
    one year regularly differ from the same statistics published a year later.
    Unfortunately, the same is true for *The Civil Service Year Book*, which,
    for example, on occasion lists an individual as a Grade 2 in one year
    and as a Grade 3 in the next year. As it is almost unheard of for a
    senior official to be demoted, one can only conclude that, at some
    stage, a mistake has been made. Since 1992, *The Whitehall Companion*
    (London: Dod's Publishing & Research) has been annually published,
    which provides far more accurate and detailed information of officials
    serving in the senior Civil Service. Unfortunately, the bulk of my own
    data-sets involved appointments between 1974 and 1990.
7   For example, the statistics presented in RIPA's (1987) *Top Jobs in
    Whitehall* (which the author privately informed me were made available
    to him directly from the Cabinet Office) vary from those presented in
    Plowden's (1994) *Minister's and Mandarins* (which the author privately
    informed me were compiled from official Government statistics).
8   In January 1996, an official from the Office of Public Service (privately)
    informed me that: 'the dates of entry to the new senior grades appear
    on the database only as "July" for each year prior to 1984. This makes
    it difficult to determine whether appointments occurred before or after
    key dates such as general elections.'
9   See chapter 2 for details of Mrs Thatcher's attack on Civil Service
    numbers.
10 In this context, what I imply by 'meritocratic' is a shift away from

the traditional type of Permanent Secretary, described earlier in the chapter.

11 Theakston and Fry (1989) also noted the degree of homogeneity in their systematic survey of the mandarinate.

12 The figures for Grade 2 appointments under Mrs Thatcher were 296 (both horizontal and vertical appointments). It is inconceivable, for example, that Mrs Thatcher would have fretted over a Grade 2 appointment to MAFF.

Chapter 5

1 For accounts of her increased intervention see Peters (1986, p. 91), Pliatzky (1989, p. 164), RIPA (1987, p. 42), Simpson (1989, p. 6), McDonald (1992, p. 87), Savoie (1994, p. 251) and the Seventh Treasury and Civil Service Report (1986).

2 The details of these appointments are discussed in chapter 9, along with the observations of the political commentators.

3 It should also be remembered that in the 1970s, during her time as Minister for Education and as Leader of the Opposition, Margaret Thatcher would undoubtedly have had contact with the generation of Assistant Secretaries and Under Secretaries, who, by the 1980s, would be in line for Permanent Secretary posts.

4 The Barberis (1996a, p. 137) survey of officials who were appointed to Grade 1/1a examined the period 1914–58. The author informed me that the departments involved in his study included what he regarded as 'mainstream, non-specialist departments'. In an attempt to attain a degree of compatibility between our two surveys, I also only included those departments I regard as mainstream. Therefore the departments which I used to compile this data-set were: Ministry of Agriculture, Fisheries and Food, Cabinet Office, Civil Service Department, HM Customs & Excise, Ministry of Defence, Department of Education & Science, Department of Employment, Department of Energy (abolished in 1992), Department of Environment, Office of Fair Trading, Department of Health & Security (and its division after 1988), Home Office, Department of Trade and Industry (divided up to 1984), Board of Inland Revenue, Overseas Development Agency, Prime Minister's Office, Department of Transport, HM Treasury, Northern Ireland Office, Scottish Office, Welsh Office and the Department of Prices and Consumer Protection (abolished in 1979).

5 Not all memoirs by ministers have directly addressed Margaret Thatcher and her relationship with the Civil Service. For example, Geoffrey Howe's *Conflict of Loyalty*.

6 For a more detailed account of the Middleton appointment, see chapter 9.

7 The only officials with experience of the Thatcher years to have written their memoirs have been Maitland (1996), Pliatzky (1989), Ponting (1986), Part (1990) and Ingham (1991). Barberis (1996b, pp. 264–6) identifies the main articles written by other senior officials who served in the Thatcher era.

Chapter 6

1 A number of officials I interviewed kindly gave me permission to cite them. A list of the names of these individuals can be found in Appendix C. However, there were a number who wished their anonymity to be protected. Where this is the case, the material I have used has remained unattributed. I also wrote to Margaret Thatcher requesting an interview. Her private secretary, Mark Worthington, wrote and replied (20 March 1995) that: 'Lady Thatcher was interested to read of your research into the changes within the senior Civil Service during her time as Prime Minister. As I am sure you will appreciate, Lady Thatcher receives a large number of requests similar to your own and as it is simply not possible for her to meet them all, reluctantly she has had to adopt a policy of declining all such requests'.
2 H. Young (1989) *One of Us*, London: Macmillan.
3 Sir William Armstrong was Head of the Home Civil Service, 1968–74.

Chapter 7

1 Private information.
2 In chapter 9, I deal with the cases of individual officials who clashed with Margaret Thatcher and were subsequently 'black-balled', preventing any future chance of promotion.

Chapter 8

1 For example, appointments to Deputy Secretary in the Cabinet Office or the Treasury.
2 Interestingly, Steven Curtis never became a Permanent Secretary and his career in Whitehall did not prosper after Margaret Thatcher left office.
3 For more information on the outcome of Warner's scrutiny, see P. Hennessy (1989, p. 598).
4 The same problem does not apply to socialisation, as this effect mainly occurred once the high-flyers had been relocated to the centre.

Chapter 9

1 Between June 1994 and September 1995 I wrote to Robin Butler on four occasions requesting an interview; no reply was forthcoming.
2 During Kemp's time at the Treasury, 1973–88, he was one of the few qualified accountants employed there!
3 See H. Porter 'Club Has Lost Its Class', *The Guardian*, 18 January 1993, or P. Hennessy (1989, p. 635).
4 Despite the fact that, in the aftermath of the Thatcher Government, a new cottage industry sprung up in ministers' memoirs, it is rare to find an ex-Cabinet Minister displaying any interest in the actual machinery of Government. Memoirs normally take the form of a modest account

of the vital role a Minister played in dragging Britain back from the abyss.

5 In his memoirs *Conflict of Loyalty*, Howe does not mention the Middleton appointment.

6 Middleton was one of the members of SASC in the 1980s.

7 As chapter 3 indicates, Mrs Thatcher would have had a formal part to play in Sparrow's appointment and, further, she most certainly would have been aware of what was going on.

8 For details of Ingham's use of the phrase 'semi-detached', see Ingham (1991, pp. 323–8), when during a lobby session, he referred to John Biffen as: 'that well-known semi-detached member of the Cabinet'.

9 For details on why Margaret Thatcher believed the CPRS had outlived its use, see Thatcher (1993 pp. 278–9).

10 For example see *The Times*, 1 November 1983 and *The Guardian*, 2 November 1983.

11 For details see P. Hennessy (1989, p. 372).

12 For further details of the circumstances surrounding the Ingham appointment see both Robert Harris's biography of Ingham, *Good and Faithful Servant* (1990) and Ingham's autobiography, *Kill The Messenger* (1991). They provide differing accounts of the appointment, but both stress that Ingham's contact with Margaret Thatcher, prior to his appointment, was limited.

13 See chapter 6 for further details of this incident.

14 For details see C. Ponting (1986) or P. Hennessy (1989).

15 Another post upgraded to Deputy Secretary, during the incumbent's tenure.

16 Peach left the service at the early age of 57, in order to take a post in the private sector at IBM, as their Director of Personnel and Corporate Affairs.

17 For details of this clash and Mrs Thatcher's reaction to Derx, see chapter 5.

18 Ibid.

19 See G. Howe (1994, p. 202).

Chapter 10

1 Of the nineties' generation of mandarins I interviewed, one had been an active member of SASC.

2 The interviewee is referring to the case of Michael Bichard, a Chief Executive of an agency, who in 1995 was appointed a permanent secretary.

3 In carrying out an identical survey, the reader must note that the methodology remained as before and, as such, the methodological problems also remain. For the names of all first-time appointees by John Major see Appendix B.

4 The reason behind this, as observed in chapter 6, is that the sheer scale of the number of appointments to be made at Grade 2 confines a Prime Minister to little more than a passing interests in appointments at this level. The reader should also note that, due to the constraint of the

unavailability of regularly updated information on the most recent appointments in Whitehall, the time-frame for my quantitative survey covers the period from November 1990 until December 1995. Also, I have provided the statistics from the Thatcher era, in order to help the reader compare the two different generations of the Conservative Administration.

5 Lankester had already, at an earlier stage in his career, surrounded himself in controversy. Whilst Permanent Secretary in the Overseas Development Agency, he sent a minute to the Public Accounts Committee expressing his belief that the Government's offer of a well-publicised grant to Malaysia, for the building of the Pergau Dam, was a misguided use of public money. As Foster and Plowden (1996, p. 232) rather severely concluded of the whole Lankester affair: 'His [Lankester's] view was upheld by the Public Accounts Committee. However innocent the circumstances leading to his departure may have been, it was impossible for many not to draw the moral that, however justified, a permanent secretary who writes such a minute censuring ministerial behaviour will be caught up with in the end.'

6 For more details on the Kemp sacking, see John Willman, pp. 67–8, in Kavanagh and Seldon's (1994), *The Major Effect*.

Chapter 11

1 A transcript of this programme has been published: P. Hennessy and S. Coates (1992), *Strathclyde Analysis Papers*, No. 11.

2 In fact, the arguments over a less critical Civil Service evolving in the 1980s can be further extended. It became apparent from the interviews I conducted that one of the reasons behind the downfall of Mrs Thatcher was that, particularly in her third term of government, she increasingly surrounded herself only with individuals prepared to tell her what she wanted to hear. This obviously included the likes of Alan Walters, Bernard Ingham and Charles Powell. Mrs Thatcher became more and more out of touch, hearing only a few selective views from a small number of her closest confidants, all singing praises in her ear. And so her and her government went off the rails, having lost contact with the political reality.

Bibliography

Allen, D. (1981), 'Raynerism: Strengthening Civil Service Management' in *RIPA Report* 2(4).

Armstrong, R. (1985), *Address to the Centenary Conference of the Chartered Institute of Public Finance and Accountancy*, 15 June 1985.

Barberis, P. (1981), *Permanent Secretaries in the British Civil Service: An Historical and Biographical Survey* (unpublished Ph.D.), Manchester: Victoria University of Manchester.

Barberis, P. (1996a), *The Elite of the Elite*, Aldershot: Dartmouth.

Barberis, P. (ed.) (1996b), *The Whitehall Reader*, Buckingham: Open University Press.

Brown, G. (1992), 'Open Arms Welcome Officer Class to Defence Industry' *The Guardian*, 10 September 1992.

Bulletin, February 1985, London.

Burnham, J. and Jones, G. W. (1993), 'Advising Margaret Thatcher: The Prime Minister's Office and the Cabinet Office Compared' *Political Studies* XLI.

Butler, D., Adonis, A. and Travers, T. (1994), *Failure in British Government: The Politics of the Poll Tax*, Oxford: Oxford University Press.

Butler, D. and Butler, G. (1994), *British Political Facts*, London: Macmillan.

Butler, R. (1990), Internal Cabinet Office Memorandum *Guidance on Guidance*, London: HMSO.

Cabinet Office (1974–96), *The Civil Service Yearbook*, London: HMSO.

Campbell, C. and Wilson, G. (1995), *The End of Whitehall: Death of a Paradigm?* Oxford: Blackwell Publishers.

Carrington, P. (1988), *Reflection on Things Past*, London: Collins.

Cassels, J. S. (1983), *Review of Personnel Work in the Civil Service: Report to the Prime Minister by J. S. Cassels*, London: HMSO.

Castle, B. (1984), *The Castle Diaries 1964–1970*, London: Weidenfeld & Nicolson.

Chapman, L. (1979), *Your Disobedient Servant*, London: Penguin.

Chapman, R.A. (1992), 'The End of the Civil Service?' *Teaching Public Administration* XII(2): 1–5.

Civil Service Commissioners (1993), *The Role of the Office of the Civil Service Commissioners in Recruitment to the Civil Service: A Note for Visitors* [internal], London: HMSO.

Civil Service Statistics (1996), London: Government Statistical Services.

Clark, A. (1993), *Diaries*, London: Weidenfeld & Nicolson.

Cmnd 2627 (1994), *The Civil Service – Continuity and Change*, London: HMSO.

Cmnd 2748 (1995), *The Civil Service: Taking Forward Continuity and Change*, London: HMSO.

Cmnd 3638 (1968), *The Civil Service Report by the Fulton Committee*, London: HMSO.

Cmnd 4506 (1970), *The Reorganisation of Central Government*, London: HMSO.

Cmnd 8293 (1981), *Efficiency in the Civil Service*, London: HMSO.

Cmnd 8616 (1982), *Efficiency and Effectiveness in the Civil Service: Government Observations on the Third Report from the Treasury and Civil Service Committee, 1981–82*, London: HMSO.

Crick, B. (1992) 'Finish with Honours Uneven' *The Guardian*, 7 May 1992.

Crossman, R. (1975), *The Diaires of a Cabinet Minister, Volume 1*, London: Hamish Hamilton.

Crossman, R. (1976), *The Diaries of a Cabinet Minister, Volume 2*, London: Hamish Hamilton.

Crossman, R. (1977), *The Diaries of a Cabinet Minister, Volume 3*, London: Hamish Hamilton.

Dowding, K. (1995), *The Civil Service*, London: Routledge.

Drabble, M. (ed.) (1985), *The Oxford Companion to English Literature*, Oxford: Oxford University Press.

Drewry, G. and Butcher, T. (1991), *The Civil Service Today*, 2nd edn, Oxford: Blackwell.

Efficiency Unit (1993), *Career Planning and Succession Planning [the Oughton Report]*, London: HMSO.

Falkender, M. (1983), *Downing Street in Perspective*, London: Weidenfeld & Nicolson.

Foster, C. and Plowden, F. (1996), *The State Under Stress*, Buckingham: Open University Press.

Fowler, N. (1991), *Minister's Decide: A Memoir of the Thatcher Years*, London: Chapmans.

Fry, G.K. (1984), 'The Development of the Thatcher Government's 'Grand Strategy' for the Civil Service' *Public Administration* 62.

Fry, G.K. (1985a) 'The British Career Civil Service Under Challenge' *Public Administration* 63.

Fry, G.K. (1985b), *The Changing Civil Service*, London: Allen & Unwin.

Gamble, A. (1994), 'State of the Art: Political Memoirs' *Politics* 14.

Garrett, J. (1980), *Managing the Civil Service*, London: Heinneman.

Gilmour, I. (1992), *Dancing with Dogma: Britain Under Thatcherism*, London: Simon & Schuster.

Gray, A., Jenkins, B., Flynn, A. and Rutherford, B. (1991), 'The Management of Change in Whitehall: The Experience of the FMI' *Public Administration* 69.

Greenaway, J. (1988) 'The Political Education of the Civil Service Mandarin Elite' in Fieldhouse, R. (ed.) *The Political Education of Servants of the State*, Manchester: Manchester University Press.

Greenaway, J. (1995), 'Having the Bun and the Halfpenny: Can Old Public Service Ethics Survive in the New Whitehall? *Public Administration* 73(3).

260   *Bibliography*

Greer, P. (1994), *Transforming Central Government: The Next Steps Initiative*, Buckingham: Open University Press.

Haldane, R. B. (1918), *Report of the Machinery of Government Committee: Ministry of Reconstruction*, Cmnd 9230. London: HMSO.

Harris, J. and Garcia, T. V. (1966), 'The Permanent Secretaries: Britian's Top Administrators' *Public Administration Review* 26(1).

Harris, R. (1990), *Good and Faithful Servant*, London: Faber & Faber.

HC (1982a), 38.Debate 6s.c. 918.

HC (1985–86), 'Annex, Minutes of Evidence and Appendices' *Seventh Report from the Treasury and Civil Service Select Committee Session*, Vol. II, London: HMSO.

HC (1985–86), 'Civil Servants and Ministers: Duties and Responsibilities' *Treasury and Civil Service Select Committee Session* , no. 92–vi, London: HMSO.

HC 92 (1985–86), *Seventh Report from the Treasury and Civil Service Committee*, London: HMSO.

HC 236–1 (1982b), *Third Report from the Treasury and Civil Service Committee 1981–82: Efficiency and Effectiveness in the Civil Service*, London: HMSO.

HC 410 (1989), *Report by the Comptroller and Auditor General: The Next Steps Initiative*, London: HMSO.

HC 535, II [part 1] (1976–77), 'Memorandum by the Civil Service Department, the Response to the Fulton Report' *The Civil Service, Eleventh Report from the Expenditure Committee, Session 1976–77*, London: HMSO.

HC 588 (1986), *The Financial Management Initiative*, London: HMSO.

Healey, D. (1989), *The Time of My Life*, London: Michael Joseph.

Heclo, H. and Wildavsky, A. (1974), *The Private Government of Public Money*, London: Macmillan.

Heiser, T. (1994), 'The Civil Service at the Crossroads?' *Public Policy and Adminstration* 9(1).

Hennessy, P. and Coates, S. (1992), 'Bluehall SW1?' *Strathclyde Analysis Papers*, no. 11.

Hennessy, P. 'Club that has Lost its Class' *The Guardian*, 18 January 1993.

Hennessy, P. (1989), *Whitehall*, London: Fontana.

Hennessy, P. (1995), *The Hidden Wiring*, London: Victor Gollancz.

Heseltine, M. (1987), *Where There's a Will*, London: Hutchinson.

HMSO (1993) [internal brochure], *Civil Service Commissioners' Guide: The Role of the Civil Service Commissioners in Recruitment to the Civil Service: A Note for Visitors*, London: HMSO.

Hogwood, B. (1993), 'The Uneven Staircase: Measuring up to Next Steps' *Strathclyde Papers on Government and Politics* 92.

Hood, C., Dunsire, A., Carter, N. et al. (1991), *Public Administration* 60(1).

Hopwood, A. and Tompkins, C. (eds) (1984), *Issues in Public Sector Accounting*, Oxford: Philip Allan.

Hoskyns, J. (1983), 'Whitehall and Westminster' *Parliamentary Affairs* 36.

Hoskyns, J. interviewed for 'All the Prime Minister's Men' *Channel 4*, 26 March 1986.

House of Commons Debates, 8 February 1966, col. 210

Howe, G. (1994) *Conflict of Loyalty*, London: Macmillan.

Bibliography 261

Ingham, D. (1991), *Kill the Messenger*, London: Fontana.

Jay, D. (1947) *The Socialist Case*, 2nd edn, London: Faber & Faber.

Jenkins, K., Caines, K. and Jackson, A. (1988), *Improving Management in Government: The Next Steps: Report to the Prime Minister (Ibbs Report)*, London: HMSO.

Jessop, B. et al. (1988), *Thatcherism: A Tale of Two Nations*, Cambridge: Polity Press.

Johnstone, D. (1986) 'Facelessness: Anonymity in the Civil Service' *Parliamentary Affairs* 39.

Jones, G. and Kavanagh, D. (1987), *British Politics Today*, 3rd edn, Manchester: Manchester University Press.

Kavanagh, D. (1990), *Thatcherism and British Politics: The End of Consensus*, 2nd edn, Oxford: Oxford University Press.

Kavanagh, D. and Seldon, A. (eds) (1989), *The Thatcher Effect*, Oxford: Oxford University Press.

Kavanagh, D. and Seldon, A. (eds) (1994), *The Major Effect*, London: Macmillan.

Keegan, W. (1991), 'The March of the Mandarins' *The Observer*, 21 April 1991.

Kellner, P. and Lord Crowther-Hunt (1980), *The Civil Servants*, London: Macmillan.

Kelsall, R.K. (1955), *Higher Civil Servants in Britian*, London: Routledge.

Lawson, N. (1992), *The View from Number Eleven*, London: Bantam Press.

Lee, M. (1990), 'The Ethos of the Cabinet Office' *Public Administration* 68(2).

Macmillan, H. (1966), *Winds of Change 1914–39*, London: Macmillan.

Macmillan, H. (1967), *The Blast of War 1939–45*, London: Macmillan.

Macmillan, H. (1969), *Tides of Fortune 1945–55*, London: Macmillan.

Macmillan, H. (1971), *Riding the Storm 1955–59*, London: Macmillan.

Macmillan, H. (1972), *Pointing the Way 1959–61*, London: Macmillan.

Macmillan, H. (1973), *At the End of the Day 1961–63*, London: Macmillan.

Madgwick, P. (1991), *British Government: The Central Executive Territory*, Oxford: Philip Allen.

Maitland, Donald (1996), *Diverse Times, Sundry Places*, Brighton: Alpha Press.

McDonald, O. (1992), *The Future of Whitehall*, London: Weidenfeld & Nicolson.

Metcalfe, L. (1993), 'Conviction Politics and Dynamic Conservatism: Mrs. Thatcher's Managerial Revolution' *International Political Science Review* 14(4).

Metcalfe, L. and Richards, S. (1987) *Improving Public Management*, London: Sage.

Middlemas, K. (1979), *Politics in Industrial Society: The Experience of the British System since 1911*, London: André Deutsch.

Morrison, H. (1964), *Government and Parliament; A Survey from the Inside*, 3rd edn, Oxford: Oxford University Press.

Office of the Civil Service Commissioners [internal guide] (1993), *The Role of the Office of the Civil Service Commissioners in Recruitment to the Civil Service: A Note for Visitors*, London: HMSO.

PA News (1996), *'£30 Billion Tag on Labour Pledges' Claims Tories*, 20

November 1996.

PA News (1996), *Heseltine Denies Tory Bid to 'Hijack' Civil Service*, 11 November 1996.

Painter, C. (1989), 'Thatcherite Radicalism and Institutional Conservatism' *Parliamentary Affairs* 42(14).

Parkinson, C. (1992), *Right at the Centre*, London: Weidenfeld & Nicolson.

Part, A. (1990), *The Making of a Mandarin*, London: André Deutsch.

Peters, B. G. (1986), 'Burning the Village: The Civil Service under Reagan and Thatcher' *Parliamentary Affairs* 39.

Pliatzky, L. (1989), *The Treasury under Mrs. Thatcher*, Oxford: Basil Blackwell.

Plowden, W. (1994), *Ministers and Mandarins*, London: Institute for Public Policy Research.

Ponting, C. (1986), *Whitehall: Tragedy and Farce*, London: Hamish Hamilton.

Priestley, C. (1988), 'Government Management Must No Longer be Left to Chance' *The Independent*, 26 February 1988.

Prior, J. (1986), *A Balance of Power*, London: Hamish Hamilton.

Punnett, R. M. (1987), *British Government and Politics*, 5th edn, London: Gower.

Pym, F. (1984), *The Politics of Consent*, London: Hamish Hamilton.

Pyper, R. (1991), *Political Realities: The Evolving Civil Service*, London: Longman.

Regan, C. M. (1986), 'Anonymity in the British Civil Service. Facelessness Diminished', *Parliamentary Affairs* 39.

Richards, D. (1993), 'Appointments in the Higher Civil Service: Assessing a "Thatcher Effect"' *Strathclyde Papers on Government and Politics*, no. 93, Glasgow: University of Strathclyde.

Richards, D. and Hay, C. (1996) 'Heseltine and the Civil Service' *The Times*, 18 November 1996.

Richards, S. (1992), 'The British Civil Service since 1979: Changes in the Management of People'. Paper prepared for *Administration Modernisation Conference*, Perugia, 12–13 June.

Ridley, F. (1983a), 'Career Service: A Comparative Perspective on Civil Service Promotion' *Public Administration* 61.

Ridley, F. (1983b), 'The British Civil Service and Politics: Principles in Question and Traditions Influx' *Parliamentary Affairs* 36.

Ridley, F. (1986), 'Political Neutrality, the Duty of Silence, and the Right to Publish in the Civil Service' *Parliamentary Affairs* 39.

Ridley, F. and Doig, A. (1986), 'Traditions, Responsibility and Politicisation; The British Civil Service Today' *The Seventh Report from the Treasury and Civil Service Committee Session 1985–86*, London: HMSO.

Ridley, N. (1991), *My Style of Government*, London.

RIPA (1987), *Top Jobs in Whitehall: Appointments and Promotions in the Senior Civil Service*, London: RIPA.

Rubenstein, W. D. (1986), 'Education and the Social Origin of British Elites 1880–1970' *Past and Present*, 112.

Russell, W. (1987) 'Butler – A Civil Servant For All Seasons' *The Glasgow Herald*, 14 July 1987.

Savoie, D. (1994), *Thatcher Reagan Mulroney: In Search of a New Bureaucracy*, Pittsburgh: University of Pittsburgh Press.

Seldon, A. (1990), 'The Cabinet Office and Co-ordination 1979–87' *Public Administration* 68(1).

Sheriff, P. (1976), *Career Patterns in the Higher Civil Service*, London: HMSO.

Silkin, J. quoted in *The Times*, 4 November 1982.

Simpson, D. (1989), *Politicisation of the Civil Service*, York: Longman.

Smith, M. J. (1996), 'Reforming the State' in Ludlam, S. and Smith, M. *Contemporary British Conservatism*, Basingstoke: Macmillan.

Tebbit, N. (1988), *Upwardly Mobile*, London: Weidenfeld & Nicolson.

Thatcher, M. (1993), *The Downing Street Years*, London: Harper & Collins.

The Guardian (18 January 1993), *Club has Lost its Class*.

The Guardian (16 July 1993), *Right of Information Access To Be Widened*.

The Observer (6 May 1994), *Senior Whitehall Mandarin Defects to Private Sector*.

The Observer (14 April 1996), *Now Only 'Yes Minister' Will Do*.

The Sunday Times (11 July 1982), *Thatcher's Mandarins*.

The Times (1979), *The Times Guide to the House of Commons*, London: Times Books.

The Times (11 November 1996), *Heseltine Challenged over the Use of Civil Service*.

The Times (21 November 1996), *Butler Defends Whitehall Role in Tory Attack*.

The Times (26 November 1986), *Pay Re-Think at the Civil Service*.

The Whitehall Companion (1995–96), London: DPR Publishing.

Theakston, K. (1990a), 'Labour, Thatcher and the Future of the Civil Service', *Public Policy and Administration* 5(1).

Theakston, K. (1990b), 'The Civil Service: Progress Report 1989/90' *Contemporary Record*, April 1990.

Theakston, K. (1992), *The Labour Party and Whitehall*, London: Routledge.

Theakston, K. (1995), *The Civil Service since 1945*, Oxford: Blackwell Publishers.

Theakston, K. and Fry, G. (1989), 'British Administrative Elite: Permanent Secretaries 1900–1986' *Public Administration*, 67.

Treasury and Civil Service Committee (1986), *Civil Servants and Ministers, Seventh Report from the Treasury and Civil Service Commission, Minutes of Evidence, Session 1985–86*, London: HMSO.

Treasury and Civil Service Committee (1994), *The Role of the Civil Service Fifth Report, Session 1993–94*, London: HMSO.

Trend, B. (1976), 'How Cabinet Government Works', *BBC Radio 3*, 12 March 1976.

Whitelaw, W. (1989), *The Whitelaw Memoirs*, London: Aurum Press.

Who's Who (1996), London: A&C Black.

Willets, D. (1987), 'The Role of the Prime Minister's Policy Unit' *Public Administration* 65(1).

Wilson, H. (1974), *The Labour Government 1964–70*, London: Macmillan.

Wright, P. 'Whitehall Watch; Recruitment the Key to a Better Foreign Office Career Structure' *The Independent*, 18 January 1988.

Young, H. (1989), *One of Us*, London: Macmillan.

Young, H. and Sloman, A. (1986), *The Thatcher Phenomenon*, London: BBC Publications.

Zebel, H. (1973), *Balfour: A Political Biography*, Cambridge: Cambridge University Press.

Index

268

Index